BARRON'S

Legal-Ease

Small Claims Court

S T E P · B Y · S T E P

BARRON'S
Legal-Ease

Small Claims Court

S·T·E·P · B·Y · S·T·E·P

Ted Rothstein, D.D.S., Ph.D.
in collaboration with
Isaac Druker, J.D., S.J.D.

BARRON'S

DISCLAIMER

This publication is designed to provide accurate and authoritative information in regard to the subject matter covered. It is sold with the understanding that the publisher is not engaged in rendering legal, accounting, or other professional services. If legal advice or other expert assistance is required, the services of a competent professional person should be sought.

The material presented in this book includes revisions made in the Small Claims Court system that were introduced up until July 23, 1996.

All inquiries should be addressed to:
Barron's Educational Series, Inc.
250 Wireless Boulevard
Hauppauge, New York 11788-3917

ISBN 0-7641-9157-8

Library of Congress Catalog Card No. 97-17748

Library of Congress Cataloging-in-Publication Data
Rothstein, Ted.
    Small claims court : step-by-step / Ted Rothstein, in collaboration with Isaac Druker, Esq.
        p. cm.—(Barron's legal-ease)
    Includes index.

    1. Small claims courts—New York Metropolitan Area—Popular works. 2. Small claims courts—New Jersey—Popular works. 3. Small claims courts—Connecticut—Popular works. I. Druker, Isaac E. II. Title. III. Series.
    KF8769.Z9R67   1997
    347.747'104—dc21   97-17748
                                            CIP

PRINTED IN THE UNITED STATES OF AMERICA

987654321

DEDICATION

Dedicated to the men and women who work to make the small claims courts of New York City a place where the little guy can find justice for a bargain basement price and to the volunteer lawyers who serve ably as arbitrators in those courts.

ACKNOWLEDGMENTS

To each of the following I offer my thanks for their editorial suggestions and constructive criticism—the core element of a manuscript that wants to be:

At the Brooklyn Small Claims Court: John Kelleher, Chief Officer; Janice Stone, Associate Court Clerk, Small Claims Supervisor

At the Superior Court of New Jersey, Hudson County: The staff of the Division of the Special Civil Part

At the Superior Court, W. Hartford, Connecticut, Small Claims Part: Carol Turansky, Court Services Clerk and Benjamin Johnson, Sidney Leonidas, Kimberly Magee, Christine Collazo, Len Rothstein, M.B.A., Barbara Joseph, D.S.W., Desirée Hamilton, Esq., Dina Dauber, Donald Aronofsky, M.S. Ele. Ed., Andrea Hanneman, Esq., Sophie Truslow, Esq., Esther Lafair, Michael Capriano, Esq., Isaac Druker, Esq.

Special thanks to Jon Rothstein whose skills, patience, and long tedious hours of work at the computer facilitated the conversion of the manuscript into book form; to Esther Lafair for her comprehensive and detailed proofreading; to Isaac Druker who, in addition to offering editorial suggestions, helped me clarify the expository text related to the legal concepts involved; finally, my gratitude, humbly offered, to my wife Frances, for among other things, her patience, attentiveness, and encouragement from start to finish of the manuscript.

ABOUT THE AUTHOR

Dr. Ted Rothstein is a specialist in orthodontics whose private practice in Brooklyn Heights was established in 1976. He earned his D.D.S. and Ph.D. (Physical Anthropology) from Temple Dental School and the University of Pennsylvania, respectively, during a 10-year sojourn in Philadelphia. He returned to Brooklyn, the home of his alma mater—Brooklyn College—to train for his specialty at New York University. He is on the staff of St. Luke's–Roosevelt Hospital Center and resigned after 15 years of service on the staff of Long Island College. Except for his actual experiences in the small claims court, where he has won all but a handful of the more than 100 hearings that he initiated, he makes no claim to legal wisdom.

Contents

Foreword

Dr. Ted has really done it. In clearly written, witty and energetic prose, he has given us a powerful every-person's-guide to the procedures of small claims court.

Small claims court was created to provide an easily accessible, inexpensive forum for the resolution of money claims. Most of us encounter these problems once or twice in our lives, if that. Professionals and small business owners, subject to the whims of recalcitrant patients, clients, and customers, tend to accept a certain number of "bad debts" as a cost of doing business.

Dr. Ted says, if you provide appropriate services or sell suitable merchandise, you are entitled to be paid. And now you can improve the odds in favor of your getting paid by utilizing his methods: (a) preventative account management, (b) mastery of the simple procedures of the small claims court, and (c) overcoming your apprehension of the potential confrontation with your debtor. Dr. Ted also shows you, step-by-step, what the paperwork looks like and how to prepare yourself substantively and psychologically for the challenge. Equally important, he guides you through the process of converting your judgment into cash, with numerous practical suggestions—for example, when to use a specialist in asset location and how to get an early settlement.

If a virtuous tone creeps into Dr. Ted's "scenarios" from time to time, it's because Ted has by now pretty much seen it all—and has succeeded. He wants you to learn the ropes, and he is willing to share his extensive experience. This book will put you in Ted's shoes and help you achieve his "win and collect rate," once you have followed his training tips. Ted tells you that endurance and know-how make you a winner.

One wonders to what extent small claims court has lived up to the expectations of its early supporters. I suspect that its use has been less than predicted; however, its very existence may nudge disputants toward settlement. It is therefore tempting to speculate whether widespread dissemination of Ted's guide may itself further alter the landscape: Won't adverse parties be more likely to resolve their differences by negotiation rather than resort to the court if both of them read Ted's book? I believe so, and I would urge everyone to have a copy on their bookshelf—just in case.

Ted has written from the perspective of his own profession—he is a dedicated practitioner at the leading edge of innovative orthodontia. This manual will particularly resonate with other health care providers, big and small. Its techniques are easily adapted to the practice of other professionals and service providers who routinely carry clients and customers for fee amounts up to the small claims court limit of $3,000. And the same is true for retailers, business persons, and trades-people who extend credit to their customers for goods sold or while a job is being done (i.e., roofers, plumbers).

On the other hand, the guide is equally useful to the individual who feels he has been poorly treated and should have something coming back—because of, for example, shoddy merchandise, failure to meet specification, default by a borrower, physical injury, or property damage. Dr. Ted's tips for spotting troubled patient or customer accounts wouldn't apply here, of course, but the principles and procedures are the same as far as using the small claims court and collecting on a judgment.

Why do it yourself, rather than go to a collection service or collection attorneys? Ted's answer is straightforward: Your claim is grist to their mill and may not receive the specific attention it needs, especially once a counterclaim is put in. On the other hand, if a shake of the tree is all that is needed to get the apple down, you can do that yourself and save the collection fee. But you have to be willing to spend a little time to prepare for the twists that sometimes make the going more difficult.

I was flattered and my curiosity piqued when Dr. Ted asked me to read his manuscript critically and provide a foreword. I don't have specific credentials as a litigator. However, as a law firm partner with 30 years of a diverse law practice in New York City, I have heard many individuals express their questions and concerns about seeking redress before our courts. For small claims, I would recommend Dr. Ted's book to all of them. In fact, every lawyer should have a supply of this book to give clients— he will gain their boundless gratitude.

Here is a guide that is easily understood by people in all walks of life. It will make you more certain about the outcome of "your day in court," and help you put the money you earned or are owed where it belongs—in your pocket.

Isaac E. Druker
Brooklyn, NY
August 1997

CHAPTER 1

Introduction

WHY YOU NEED THIS BOOK

Most of us know absolutely nothing about the law except what we may happen to see in the movies or on television. In real life we are horrified at the prospect of becoming entangled in any legal process for fear that it will take over our lives and empty our wallets. We are so paralyzed by legal matters that we are often willing to pay someone thousands of dollars to have the assurance that everything is under control.

The truth is that much of the legal machinery you need to know about is understandable, especially as it relates to small claims court. Making it understandable to you, I hope, will embolden you to initiate a claim against anyone who owes you a fee or debt that you are aching to collect, and until now, didn't know how to go about doing so legally. My story may be particularly familiar if you are a small-business person like myself. If you are not, it makes no difference because the principles of getting your money are exactly the same.

At the beginning of my clinical studies at Temple University Dental School, 31 years ago, Dr. Harold Lantz, professor of removable dental prosthetics (dentures), began his initial lecture to a classroom filled only with young men with perhaps the least understood, but most prophetic words pertaining to my career in dentistry. "Boys," he began in his most pronounced Pennsylvania Dutch Amish accent, "the first and most important lesson you must learn in making dentures is first get the gelt." Many of the Jewish students roared with laughter, for the good doctor had used the Yiddish word for *money.* These words, spoken in his not-often-heard accent, have remained indelibly in my mind.

Unfortunately, the doctor's warning to "first get the gelt" turned out to be the sum and substance of the principles of practice management offered in my dental school back then.

I became a specialist in orthodontics in 1973. As such, my services are contracted for, and fee payment plans are structured with an initial payment followed by 18 to 24 monthly payments. This arrangement is unique among the various branches of dentistry and medicine, which generally require immediate payment, or the commitment of a third-party payer, for services rendered. In 1976 I first opened the doors to my office notwithstanding my abysmal lack of business knowledge. What I lacked in business acumen I made up for in dedication to work and devotion to my patients.

Guided then only by lofty principles, I delegated the responsibility of fee collection to the office manager, whose skills in such matters were generally learned on the job. Computers were rarely heard of and, like most professionals, I kept track of patient accounts by using handwritten ledger cards, as is still done by many professionals today. Painfully I learned such a system does not permit an instantaneous global view of who owes what and for how long they have been owing it. Besides which, devoted doctors in general are notorious for being bad businessmen—this is no myth.

DOES THIS SOUND LIKE YOU?

Some professionals are laid-back about patients or clients who owe them money for services rendered. I was one of them for the first five years of my practice. My fee-for-service contract was far more elementary than its present successor. I lacked the experience and the necessary management skills to realize that collection problems were becoming a reality in my practice. Fortunately, most patients paid their bills. As my practice grew, I began to realize that overdue accounts receivable were taking hold. The problems seemed to grow on the fringes of the practice, in the periphery of my vision, so to speak. When collection problems take hold they are like algae in a hobbyist's aquarium, barely noticeable until you look carefully and observe they are colonizing the whole tank. I casually named the collection problems the "bads," not yet realizing what lay ahead. A decade passed before I learned that Experian (formerly TRW), one of the most well-known, revered (and feared) credit collection agencies, refers to its clients that have an unsound credit history by the same term.

My accounts receivable problem began and continued to grow. Successive office managers inherited the old bad accounts and in the course of their tenure (with the best of intentions) allowed new ones to sprout like weeds. I learned that accounts receivable problems vary with practice management policies and strategies, which are commonly controlled by the aptitudes and preferences of the staff in charge of accounts receivable.

Before computers it was very difficult to keep track of accounts that were 30, 60, and 90 days overdue. During the past seven years I have become dependent on not less than four computers to assist

in managing the various aspects of the office. It became easier to spot the bad accounts; one had only to look over the monthly practice statistics report, or the "on-demand" report of the "90-day overdue" patients, to know what new bad accounts had emerged. My computer reports forced me to see my patients in the cold light of financial reality. Each bad account I identified became an object lesson in poor practice management.

Slowly I identified those practice policies and personal attitudes about collection that were my undoing. Then I began to correct the policies that were underlying and nurturing my growing accounts receivable problem. Eventually I developed criteria for initiating litigation and instituted interceptive and preventive measures to minimize the new bad accounts.

But my collection problem had grown uncomfortably large, and I attacked the problem using a variety of strategies. Caught between a rock and a hard place, and being neither passive by personality nor willing to forgo my fee, I turned to the court, no doubt also motivated by its proximity to my office and home. Gradually, I focused primarily on the small claims court because there I had the most control of the outcome.

I came to realize how ineffectual most collection agencies are. I remember one agency that collected some fees for me and then went bankrupt, taking my share along with it.

This was the moment of truth for me. Collection attorneys were also out of the question because they wanted 35% to 50% of the *gelt* I worked so hard to earn. Taking my uncollectible accounts receivable as a tax write-off occurred to me early on as a solution. While my accountant has patiently tried to explain to me why this is not possible for a cash-based business, I accepted what he said; afterall, I'm an orthodontist not an accountant.

My experiences over 15 years number well over a hundred cases in the small claims court. An attorney, a patient of mine, ventured to say that I was perhaps one of the most proficient, if not the most experienced, nonlawyer using the court.

This guide contains the details of all the procedures involved in the small claims process and the myriad pitfalls that I have experienced. You can avoid many of these pitfalls if you take heed of the precautions I outline. I hope my experiences will encourage you to use the small claims court with less timidity.

The litigious approach admittedly is an in-your-face way of getting your debtor's rapt attention and may not be suitable to some service providers or persons whose personality types are less than comfortable in a confrontational situation. Being prepared may give you more confidence to resolve and overcome this problem.

The sum of my experiences in court has reinforced my belief that in some cases the only way to confront the nonpayment issue is in the impressive, formal environment of small claims court. In essence you are alerting the debtor that he is responsible for his bill and that you are serious about collecting on it.

THE GOALS AND APPLICABILITY OF THIS BOOK

The guide's contents will provide you with the "tools" and understanding you need to navigate the do-it-yourself *pro se* court system with minimal discomfort and to let you emerge unscathed with the payment due for your services or goods. The principles are no less valid for money lent to a "friend" or the expense you incurred when your neighbor's dog chewed up your garden.

This book was originally conceived for professionals, but it gradually became clear to me that anyone can use the principles outlined in the book to sue in the small claims court if there is a legitimate reason or cause of action. The principles are the same whether you are suing the dry cleaning store that damaged your clothing, the fellow who damaged your property, or the air-conditioning guy who sold you that rebuilt model for new. The real difference in all these cases is mainly the proof or evidence that is needed to support your claim.

The information provided in this book is generally applicable to every small claims court in the United States. The forms, fees, procedures, and terms may vary from one locale (county) to the next and from time to time may vary even in the same locale. For example, on a visit to Oregon I discovered that in Deschutes County not only must the plaintiff pay a filing fee of between $36 and $73, but the defendant must also pay a fee of between $20 and $34 if he demands a hearing. Also, outside of New York City, you are likely to request a "continuance" rather than an "application" when you need to postpone your hearing to a future time.

The residents of Connecticut, New Jersey, and New York will be pleased to find the location and telephone number of every small claims court in their state in Appendix B. This information alone facilitates entry into the process because they can write to a particular court and request the initial claim form and specific instructions for their area.

The book is generally specific for the states of New York (population 18,136,000), New Jersey (population 7,945,000), and Connecticut (population 3,295,669) because these states have unified statewide codes for their courts. Connecticut, for example, seems to be the most unified in that each of its 22 geographical areas' superior courts (small claims division) uses the same forms (shown in this book), starting with the initial claim form [FORM 53]. The same is true for the small claims courts of the five boroughs of New York City (population 7,322,564) because they share forms in common such as [FORM 1]. Forms are shown from New York's Westchester (population 890,918), Nassau (population 1,305,000), and Suffolk (population 1,321,000) counties, but each major district within these counties may have minor local variations in their forms. The forms for New Jersey's Bergen (population 845,000) and Hudson (population 550,000) counties are specific to those counties.

My observations on-site were mostly gleaned from experiences in the Brooklyn Small Claims Court, which serves a population of 2,300,664. Indeed Brooklyn is considered to be the fourth largest "city" in the world. (Court statistics indicate that the small claims court in Queens heard the most cases of all the boroughs—an astounding 17,374 cases out of more than 60,000 claims filed throughout the five boroughs in 1996.)

It is said that "to be forewarned is to be forearmed." This guide is an attempt to help you provide yourself with that forewarning to be well armed.

Because I am not a lawyer, this guide is not meant to provide legal advice. Rather, it is a compendium of my experiences, designed to illuminate your understanding of the small claims court process. If you come across problems not addressed in this book consult a lawyer. You can have a 30-minute consultation with one for $25 by calling the Brooklyn or Manhattan Bar Association (see Appendix A for the addresses and telephone numbers of the bar associations of these boroughs and those of the other major geographic areas covered in this guide).

Finally, I recommend reading chapter 7, covering sections 1801-1815 of the New York City Civil Court Act. These sections cover in detail the rules that govern small claims (see Bibliography).

HOW THIS BOOK IS ORGANIZED

This book is divided into two parts: winning your judgment, which outlines the steps you would follow prior to the courtroom hearing and details what you may encounter at the hearing. The section on scenarios illuminates the unexpected twists and turns that can create anxiety for the uninitiated do-it-yourselfer. The second part, collecting on your judgment, demonstrates specifically how to put your judgment into effect. Your judgment gives you the right to subpoena information about the debtor, garnish the debtor's salary, place a levy on his bank account, seize his property, and mar his credit. This section gives special attention to the counterclaim and shows specifics on how to appeal a case to a higher court. Sometimes you will be referred to a specific appendix for the how-to on a particular objective, but usually you will be guided to a specific legal form because these are really the tools that drive the process forward. The forms do not bear page numbers because they are actual forms, and some of them may be copied and filed as they are. There are 70 forms labeled sequentially 1 through 70. Most of them have a back side that complements or supplements the front side.

Begin with Chapter 5: "Twelve Scenarios After You File an Initial Claim Form," which covers various unexpected twists and turns.

Chart I (see page 46) provides a schematic overview of the decisions and actions you will encounter when you use the small claims court as the collection tool. Chart II (see page 47) summarizes what you can effectively do to get the fee or debt you are owed once you have obtained a judgment in your favor.

Finally, the guide includes a detailed index to make it easier for you to find information.

It helps to be familiar with the basics when you navigate new waters...

What is a *judgment* anyway?

CHAPTER 2

The Legal Terms Step-by-Step

A good sailor knows the name of every part of his sailboat. The small claims process is laden with legal terms that are essential in navigating this rarely explored and generally incomprehensible environment. These terms are the foundation of the small claims process. By understanding these terms in the order they occur you can better grasp the process step-by-step. You shouldn't feel compelled to memorize them, just know that they are the trappings of the environment you are about to enter, so take some time to familiarize yourself with them, because they are the parts of the system you will be navigating in.

THE TERMS STEP-BY-STEP

ALLEGED DEBTOR:
Synonymous with the term defendant. The person to whom a service was provided or goods were sold and who wrongly refuses, fails, or neglects to pay for that service or those goods. Also includes a seller of faulty goods, or one who has injured or wronged you in any way for which money damages would compensate you for your loss.

CAUSE OF ACTION:
A *right of action* is the legal right to sue; a cause of action is what gives rise to a right of action. If the Statement of Claim (see page 6) fails to set forth a proper cause of action, it will be dismissed. "Jones failed to pay for the services I rendered pursuant to the retainer agreement between us" is a cause of action. [FORM 1] presents a list of causes of action.

CLAIM:
The assertion of a right to money or other property; all of the events and facts giving rise to a right enforceable in court.

STATUTE (PERIOD) OF LIMITATIONS:
The amount of time the law allows you to begin legal proceedings to collect the fee or debt that is due you under the contract (written or oral) with the debtor. After this time (typically six years) you lose your right to sue for collection.

SMALL CLAIM:
When one person sues another person in a small claims court. The maximum amount that can be awarded in New York is $3,000; the amount varies according to the state.

INDIVIDUAL CLAIM:
A small claim initiated by an individual, as long as that individual is not acting on behalf of or representing a corporation or partnership. It remains an

individual claim even when the claimant initiates a small claim against a corporation of any kind.

COMMERCIAL (CORPORATE) CLAIM

A small claim initiated by a corporation or partnership of any kind. A commercial claimant must have its principal office in the state where it desires to initiate suit. The claim remains a commercial claim even if the claimant initiates a claim against another corporation of any kind, or an individual who is not incorporated.

SMALL CLAIMS COURT:

A court that is usually a subdivision of civil court where one can sue for an amount not more than $3,000 (New York), $2,000 (New Jersey), $2,500 (Connecticut). Proceedings are informal, with parties usually representing themselves. A jury is never present. (In New York City the defendant can pay an additional fee of $55 to have the case heard and decided by a jury.) The suit cannot be for the return of property or the performance of services; money damages are the only form of restitution in small claims court.

PRO SE:

A Latin term meaning for self. In legal usage when this term is added to one's signature as in "Dr. Ted Rothstein, *Pro Se*," it means that the person is acting on behalf of himself in a legal capacity, or simply that he has not hired an attorney and is acting as such. See [FORMS 19, 25].

STATEMENT OF CLAIM:

Also referred to in this guide as the Initial Claim form—see [FORMS 1, 3, 4]. It is the first form that you file at the clerk's window. It signifies that you are an aggrieved party with a cause of action (a complaint) and you are seeking the legal remedy offered by way of a court hearing to obtain the payment due you.

INSTRUCTIONS TO THE CLAIMANT:

See [FORM 5]. The form the small claims court clerk gives you when you file the Statement of Claim (initial claim) form. It provides you with the official identification (index, docket) number of your case, the name of the defendant, and the date of your hearing.

PLAINTIFF (CLAIMANT):

The person who starts the small claims action. The plaintiff in a small claims action may bring an attorney with him to court to represent and advise him. The plaintiff may also represent himself (see *Pro Se* above).

DEFENDANT

The one who is sued and called upon to make satisfaction for a complaint filed by another—the defendant can also choose to represent himself or have an attorney represent him (see *Pro Se* above).

SUMMONS:

See Notice of Claim and Summons.

NOTICE OF CLAIM AND SUMMONS [FORM 6]:

The notice that the clerk at the small claims court window serves on (sends to) the person who you claim owes you money when you file the Statement of Claim (see [FORMS 1, 3, 4]). The summons requires the defendant to appear in court on a specified day and time to defend the claim referred to in the Notice of Claim and detailed in the Statement of Claim. The defendant's failure to appear can result in the penalty of having a judgment [FORM 14] entered against him. [FORM 6] is also the form you receive if the person you are suing makes a counterclaim against you.

DEFECTIVE SERVICE

As applied to serving the Notice of Claim (see above) on the defendant, detective service occurs when for one reason or another (incorrect or incomplete address) the notice could not be delivered to the defendant and was returned to the court clerk. Defective service may also refer to the service of other documents such as subpoenas. (See [FORM 42]).

COUNTERCLAIM:

When the defendant responds to the plaintiff's Statement of Claim by filing his own Statement of

Claim, in which he asserts a cause of action to oppose the plaintiff's claim; the counterclaim arises from or is logically related to the plaintiff's claim.

SUBPOENA FOR RECORDS, WITNESS, or INFORMATION:
A document that either the plaintiff or the defendant can obtain at minimal or no cost from the small claims court clerk's window. This form is a notice (demand-request) served on another person (or business entity) to compel the person to hand over documents he possesses [FORM 10], appear as a witness at the hearing [FORM 9], or provide information he may possess about a party's assets [FORM 22].

SERVE (as in "to serve a subpoena"):
To deliver in person by someone called a process server or have delivered by mail (certified, return receipt requested, or registered) a subpoena or other legal documents to a person or official representative of a business named in that document.

CALENDAR CALL:
In the courtroom the calling out of the names of the plaintiffs and defendants in each case (by an officer of the court) to determine if they are present at the hearing.

"APPLICATION" (as used in small claims court, Brooklyn, NY):
The word that, when called out by either the plaintiff or defendant in response to the calendar call for their case, means that the plaintiff or defendant wants to request a postponement of the hearing to a future date. The more widely used legal terms for postponement are *continuance* and *adjournment.*

"BY THE COURT" (as used in small claims court, Brooklyn, NY):
The words that, when called out by the plaintiff or the defendant in response to the calendar call for their case, request that the case will be heard by a judge (whose decision can be appealed, see Judge) rather than an arbitrator (whose decision is irrevocable).

JUDGE:
A public officer appointed to oversee and to administer the law in a court of justice; in some courts is called a magistrate or justice; the chief member of a court who has control of the proceedings and the decisions about questions of law or discretion. *Judge, Justice,* and *Court* are commonly used synonymously or interchangeably. The decision of a judge can be reversed by an appeal taken to a higher court. (See Arbitrator below.)

ARBITRATOR:
Usually a volunteer lawyer in a small claims court who hears the facts put forth by the plaintiff and/or the defendant, in order to determine if the plaintiff's grievance is such that he deserves to have a judgment (decision) awarded in his favor. The arbitrator's decision is not appealable and may be vacated only in rare situations. These include, for example, corruption, fraud, misconduct, or partiality of a supposedly neutral arbitrator. Other situations are set forth in Article 75 of the New York Civil Practice Law and Rules. (See Judge and Vacate.)

HEARING:
A proceeding that takes place in front of an arbitrator or judge (usually an arbitrator in small claims court) wherein evidence is taken for the purpose of determining issues of fact upon which the legal conclusion (decision) will be based.

HEARSAY:
A term applied to testimony, given by the plaintiff or defendant or any third-party witness, based on what someone else said or wrote, rather than experienced firsthand, and generally inadmissible because the person who said or wrote it is not present to be cross-examined.

OBJECTION:
A device that permits the plaintiff or defendant, believing that the witness, testimony, or questions being asked are improper or inadmissible, to stop the proceeding and request that the judge rule on that which is in question. It is accomplished by saying the words "I object" out loud. The objection is

important in that it will appear on the record for purposes of appeal.

INQUEST:

The name given to a trial (hearing) of an issue of fact, when the plaintiff alone presents the case to an arbitrator or judge because the defendant failed to appear.

(NOTICE OF) JUDGMENT [FORM 14]:

The decision of the judge or arbitrator after all the facts have been presented. In small claims court: a monetary award to the plaintiff; a statement that the plaintiff's claim is dismissed (judgment in favor of the defendant); or a monetary award to the defendant on the merits of his counterclaim.

SUBSTANTIAL JUSTICE:

Justice administered according to the rules of substantive law, which is that part of law that creates, defines, and regulates the rights and duties of parties, as opposed to procedural law, which pertains to and prescribes the practice, method, or legal machinery by which substantive law is applied. The concept of *substantial justice* directs judges and arbitrators to set aside procedural hurdles, which might otherwise dictate a harsh result in favor of a right sense of justice.

DEFAULT JUDGMENT:

A judgment entered in favor of the plaintiff when the defendant fails to appear in court for the hearing. This judgment is awarded after an inquest on the merits of the evidence presented by the plaintiff, which may include oral argument, documentation, and witnesses.

EXECUTION:

The completion of the legal process of enforcing (by a sheriff, marshal, or constable) the collection of the monetary award granted in the judgment.

GARNISHMENT OR INCOME EXECUTION (ATTACHMENT):

The form (court order) provided to the sheriff, marshal, or constable by which he is empowered to initiate a garnishment (seizing, attachment) of part of the debtor's salary to satisfy the judgment that the plaintiff has won. (See [FORMS 18, 19]).

PROPERTY EXECUTION:

The form (court order) provided to the sheriff, marshal, or constable by which he is empowered to seize and sell a debtor's property or remove from the debtor's bank account that sum of money that satisfies the judgment the plaintiff has won. (It is also called a Writ of Execution, an Execution Against Property, and an Execution with Notice to Garnishee—see [FORM 25]).

SHERIFF:

The chief executive and administrative officer of a county (Brooklyn, Queens, Nassau, Westchester, Bergen, and so on), chosen by popular election. His principal duties are to aid the criminal and civil courts of record, such as executing judgments, serving process, summoning juries, and holding judicial sales. In New York City, chief sheriff is a mayoral appointment and borough sheriff is a civil position obtained by a civil service test.

MARSHAL:

The name of a law officer in some cities (i.e., the City of New York) having powers and duties corresponding generally to those of a sheriff or constable.

VACATE:

To render void, to set aside, as "to vacate a judgment." A default judgment may be vacated—for example, when the defendant claims he didn't receive the Notice of Claim and Summons or when either party has a reasonable excuse for failure to appear on a scheduled court date. Consequently, the judgment is nullified and a new hearing date will be scheduled.

APPEAL:

When you believe that a decision made by the judge in small claims court is incorrect or substantially unjust (see Substantial Justice), you may appeal the case. That is, you may request that a higher court review the record of your hearing for the purpose of obtaining a reversal of the lower court's decision or the granting of a new trial (among other remedies you can seek).

NOTICE OF APPEAL [FORM 27]:
The first document you must file in order to secure your right to appeal. In New York, it must be filed 30 days from the time you receive the Notice of Judgment from the small claims court.

TRANSCRIPT:
An official copy of the record of the proceedings in hearing or trial. A word-for-word typing of everything that was said "on the record" during the trial—that is, all the spoken words of the judge, plaintiff, defendant, and other witnesses, in written form.

TRANSCRIPT OF THE RECORD:
A transcript that has been specially prepared ("perfected" and "settled") to allow the appellate court to review the history of the case.

PERFECT:
As in "to perfect a transcript of the record" is to correct any errors that may have been introduced at the hearing or by the person who transcribed them.

SETTLE:
As in "to settle a transcript of the record" is a formal process whereby the plaintiff and the defendant meet before the judge who heard their case to work out any disagreements regarding the accuracy of the transcript.

BRIEF (LEGAL BRIEF):
A formally structured, written argument, concentrating on the facts at issue, and the legal points and authorities, which a lawyer or *pro se* plaintiff or defendant uses to present a case to either an appellate or trial court. It includes a statement of the questions of law involved, the law that the lawyer should apply, and the result that the brief writer desires.

APPELLATE TERM COURT:
The division of the supreme court that hears cases on appeal from the small claims court (in New York State).

CHAPTER 3

Deciding Whether Small Claims Court Is the Right Approach for You

Regardless of what your small claim is, if you are faced with the problem of collecting a debt or fee, you have alternatives. One of the most commonly chosen options is to turn over the problem to a collection agency, a tactic I employed several times without much success.

Pay no attention to the fact that they take 20% to 25% if their collection efforts are successful. According to the *Nilson Report*, an industry newsletter published in Oxnard, California, collection agencies retrieve a mere 7.5 cents out of every dollar they attempt to collect.

Savvy debtors are well aware that they are amply protected from certain abusive practices of collection agencies by the 1977 Fair Debt Collection Practices Act. As a consequence of the act, while an individual creditor may call a person at work or at home after 9:00 P.M. or threaten to sue, a collection agency is legally prohibited from doing the same.

My experiences with collection agencies demonstrate that they are capable of collecting the fees or debts that are generally collectible to begin with. However, the small claims court system enables people to "get the gelt" for themselves without recourse to a collection agency, which will pocket an unearned share of the money.

For the committed do-it-yourself (*pro se*) creditor, a review of your circumstances is a prerequisite. Inherent in any decision whether or not to commence a legal battle or flee from it are some basic considerations that must be examined. It is foolhardy to engage in a small claims litigation without examining the factors that will have some bearing on whether you will ultimately prevail.

Insofar as possible you should review the factors that may determine (1) whether you have a reasonable chance of winning a judgment in your favor and (2) whether you have a reasonable chance of collecting. Here are some considerations that may have a bearing on the outcome.

CONSIDERATIONS IN CHOOSING NOT TO INITIATE A SMALL CLAIMS COURT ACTION

The considerations listed here are applicable to all potential claimants. I believe that many claimants should and will avoid pursuing the small claims court approach simply because their personality type renders them highly uncomfortable in situations that may involve direct confrontation. It is for that same reason that the service provider is often loath to actually call the debtor himself to request payment, an elementary approach that is often effective. In fact I highly recommend such an action as a first step because what the debtor says during that call may well provide the incentives to either initiate or refrain from initiating an action.

You will probably want to avoid small claims court if:

- Your debtor is a lawyer—specifically, a collection lawyer.
- You are not willing to accept the small claims court maximum ($3,000 New York, $2,000 New Jersey, $2,500 Connecticut) as sufficient compensation.
- Your debtor has no assets (i.e., is not employed, has no property, has no car or checking account, or has already named you as creditor in his bankruptcy action).
- You imagine the debtor is homicidal or sociopathic.
- You may be vulnerable to a counterclaim with some substantive merit, or you believe the debtor may be able to support bringing a speculative counterclaim with adequate evidence, including documentation and testimony from witnesses or experts.
- There may be a justifiable reason for the nonpayment which, if the defendant were to document it at a hearing, would allow him to prevail. Moreover, never underestimate your adversary's ability to fabricate the truth. Gather your supporting documents thoroughly, as though he were going to be present at the hearing with evidence supporting his position. (My experiences indicate that the defendant will show up 5% to 10% of the time and then only because he believes he is legally obliged to be present, rarely to contest the validity of your bill.)
- The debtor has referred many patients/clients/customers and by forgiving the bill your return will be even more referrals.
- Your debtor is aware of facts, or even rumors about you, that could be brought to light by a public proceeding.
- If you feel an investigation by the Office of Professional Discipline, or the peer review committee of your local professional association, licensing authorities, or other patient, client, or customer claim review board will not vindicate you.

I recall being paid with an American Express card for the service I provided. The bill was in dispute and my patient stopped payment. In this case I was eventually paid, but I had to spend much time explaining to the review board person at American Express that my charge was appropriate for the services I rendered.

- You don't have an accurate home or work address for the debtor and you're not willing to spend $100 for a skip-trace agency to locate your debtor's place of employment. (The minimum fee is $25 to initiate a search, whether it's successful or not.)
- You don't know the defendant's social security number (not a must, but can be helpful in locating a person or his assets).
- You don't have a signed contract with the defendant.
- It doesn't bother you to lose the amount of money involved, or it's not worth the time and trouble. (However, if you considered buying or have bought this book, you are just the person it does bother.)
- Your records, documents, and contracts are not sufficient to prove your claim. Of course this does not preclude you from bringing a claim. Insufficient documentation has caused me to lose a case I should have won, but just initiating a claim that never reached hearing status prompted more than one debtor to make payment.

CONFRONTATION: AN ENLIGHTENING STORY

In more than one instance, on the night of my court hearing, I arrived at the court and sat down to await the "calendar call." As I surveyed the scene, I realized I had unintentionally seated myself next to my patient. At first I was startled, but managed to seize the moment, and began to exchange pleasantries. In so doing, I discovered that my patient had come to court that night, not to contest, but to arrange a settlement. He had been too embarrassed to contact us by mail or telephone at the office. We continued on to the hearing where the arbitrator formally witnessed the settlement agreement and wrote the terms of our settlement into the judgment.

This event reinforced my belief that in some cases the only way to confront the nonpayment issue is in a formal environment such as that offered by the small claims court. In essence you are fully awakening the debtor to responsibility for his bill and the seriousness of your intentions to collect it.

CONSIDERATIONS AND CRITERIA IN CHOOSING TO INITIATE A SMALL CLAIMS COURT ACTION

As noted previously, small claims actions involve the settlement of disputes by a demand for money not in excess of the limit that each state puts on its small claims court (New York, $3,000; New Jersey, $2,000; Connecticut, $2,500). You may not file a small claim with the objective of obtaining performance of a service or the return of property.

The following list may help you decide if your claim falls under the realm of the small claims court. The following are typical of small claims:

- breach of written or oral contract;
- claims for return of money used as down payment;
- claims for property damage resulting from a motor vehicle accident;
- claims for damage or loss of property left in someone's care;
- consumer complaints for faulty merchandise or claims under warranties;
- claims for payment of work or services performed;
- claims for faulty workmanship by a tradesman;
- claims based on bad checks; and
- claims between a landlord and tenant for rent, money damages, or for the return of all or part of your security deposit.

A more complete list of complaints may be seen on [FORM 1]. The author's typical complaint is "nonpayment for professional services rendered."

OBSERVATION *The criteria listed below are pertinent to all providers of services and sellers of goods, but in some ways relate specifically to the nature of the author's profession and the peculiarities of his personality and way of doing business. For instance, he might choose to initiate a claim against one debtor and be motivated by one criterion alone. With a different debtor, multiple criteria might come into play.*

- The debtor owes you more than $500. In my office that means my patient received five bills and ignored them while receiving two or perhaps three adjustments of his braces. Today, the computer report that outlines my daily appointment schedule also highlights any patients in arrears, and both I and the front desk manager are able to see exactly how many dollars overdue the patient is in each of the 30-, 60-, and 90-day categories respectively. Persons in the 60- and 90-day categories would then receive more focused attention and efforts would be made to discuss the problem with them.
- The debtor owes you nearly $3,000—the limit for small claims in New York. The limit used to be $2,000. If this debtor's debt approaches the small claim's limit, initiate your suit now. Debt beyond $3,000 must be sacrificed or else you must sue in civil court. I recommend an attorney for that. I allowed patients to accumulate debt in excess of $2,000 on two occasions in my professional career. The first time the patient declared bankruptcy; the second time the patient left for parts unknown, and the skip-trace agency I hired is still looking for her.
- The debtor has a 60- or 90-day balance for at least 3 months. The chances of collecting an account over 90 days gets progressively slimmer with each month beyond 90 days.
- The debtor's previous commitments to pay were not honored. Every attempt at collection should end with the debtor's explicit oral (or even better, written) commitment to make payment in part or in total by a specific date. Furthermore, every commitment should be documented on the debtor's ledger card. One or more disappointments should be taken as a telltale sign of an impending problem.
- Your debtor has changed his telephone to an

unlisted number. This criterion coupled with an account balance in excess of $500 for more than 90 days galvanizes me to mail a letter that starts, "Regarding your bill...," and I write beneath my return address the phrase "Forwarding and Address Correction Requested." This technique lets you know if you have a genuine problem when your postman returns the letter to you, and it says "No Forwarding Address."

- Your debtor has changed address and place of employment or both. This happens all the time, but if you accepted a personal check for $850 as "payment in full" and the check comes back to your office marked "Account Closed" and the telephone number is now unlisted, you should begin to have that "time to take action" feeling.

- The messages you leave on the answering machine or with the secretary as well as your written communications are ignored. This criterion alone once caused me to initiate a claim.

- Debtor does not respond within 10 days to your second, "final," really serious "pay me now or I'm going to small claims court" letter.

    Without another moment's delay turn to [FORM 1]—the Initial Claim form in this guide and complete it. Call the small claims court of your preference (see Appendix B) to find out which date is being given out on the summonses they are "selling," and send the most expendable member of your team to buy a summons from the clerk at the small claims court window. Better yet, because you are allowed to buy two summonses, search your records for another debtor and really make your day in court.

- You have reason to believe your debtor is in the process of moving to a more remote location.

    Your last bill for $675 is returned to you stamped "Addressee moved—no forwarding address," or when you call the home you hear the robotic operator say: "The number you have called has been disconnected." These are telling indications for some action on your part.

- The debtor claims he does not owe the amount in dispute, but is not willing to provide evidence such as canceled checks even after you have offered to pay the expense of a bank record search.

E.B. insisted relentlessly she paid the balance of $1,150 on her daughter's bill. "Show me the canceled checks," I said. "It's not cheap to have the bank do a record search on an account older than six months—I can't afford it," was the reply. To which I responded, "I'll reimburse you if it turns out you paid me." Result: Her salary was attached. See [FORMS 18, 19] and Appendix G.

- The statute of limitations has not expired. Your debtor owes the money for a long time, but less than six years, the statute of limitations for payment due on contract—(i.e., how long after the date the amount was due under the contract before you lose your legal right to initiate a suit).

    The moral of this criterion is this: Act promptly to obtain the judgment and take significant action to obtain payment. If you seem to be at an impasse in obtaining payment, put the judgment you were awarded in your "Judgments" folder because things happen and your judgment remains in effect for 20 years.

- You have that "helpless-no next step-dead-end" feeling.

    It's not without reason you feel that way. Pull out the ledger card where you entered the history of the financial transactions and you'll know why (if you kept good records of the debtor's commitments and excuses). I remember patient D.P., whose ledger card resembled a rap sheet. With each hard luck story I renegotiated the contract downward, and then she disappeared into thin air.

....
PLANNING TIP *All calls and letters to the debtor should be documented. In addition, the debtor's commitments (promises of amounts and the dates by which the debtor will pay) should be documented. This enables you to see the pattern of events unfolding before you and permits you to plan your strategy.*
....

WHY DO IT YOURSELF (*PRO SE*)?

- It's not the principle of the thing! You care about the money—it's your vacation, mortgage payment, and so on, and you want it because it's due you. You're angry that still another person is trying to avoid paying you. You are now determined to do something decisive about the money that is due you.

- Your fear that the other party will bring a lawyer and you will be defenseless is unfounded:
  (1) because lawyers are very expensive, and
  (2) because my experiences in over 100 cases are proof that the debtor seldom comes to court and none has ever brought a lawyer.

- Even if they have legal representation, it does not imply a disadvantage because it's your proof that wins the case. Besides which, few and far between are the lawyers who would take the case if it were a small claim—it's not worth it for the lawyer.

- You want to retake control of your destiny. Attorneys typically charge $150 to $200 per hour. Here are some billing items you might see: prehearing case preparation; the time spent with you on the telephone (same rate as above!); research, travel time, and other expenses incurred (postage, copies, and so on); posthearing collection letters written to the defendant and legal forms prepared for the marshal or sheriff to reel in your court award. And never forget that the attorney's billing meter keeps running even while he's waiting for your name (among 60 to 90 other names) to be called in court or for your hearing to begin. Finally, you may sometimes find your hearing has to be postponed, adjourned, or completed at yet another court session. As you mentally watch the attorney's bill absorbing your court award, your enthusiasm for the process will evaporate.

- If you and the debtor both bring lawyers, the judge has the discretion to refuse to hear the case in small claims court. I have witnessed a case that ended exactly that way: The parties were advised by the judge to have their case heard in the next higher court, which is civil court.

....
WARNING *For residents of New Jersey and Connecticut it makes no difference because their small claims cases are always heard during day court. In New York, small claims cases typically start at 6:30 P.M., while civil court cases are held during the day, which means you are obliged to take time off from work.*
....

- The hearing itself is informal and does not require that you conform to a strict set of rules, such as those an attorney is expected to abide by in a higher court.

- Your collection agency isn't aggressive or effective enough.

- The collection attorney wants 35% to 50% of the collection.

- You're willing to go to the court and do the work yourself—indeed you really wanted to be a lawyer in the first place.

- You know exactly where the debtor works or banks and/or what property he owns. This is the best reason of the lot. The game's over; you won.

- In New York you can now sue for up to $3,000 per claim and as many as two, three, and five people at a time depending on the county court you are suing in. In brief, it's worthwhile. (Nationwide, the amount you can sue for ranges from $2,000 in New Jersey to $5,000 in Colorado.)

- You have a collection of accounts receivable amounting to thousands of dollars and you are angry.

- Finally, you should file a small claim because you put your heart and soul into providing what the customer requested, or you helped someone with a loan when they really needed it. You really don't care about the money—it's the principle of the thing. Besides, now you have a step-by-step guide book with all the forms, so if you don't act, you will not be able to forgive yourself.

WHEN YOU SHOULD CONSULT AN ATTORNEY

There are times when it may be necessary or advisable to consult an attorney. For example, if your case involves personal injury and medical expense. Also if your case involves damages resulting from a traffic accident. If the defendant is insured, he probably will be represented by an attorney provided by the insurance company, and you may also wish to have an attorney. Finally, if you have difficulty filling in the forms or have unanswered questions about preparing your case, you should see an attorney.

THE KIT OF FORMS FOR SMALL CLAIMS COURT BY STATE: NEW YORK, NEW JERSEY, CONNECTICUT

This compilation of forms should help you in every stage of the process to recover payment due you. The forms are copies of actual documents, some of which you may copy and use as is. The forms are both utilitarian and educational. You have them right at hand, so you don't have to expend energy obtaining the forms from the small claims court clerk. Furthermore, some have been completed to show you how it is done. For example, the blank T 239 Income Execution form [FORM 18] may be difficult to read, no less to understand. Once you see it filled in [FORM 19], it is easy to read and comprehend. I have seen the clerk at the small claims court window reject a form as easy as the Initial Claim form [FORM 1] because it was not completed correctly.

The forms are presented in approximately the same order of need as if you were actually proceeding to a recovery of a specific payment due for services rendered or goods sold and delivered. While many of them can simply be copied, others may have to be initially purchased for a small sum. The kit includes among others the following forms: (The complete list of forms can be seen on pages 140–247).

New York:
- Initial (Statement of) Claim form (NY)—a form for further copies
- Initial (Statement of) Claim form (NY) for those who are incorporated or for professional corporations—a form for further copies
- Initial Claim form—a completed sample
- Instruction to Claimant form indicating the index number, date, and time of your court session—a document the clerk gives you upon filing your Initial Claim form
- A Notice of Claim and Summons to appear in court (what the debtor receives after you file your Statement of Claim)
- Subpoena for Records and Affidavit of Service for the Subpoena—an example of an actual form that was completed and served
- Instructions for Service of the Subpoena
- Notice of Judgment

- Sample letter sent to a debtor after receiving a judgment
- Sample montage of court papers sent to a defendant either prior to or after the plaintiff received a judgment in his favor
- An actual Transcript of Judgment to be filed in the county clerk's office
- A blank specimen T 239 Income Execution form—this document empowers the marshal to compel your debtor's employer to begin salary garnishment.
- A completed T 239 form—an example of an actual completed form
- Information Subpoena and Restraining Notice showing the questions a bank must respond to before freezing your debtor's assets
- A specimen B 320 form showing how to fill in an Execution with Notice to Garnishee; this document empowers the marshal or sheriff to freeze and seize the assets of your debtor's checking, saving, or certificate of deposit account up to the amount of his debt
- Completed B 320 form to demonstrate how it is filled in
- A sample specimen B 110 form showing how an attorney filled in a General Release Form—Individual; this document, provided to the debtor after he pays you, is your acknowledgment of his payment to you
- A completed example of Form B 493 stating your intention to discontinue your litigation in view of a mutually agreed upon settlement
- A legal excerpt copied directly from the original text supporting your legal right to have the debtor provide you with information about where he banks and where he is employed (useful only when he appears in court)
- A completed specimen of Blumberg Form T 471 (Notice of Appeal), the first form you must file (within 30 days of the time you receive the judge's decision from your hearing) if you want to appeal a decision
- An affidavit (a sworn statement) submitted to the county clerk's office supporting your motion (request) to have the Civil Court of the City of New York recognize your out-of-state judgment and

attesting that you received your judgment after trial (the defendant was present at the hearing)

New Jersey:
- Initial (Statement of) Claim form (Bergen County, NJ)—a form for further copies
- Initial (Statement of) Claim form (Hudson County, NJ)—a form for further copies
- A notice indicating that the Summons and Complaint could not be served on the debtor
- The Notice of Appeal form used by would-be *pro se* appellants
- The income execution forms supplied on request from the Bergen County Court, consisting of a Notice of Motion for Wage Execution and an Order, Certification and Execution Against Earnings
- A blank Statement of Docketing form (Hudson County, NJ); when registered in the Superior Court in Trenton, NJ, it permanently registers the judgment you won statewide as part of the property execution procedure
- A fictitious completed example of a Notice of Motion (for Summary Judgment) form, that is, a request (motion) from a *pro se* plaintiff, asking the judge for a summary judgment in order that the plaintiff may have his out-of-state judgment recognized in New Jersey

Connecticut:
- Instructions to the plaintiff regarding procedural rules for using the Small Claims Division of Superior Court G.A. 1. (Stamford-Norwalk, CT)
- The front page of Connecticut's Initial Claim form including instructions how to fill in the blanks
- A copy of the form used in Connecticut to garnish a person's salary—Wage Execution Proceedings Application, Order, Execution
- A copy of Connecticut's Wage Execution form demonstrating how to fill it out

- A copy of a form used in Connecticut that must accompany the wage execution when the person you are suing is not incorporated, entitled Exemption and Modification Claim Form Wage Execution
- A copy of the form used in Connecticut to place a levy on a debtor's bank account—Bank Execution Proceedings Application and Execution
- UCC-1 (Uniform Commercial Code) form—the form used in Connecticut to register a judgment on a person's credit report (Experian, formerly TRW; Equifax; Transunion) and put a lien on their property statewide

PLANNING TIP *Blumberg forms can be obtained from Blumberg Office Products, 80 Exchange Place, New York, NY 10004; (212) 509-1203, Fax (212) 344-4141, (800) 221-2972. Some large stationery stores also sell these forms for $1 to $2 each.*

In New Jersey, forms can be obtained from All State Legal Supplies at 3 Commerce Drive in Cranford, NJ 07016; (908) 272-0800. They offer the service of an in-house form attorney who can help to clarify some questions about New Jersey forms (extension 232). Large stationery stores, especially those around the Hackensack and Jersey City court areas, stock many of these forms. One such store is Silvers on Newark Avenue in Jersey City, (201) 963-1700.

Both Blumberg and All State will mail you a catalogue of their forms as well.

In Brooklyn, you can obtain forms from Court Street Office Supplies located on 44 Court Street, within three blocks of all the courts, (718) 625-5571 or (718) 625-5778.

Finally, in Connecticut, you can have the necessary forms mailed to you at no cost. See Appendix B.

CHAPTER 4

Preparing and Filing a Claim

Т he process can be broken down into four basic parts: preparation, filling out the Initial Claim form, filing the Initial Claim form, and having your hearing in small claims court.

PREPARATION

Above all, never be reluctant to call the court clerk to obtain new information or verify current beliefs. When you call, state who you are and what your objective is. For example: "Hello this is Ms. Demonet, I am an individual, nonincorporated person, and I live in Downtown Brooklyn; the party I want to sue in small claims court is an incorporated entity who resides in Queens. What is the closest court to me in which I can file an Initial Claim form, and what is the fee for filing?" Appendix A and B will provide you with all the telephone numbers for the various courts as well as other essential information to make the going smoother.

Before filing your claim, verify the following information:

- That the person you are suing is not a minor— i.e., under 18 years old;
- That the person you are suing is the person who is responsible for the payment of your bill or can be held coresponsible for the payment of your bill;
- The correct name and address where the person you are suing works or where the person lives;

you must have at least one of these two items, otherwise the Initial Claim form cannot be filed. (A post office box number is not acceptable.)

PLANNING TIP *One approach that I have used successfully is a search of the voter registration records: Every county has an office for its board of elections, which keeps a record of the name, address, and birth date of every registered voter in that county. Under the Freedom of Information Act you are legally entitled to have this information. You can go to the office of the Superintendent of the Board of Elections (or mail in your request, cost $1 to $3) and ask for the current address of the plaintiff. At the borough office in Manhattan (200 Varick St., 10th fl., New York, NY 10014, (212) 886 3800) you can do a computer search of the voter records of all five boroughs of New York City (free of charge). In Brooklyn this same search can be done at the Board of Elections at 345 Adams St., 4th fl., New York, NY 11201, (718) 330-2250, also at no cost and at the Board of Elections in the Bronx, Queens, and Staten Island. Readers may turn to question 11 in Chapter 9—Questions and Answers of this manual for other helpful tips.*

- The person's employer's name and address. You must have this item, or obtain it later, to garnish the debtor's wages.

• The correct name of the person you intend to sue.

If you are suing an individual, be certain you use the correct first and last name. Nicknames and initials are not accepted. On the other hand, if you are suing a corporation you may wish to sue both the corporation and its manager-owner.

If you are suing an (unincorporated) proprietorship, you would sue John Smith d/b/a (doing business as) Smith Hardware. The name of the person under which an unincorporated proprietorship is registered can be found in the county clerk's office in which the business is located. All legitimate business owners must register their businesses. The owner must file an X201 Business Certificate, also known as a d/b/a/ or assumed name certificate, in which he provides the name of the principal owner(s) and the real name under which the business operates. For example in the county clerk's office in Brooklyn you can use the computers they provide at no cost to access the information on the business certificate if you have either the name of the business or its address. The clerk's office started computerizing this information beginning March 1992. If however a business was opened prior to this time, it was registered by name in alphabetical order in large registry books, which makes it a bit more difficult to gather the real name of the business and its owner. You must first get an index number from the large registry book and then go to another nearby room to pull the business certificate to see it. See Appendix A for the addresses and telephone numbers of all the county clerk's offices. In Connecticut such information is also kept on record in the town hall.

When you sue a corporation or partnership, keep in mind that some of them use assumed names and that obtaining the correct name of the entity will make later proceeding much easier.

....

NOTE *When you sue a corporation, you must first obtain the name under which the corporation is registered. This information is readily available from the Secretary of State, who keeps records of all corporations doing business in the state. (See Appendix A).*

....

• That the court you want to sue in has the jurisdiction, or power to hear the case, and whether there are other more convenient courts that you could use.

Rule 1: If you, the plaintiff, rendered your services in, or are a resident of, any of the five boroughs (counties) of New York City and the defendant either lives, works, or does business in the same borough, you must file your claim in that borough. For example, you are a professional with an office in Queens County, NY, where you provided a service for a person who didn't pay your bill and who also lives in Queens. You would begin your case by filing your claim in Queens.

Rule 2: If you live, work, or transact business in any borough of New York City and the defendant lives, works, or does business in a different borough of New York City, then you can choose either the small claims court in your borough or the small claims court in the other person's borough to file your claim (whichever is the most conveniently located). The form used for all the five boroughs is identical. For example, you live in Brooklyn, NY, and you lent money to a friend who lives in Queens County who refuses to repay you. In this instance you could file in Brooklyn or Queens.

Rule 3: If, however, you live, work, or do business in one of the five boroughs (counties) and the defendant lives, works, or does business in a county other than the counties of New York City, you must file your claim in the court(s) of the county that has legal jurisdiction over that person. For example, if you live in the Bronx, NY, and do some repair work for a person who lives White Plains, NY (Westchester County), you have to file your claim in the court in White Plains.

Rule 4: When you or the defendant lives or works outside of the five boroughs of New York City you must file your claim where the defendant lives, works, or transacted the business. For example, if you live in Jersey City, NJ (Hudson County) and buy a television set in a store in Manhattan, NY (New York County) that is defective, but the seller refuses to take back the set, you would file your claim in the small claims court in Manhattan.

Rule 4 also applies if both parties live, work, or do business outside of New York City. For example, you are a house painter and your business is registered in Great Neck, NY (Nassau County, Long Island). You finish a job for person whose house is located in Deer Park, NY (Township of Babylon in Suffolk County, Long Island). You must file your claim in Suffolk's Second District Court, the court that has jurisdiction over all towns in the Township of Babylon. (You file your claim in the county court that has jurisdiction over the defendant.)

When in doubt, call the small claims court clerk of the court you think could have jurisdiction and ask. This simple expedient will save you an unnecessary trip to a courthouse where the clerk will tell you of your error. Even worse, if the claim is incorrectly accepted at the small claims court window, the defendant can request that the case be dismissed at the hearing because the court does not have jurisdiction over your claim.

A notable exception is Westchester County, which is composed of 6 cities, 19 towns, and 19 villages. Each city, town, and village is an independent jurisdiction. You have the option to file the Initial Claim form in the court of the city, town, or village where the debtor lives or works (whichever is most convenient to you). However, you may also file the Initial Claim form in any one of the six major city courts in the county of Westchester (see Appendix A under WESTCHESTER for a list of those cities). Many, if not all, of these courts permit you to mail in the Initial Claim form, which you can obtain by request over the telephone, or by mail (enclose a self-addressed, stamped envelope and state if you are suing as an individual or a corporation). If in doubt about the proper court to file your claim in, call any small claims court in the county where the debtor lives (see Appendix A) and get the advice of a small claims court clerk.

NOTE *See Appendix A: SUFFOLK COUNTY for exceptions involving plaintiffs who are incorporated individuals or entities.*

Be sure of the following:
- That you have the debtor's correct Social Security number (very helpful, especially in beginning the garnishment process and locating the place of employment and other useful information)
- That you have a proper Statement of Claim (cause of action): See [FORM 1] for a list of most, if not all, of the causes of action in small claims court
- That you have assembled the proof that you are going to place before the judge or arbitrator to substantiate your claim of monies owed to you. A winning case can be built using:

1. Signed contract or documents showing the agreed upon fee for the service or cost of the goods; lacking a valid contract, a written version of your oral agreement with the defendant
2. The defendant's ledger card (statement of the account) showing payments made and the balance due
3. Canceled checks and checks returned for insufficient funds, account closed, etc.
4. Treatment or account transaction information
5. All bills and receipts that were incurred as well as any other documents that are relevant to the case (e.g., letters to and from the plaintiff or defendant)
6. Witnesses who are willing to come to court to give relevant testimony on your behalf as well as witnesses who may be unwilling to be present (see Subpoena to Testify)
7. An itemized bill or invoice, receipted or marked paid; or itemized estimates from at least two other places of business for plaintiffs who are seeking reimbursement for replacement of goods or repair of the damage or defective workmanship
8. Photographs when applicable
9. The item or object in dispute.

If possible, the plaintiff should make efforts to identify the reasons why the defendant is refusing to pay the bill or otherwise compensate him. This will help the plaintiff determine what is the best proof to document his claim. In my early case presentations at hearings before the arbitrator I would bring far more than was needed. Slowly I learned that arbitrators were not inclined to examine dental models, X rays, and photographic documentation. In plaintiff-defendant cases where workmanship is at issue, if the defendant actually comes to the hearing to contest your claim, he must support his claim in a substantive way. That cannot be done by simply making allegations or offering letters obtained from so-called experts. The experts must be present to give testimony. In essence each provider of a service must decide the nature of the proof required to support his case. Rarely, if ever, will that proof need to be of a technical nature, at least not in small claims court.

- Finally, it is wise to have recently sent a request for payment of services; regular mail will do. Certified, return receipt will prove they received it.

WARNING *If you are an incorporated entity or business, it is mandatory that you first mail (certified, return receipt requested) a "demand letter" to the debtor. In the demand letter you make your request for payment and state your intention to sue if you are not paid (see [FORM 2]); then you may file the Initial Claim form [FORM 3]. The demand letter must be sent at least 10 days before filing the Initial Claim form. A letter that is sent more than 180 days before filing the claim is not valid. There is an affidavit on the back of the Initial Claim form that you must sign attesting to the fact that you have sent a demand letter.*

Once you have found out the information listed above and have assembled your supporting evidence you are prepared to initiate your claim.

FILLING OUT YOUR INITIAL (STATEMENT OF) CLAIM FORM

With few exceptions I have filed my claims in Brooklyn Small Claims Court, mainly because it is conveniently located to my office and my patients either live, work, or do business in the five boroughs of New York City. Consequently I keep a completed Initial Claim form (see [FORM 4]) on hand for when the occasion arises. Other readers may need to file a claim in a court other than Brooklyn, and will therefore require the Initial Claim form of that court (see [FORMS 1, 34,

35] to see examples of Initial Claim forms from the small claims courts of Brooklyn, Mount Kisco, and Pelham in Westchester).

PLANNING TIP *The forms of specific courts can be obtained with a written request to the small claims court clerk that includes a self-addressed stamped envelope. The request must state whether you are suing as an individual (a nonincorporated entity) or as an incorporated entity. This will determine the type of form you receive and the filing fee you pay. When you request the Initial Claim form ask for any instruction forms or pamphlets that can guide you. One advantage of going to the small claims office and obtaining, filling in, and filing the Initial Claim form is that you find out immediately if you made a mistake.*

Except for Connecticut and the City of New York, the Initial Claim form differs in appearance depending on the small claims court from which it is sent. Some Initial Claim forms appear complex and can be intimidating at first blush. However, all ask for only seven pieces of basic information.

Because you may make mistakes in filling out the form, make a few copies of it for practice, then complete each line with exactly the information that is being asked for—no more and no less (see [FORM 4]).

You must provide only these seven pieces of information:

- Your name (the plaintiff), address, and telephone number
- Name of the person or business you are suing (the defendant) and his address and telephone number if you can provide it. (The address you provide is the place where the small claims court will serve the summons. A post office box is never acceptable.)

WARNING *The name of the person or business you are suing must be the exact, correct legal name. If you make a mistake and list the wrong name you may not get your money. You may not use abbreviations, initials or nicknames: Richard Jones cannot be sued as R. Jones or Dick Jones. The same is true of business names.*

- The amount for which you are suing[1]
- The date the payment was first due (the date of occurrence of the event or transaction)
- The reason for your suit (the cause of action):

    "Balance (or payment) due for professional services rendered" or "goods sold and delivered" or simply "failure to return money." (Spare yourself the unnecessary trouble of writing a lengthy and detailed description of the problem. You may ask the clerk at the small claims court window to help you if you cannot find the words to state your cause of action.) See [FORM 1] for a list of them.

- The current date
- Your signature
- In Connecticut you can also attach any documentation (proof or evidence) that will help you to substantiate your claim.[2]

    Many claim forms, those from Connecticut in particular, include a section in which you are asked to acknowledge that to the best of your knowledge the person you are suing is not a member of the military services.

PLANNING TIP *You are allowed to initiate up to two small claims actions at a time (three in Manhattan and five in Staten Island) at a cost of $10 per "individual" claim not in excess of $1,000, and $15 for any claim between $1,000 and $3,000. Avail yourself of the opportunity to bring two or more claims whenever possible. (See Appendix A for all other courts.)*

EFFICIENCY IN FILING YOUR INITIAL CLAIM FORM AND SCHEDULING YOUR HEARING

Call your small claims court office the day before you intend to file your claim and inquire what date the small claims court summonses are being issued for on that date.[3] This information alerts you to possible scheduling conflicts. You don't want to find out at the last minute that either you or the person you're sending to represent you can't make it that night, thus forcing you to have to refile your claim and waste five to seven weeks! Before getting on line to file your initial claim, go to the front of the line at the small claims court clerk's window where you will find conspicuously posted a calendar showing the hearing date of the summonses they are issuing at the moment.

FILING THE INITIAL CLAIM FORM

In the forms section of this guide you will find the Initial Claim form used by the small claims courts of all the courts of New York City [FORMS 1, 3]; the courts of Bergen [FORM 40] and Hudson [FORM 41] counties, New Jersey;) the courts of Nassau County [FORM 32]; the courts of Suffolk County [FORM 33]; and all the courts of Connecticut [FORMS 53, 54].

Useful information provided by some of the small claims courts offering generally helpful information and help with completing forms (NY, Suffolk County; NJ, all; CT, all) is shown on [FORM 33], [FORM 39] and [FORM 51] respectively.

---

1 The maximum amount you can sue for is $3,000 in New York State Small Claims Court. (It is also the maximum amount you can be countersued for in small claims court.) Consider the benefit of suing for the maximum even if the amount you are due is less than that. The judge or arbitrator will rarely award you an amount less than your documentation clearly shows is due. He must award you the amount that you can prove by clear and convincing evidence. Judges and arbitrators may sometimes award a judgment amount less than what you claimed, if in their opinion, your case is not compelling. There is no penalty for asking for the maximum, and sometimes the debtor may be intimidated enough to begin a prehearing dialogue to settle your differences.

2 In Connecticut, when you file your Initial Claim form [FORM 53] the debtor is sent a summons to appear in court. The debtor may choose to defend his position, in which case he responds to the summons by notifying the court that he is going to appear at the hearing. Upon receipt of such notice the court issues the plaintiff and the defendant a hearing date and the case is heard before the judge. However, the debtor may choose not to respond to the summons, in which case the judge upon reviewing your papers (Initial Claim form and documentary proof) may decide on the merits of the evidence presented in them, and that your presence at a hearing is not necessary. The judge may then award you a default judgment with which you may proceed to begin collection. In New York and New Jersey, you must always attend a hearing to present your argument.

3 Sometimes when you arrive at the window you will find that they have sold out of the day they quoted you and are now issuing summonses one day later than you expected. They "sell" 60 to 90 summonses for each court session in Brooklyn's small claims court.

Initiating the small claims action entails filing the Initial Claim form [FORM 1] if you are filing as an individual and [FORM 3] if you are filing as a corporation. [FORM 4] is a completed example of [FORM 1]. The top half of the form can be filled in with your name and address and filed for repeated use. In recent months the clerks have begun requesting verification (a "business certificate," or a business card or letterhead for a professional) showing the real name of the business. This policy was initiated to prevent some unscrupulous incorporated businessmen from filing an individual claim (at a cost of $10.00 per claim not in excess of $1,000, and $15.00 for any claim between $1,000 and $3,000), when they should be paying $22.84 for the cost of a commercial-corporate claim.

The bottom half of the forms (defendant's information—see [FORMS 1, 3]) requires your special attention only when you are initiating a claim against a corporate name or a non-incorporated business. As mentioned earlier, if you are suing a (nonincorporated) proprietorship, you would sue William Smith d/b/a (doing business as) Smith Hardware. The person in whose name a business is registered can be found in the county clerk's office of the county in which the business is located (ask to see the assumed name or d/b/a certificate).

When you sue a corporation or partnership, keep in mind that some of them use assumed names and that obtaining the correct name of the defendant will make later proceedings much easier and will avoid having the case dismissed on a technicality. Information about the true name of a corporation and the person whom you initiate the claim against (the registered agent) and the true address of the corporation can be easily obtained by writing to the Secretary of State and requesting a corporation status report for a fee that varies from free in New York to $5 in New Jersey. See Appendix A for Secretary of State information.

The completed form must be filed at the small claims court clerk's window. You need not go yourself; a staff member or relative can file for you.

The window opens at 9:00 A.M. and closes precisely at 4:30 P.M. Monday through Friday. Furthermore, when you arrive you can usually expect to find a line of at least 4 to 10 persons. Multiply the number of people on the line by five and you have calculated your waiting time. Stand near the window and watch the show for a few minutes and you will realize how exasperating it must be for the clerk at the window, who has to serve a public that is woefully unprepared.

The lesson here is to come prepared with your accurately completed claim form, and the exact fee in cash. No checks or money orders are accepted. Get on line 30 minutes before the window opens. Each borough's small claims court operates a window that stays open late (see Appendix A) one night a week. For example, in Brooklyn, the small claims court window is open Thursday from 9:00 A.M. to 8:30 P.M. I've been there at 7:00 P.M. and have been pleasantly surprised to find only one person ahead of me.

OBSERVATION *Unfortunately for the residents of New Jersey and Connecticut, small claims courts have no evening sessions, nor does the small claims court clerk's window stay open late to enable the filing of claims. They do however permit you to file by mail, but you must be careful to compute the correct filing fee, which increases by $2 for each additional defendant you add to your claim. In addition, there may be an additional mileage fee (see example, Morris County, NJ [FORM 43]) for the distance your summons must travel from the court of origination in order to reach the defendant. Call the small claims court clerk for the exact amount of the filing fee.*

The clerk behind the window will conclude the transaction by giving you an Instructions to Claimant memorandum [FORM 5], which shows your case (index, docket number, and the date of your hearing. A typical case number looks like this: SCK 9865/97 (Small Claims Kings County, 9865th case, in the year 1997). The clerk then sends a Notice of Claim and Summons to Appear [FORM 6] to the person you are suing, which provides them with the same information.

PLANNING TIP *If you have the patience, and your faith in the mail service is intact, filing the Initial Claim form* *in person at the small claims court window can be avoided by mailing the completed form, with a stamped self-addressed business-size envelope and the filing fee. Call the small claims court clerk in advance to verify the correct amount of the filing fee for your kind of case (for example, individual versus individual, or individual versus corporation) and what form of payment is acceptable (for example, personal check, money order). If you have done it all correctly you will receive by mail a memorandum such as the one shown in [FORM 5] that notes the date, time, and location of your hearing. On the other hand, if you made a mistake your papers will be returned to you with your errors noted for you to redo. Never be reluctant to call the court for the status of your paperwork, but allow 10 to 14 days for mailing and processing by the court.*

....

OBTAINING DOCUMENTS HELD BY THE DEFENDANT OR OTHER PERSONS THAT YOU BELIEVE WILL HELP YOU PROVE YOUR CASE

Upon occasion the defendant or some other person has in his possession a document that will be useful in helping you to prove your case. Appendix D and [FORM 10] are provided to familiarize you with the look and use of the Subpoena for Records. The use of this instrument is at first a bit intimidating because it has to be served (delivered to) on the defendant in person by someone other than you, and there are specific rules for the way service has to be performed. See [FORM 8], for the specifics in New York City.

Compelling an Unwilling (and Possibly Helpful) Witness to Testify

In a court hearing neither the plaintiff nor the defendant is permitted to introduce what is known as hearsay evidence (information that was heard/said/written by another person). Such evidence is generally inadmissible because it is indirect testimony—that is, information offered as evidence that does not come directly from the experience of the plaintiff or the defendant and as such does not permit cross-examination. Consequently, if there is another person whose testimony is important, and perhaps even vital, to corroborate and help prove your claim, you can compel that person to come to your hearing and

give testimony. (See also question 6 in Chapter 9—Questions and Answers and Chapter 7—Countering the Counterclaim).

To accomplish this you will need to obtain a Subpoena to Testify (see completed example [FORM 9] and Appendix C Subpoenas in a Nutshell for related information) and have it served on the party you want to testify. You can obtain a Subpoena to Testify at the small claims court clerk's window. The clerk will prepare it for you upon request at no cost. You must supply the clerk with the index number of your case and the name and the address (no P.O. Box numbers) of the party you want to subpoena. The subpoena must be served in person on the party you want to testify and it must be hand-delivered to that person. The server must give the person being served a fee (legal payment to testify) of up to $15, depending on the state. (See Appendix C). The server must then complete an Affidavit of Service, have it notarized, and return it to the plaintiff. The plaintiff can mail or bring it to the small claims court clerk who will make it part of the case record. (See [FORM 8] for explicit instruction for service of this subpoena and [FORM 9] to see a completed example of an Affidavit of Service.)

....

WARNING *You cannot obtain the Subpoena to Testify until the clerk is certain that the summons is in the defendant's possession. When the small claims court clerk files your claim, he sends the Notice of Claim to the defendant by regular mail and certified mail, return receipt requested. It typically takes 7 to 14 days and sometimes much longer for the receipt (showing that delivery was accomplished) to be returned to the clerk of the court. Therefore, the clerks will routinely advise you to check at the window 10 days before the date of your hearing to verify delivery of the summons. The clerk may be reluctant to search your file if you request it by telephone (because big city courts are usually pressed for time and short-staffed). I recommend waiting three weeks before calling to verify whether the clerk has received the certified return postal receipt indicating delivery of the summons (be prepared to give the case, index, and docket number).*

....

USING THE COURT CALENDAR TO YOUR ADVANTAGE

When you arrive at small claims court the night of your hearing, there will be posted outside the door of the main courtroom a list (the "calendar") in numerical order of the cases being heard that night.[4] It looks like this:

1. Plaintiff—(Your Name) vs. Defendant—(Debtor's Name)
2. Etc., Etc.

If an error in scheduling has been made and your name does not appear on the calendar, there is an information officer stationed outside the courtroom who can advise you.

....

PLANNING TIP *To avoid errors in scheduling you can call the small claims court the day before your court hearing and inquire, "What number am I on the calendar for the hearings tomorrow night?"*

....

PREHEARING ATTEMPTS TO SETTLE

You can also call the debtor the day or evening before the hearing, to remind him that the hearing is on schedule and that you will be present. And then you can add, "Maybe we can arrange a settlement now."

If the defendant shows up (5% to 10% occurrence), there will be a 30 to 45 minute opportunity to locate and approach him to try to settle your differences before the hearing. Try it. Sometimes the results are surprising.

A MICRO PREVIEW OF A TYPICAL EVENING IN SMALL CLAIMS COURT

Almost all of us get anxious and tense about going on stage. I was no exception. I recall how nerve-racking it was the first dozen times I went to my hearings. I sympathize with persons who are easily flustered because I'm one of them. For those of you who like a bit of rehearsal before going on stage, here's what you can do:

1. In the main courtroom where they call the calendar:

   (Observe for 30 minutes.) The court clerk begins reading off the names in the new cases. He calls the plaintiff's name, who responds by repeating his name to announce his presence, and then calls the defendant's name, who repeats his name to announce his presence. Note how the clerk directs the adversaries to go to another waiting room where they are then assigned to an arbitrator's or judge's courtroom. Also note the small variety of alternative responses such as "application" (one of the parties wants to postpone the hearing) and "by the court" (one of the parties wants the case to be heard by a judge rather than an arbitrator.

2. In the waiting room where you are assigned to a small courtroom:

   (Observe for 10 minutes.) Listen for the plaintiff's and the defendant's names being called to come forward to the clerk's desk to complete envelopes with their names and addresses in which they will receive the decision of the court, and to be directed to a specific courtroom for the hearing.

3. In the hearing rooms (small courtroom) to observe how one or two different arbitrators handle cases:

   (Observe for 30 to 45 minutes.) Plaintiff presents his story and supporting documents. Defendant (if he appears, which is rare) presents his side of the story and his documents. Plaintiff is then allowed to interrogate defendant and defendant is allowed to interrogate plaintiff. The arbitrator asks questions to clarify issues. You may note that some judges and arbitrators are patient while others are more stern and severe in their approach.

....

NOTE *In most courts, outside of New York City, the entire procedure takes place in one courtroom.*

....

....

4 Check it to see if your case is listed and what number it is. If you are first, your case is called first and your hearing will be finished before 7:30 P.M.; if you are 65th on the list, you may not finish your hearing until after 9:00 P.M. To some extent you can control your position on the calendar: You can call the clerk at the small claims window and say, "I'd like to be near the head of the calendar; are you about to start giving out summonses for a new day?"

CHAPTER 5

Twelve Scenarios after You File an Initial Claim Form

Before I review the 12 scenarios that can occur, I will first briefly describe number 8c, which is by far the most common scenario and occurs 95% of the time. It is described in more detail below:

You appear at the calendar call and your name is called. The defendant is absent, the clerk of the court instructs you to go to a special room to be assigned to a courtroom where an inquest[5] is held in the presence of an arbitrator. You present your case in two to four minutes. If your case has merit, you receive a judgment in your favor, in the mail 3 to 10 days later, for the amount you claimed.

THE SCENARIOS

1. You receive a check in the mail for payment in full.
2. You receive by regular mail and by certified mail a notice from the court that the defendant is countersuing you [FORM 6]. Do not be alarmed, defendants' counterclaims rarely have merit in that they cannot be documented or substantiated. (See Chapter 7—Countering the Counterclaim).
3. Your debtor calls before the hearing date to make a settlement offer of $2,500. You say: "I wanted $3,000, but I'll split the difference." He agrees.

4. It's one week before the hearing and no bites, not even a nibble. You call or write the defendant indicating your willingness to settle for an amount, let's say 25% less than what's due to the hearing. "This way we can both avoid the inconvenience of additional costs and having to go to court." He agrees. You say promptly: "I'll send a messenger this afternoon. I'd like to be paid with a certified bank check. I'll sign a General Release [FORM 13] (Blumberg Form B 110—see Appendix K) and have it sent to you when I receive the payment." Here you pause and wait for the response.
5. You decide to discontinue (not to go forward with) the case, for whatever the reason.

    No problem. You do not have to appear in court. When your name is called by the court clerk at the calendar call the night of the hearing and nobody responds, the clerk will say, "Case is dismissed," and for the sake of the defendant will continue, "The plaintiff has the right to sue you again; watch out in the mail for another summons."
6. You settled with the debtor, but mistakenly thinking you had to be in court, you came for the hearing; or you settled just before the calendar call. When your name is called at the

---

calendar call you respond by saying "Case settled." You leave and never make that mistake again.

7. You are present at the calendar call AND the defendant is also present, but you are not yet ready to have your case heard—you forgot, or are missing, an important document that supports your case. When your name is called you respond by saying the word *application* (the legal term more commonly used outside of New York City is *continuance*). You are telling the court clerk that you want to postpone your hearing to a future date. He will respond by saying, "Wait here until your name is called again." Your name will be called 30 to 60 minutes later, and you will be asked to approach the bench. The presiding judge will ask the reason why you want to adjourn the hearing date. Any "reasonable" excuse will suffice. For example: "I need more time to gather evidence" or "I realize I need to consult a lawyer" or "My witness is sick and can't be in court today." You and the defendant must now arrange a date to return for a hearing, usually 4 to 7 weeks in the future. Your case will then be placed on the "Adjourned Calendar," which means that on the date of the hearing, your case and other adjourned cases will be called before all other cases being heard for the first time.

I have never needed to request an adjournment. However, there have been occasions when the defendant has made such a request and the judge has granted it. Request for adjournment must be done in person before the judge (see exception below). The judge will usually grant the debtor's request for an adjournment if it is reasonable and a first-time request for an adjournment. But if the judge thinks the request lacks merit, he may note on the case folder that no further requests for adjournment will be permitted. If he does not make a note, you should request that he does. (Judge, I request that the defendant's request for adjournment be noted as final and future requests be denied.) This minimizes the possibility that the defendant will adjourn the hearing again and again.

8a. You are present at the calendar call and respond by saying your name, but the defendant does not respond to his name; however the clerk continues with, "Wait here until your name is called again." About 30 minutes later your name is called and you are invited to come forward for a brief chat with the clerk who tells you that the defendant requested an adjournment by mail. When this happened to me the excuse used by the defendant was that she was enrolled in a class that met one night a week and it would be a hardship for her to miss the class. (Her request was accompanied by a supporting document from the school.) You should ask to see the written request on the chance that it is bogus. And if it is, you should ask that the adjournment be denied, and that you be permitted to have your inquest that evening. There is virtually nothing you can do to protect yourself from this happening. After all, the debtor is not obliged to let you know that he is requesting an adjournment.

8b. Another variation takes place when you are present at the calendar call and respond by saying your name, but the defendant does not respond to his name; however the clerk continues with: "The service of the summons was defective and was returned to the clerk's office undelivered, wait here until your name is called again." When you are called again the clerk will take you aside and explain why the summons was defective (undeliverable to the defendant), and tell you what you must do to correct the problem, which is, typically, to obtain a good address for the defendant. (In 1996 about 60,000 initial claim forms were filed in the five boroughs of New York City. Of those about 16,700 were returned to the court undelivered.) [FORM 41] shows a form that the Hudson County court mailed to me after the constable tried four times to deliver the summons (see Notice of Claim, [FORM 6]) without success.

8c. A third variation occurs when you are present at the calendar call and respond by saying your name, but the defendant is not there (95% occurrence). The court clerk will now say, "Go to room

(509 in Brooklyn) for an inquest." In room 509 you will wait 10 to 40 minutes until your name is called again. Then you will be asked to come forward to sign your name (the plaintiff's name) and address on an envelope, in which you will receive 3 to 10 days later the results of the hearing. You will also be handed several official court papers and will be told to go to a specific courtroom for the hearing. With rare luck you are next. Each case before you takes 3 to 20 minutes.

When your hearing begins, the arbitrator asks you to swear to tell the truth. The arbitrator then asks you: "What is your case about?" You identify yourself and proceed to tell the arbitrator what happened between you and the debtor, being brief and clear with reference to the documents in your possession supporting your position (usually two to five minutes). The arbitrator may ask you some questions, especially if there are any discrepancies between the amount you sued for on your initial claim form and what your bills or other evidence show, so be prepared to explain. The arbitrator will conclude by saying: "You will receive my decision in the mail."

9. You are present and the defendant is also (5% to 10% occurrence). This time you present your case exactly as you did before; then the defendant presents his side. Even if you believe that the defendant is making false or distorted statements, keep your cool; the arbitrator is no fool. Have pencil and paper ready to take notes and prepare questions. Your debtor will not be allowed to submit written testimony that comes from other people, even if it is in the form of an *affidavit* (a written statement from a witness signed under oath in the presence of a Notary Public). He must present his case by supporting documents and actual witnesses. It is those documents and their testimony that win or lose the case.

10. A rare scenario, which happened to me on two occasions, plays out as follows: The defendant does not appear at the hearing. You present your

documentation and receive your judgment. Ten days later you receive a notice from the court saying that the defendant has petitioned for another hearing and that the judge or arbitrator has granted it and specified a rehearing date.

Vacating a judgment, as this action is known, is of course a two-way street. If you were sued and were unable to appear on the court date (or simply forgot about the hearing), and the arbitrator ruled against you, you would petition the court to vacate the judgment against you.

11. The cross-claim. Supposing you had to sue not one person who owed you money, but two persons who jointly owed you money (now there are two defendants involved in your claim). If defendant A believes that defendant B has the obligation to pay the entire debt to you, defendant A may file a "cross-claim" against defendant B, claiming that B alone is responsible for the money owed to you. Consequently your case and their case against each other will be heard at the same time.

12. The second scenario is called a third-party claim. For example, you sue someone who you believe is responsible for the payment of your debt (the defendant). However, the defendant believes there is a third person (not named as a defendant in your case) who is responsible for all or part of the money you may receive from the defendant. So the defendant initiates a claim against the third person and this new claim becomes a part of your hearing with the defendant. The practical difference to you between the third-party claim and the cross-claim is that where a third-party claim is made, you don't know of the existence or identity of the third party, or who the third party is until you initiate your suit.

The schematic overview of the entire process from unpaid bill to collection of fee is shown in CHART I on page 46, and offers a global view of the process.

Oyez! Oyez! The courtroom will now come to order!

CHAPTER 6

All About the Courtroom Hearing

CHOOSING TO HAVE YOUR CASE HEARD BY A JUDGE OR AN ARBITRATOR

Even before you arrive at the court you should consider whether you want your case to be heard by a judge or an arbitrator. In some instances you have the choice. That choice is made during the calendar call (see Chapter 2—The Legal Terms Step-by-Step). When your name (as the plaintiff) is called, if you respond with nothing but your name (as is customary) and the defendant does likewise, your case will be automatically heard by an arbitrator. If, however, either you or the defendant responds by saying "by the court" following your name, your case will be automatically heard by a judge. Here are some facts to help you decide which one to choose:

Judges can and do make errors in their decisions. That is why there are appeals courts. Arbitrators also make errors in their decisions, but when they do their decision is final. So, if you fear you might lose and you do not want to lose the right to appeal your case, when your name is called at the calendar call you should respond to the clerk by saying your name and the words *by the court*. For this dubious advantage you may have to wait an additional 30 to 50 minutes, and if there is an overabundance of cases, you further run the risk of not being heard at all that night. While there are many arbitrators, there is usually only one presiding judge. What allows you to appeal

your case, should you lose before the judge, is the presence of a court stenographer (nowadays, a machine, faithfully recording the dialogue of the case on tape for posterity). If you're obstinate and up for the challenge, you can obtain from the clerk at the small claims court window (Room 201 in Brooklyn) an instruction sheet explaining in the most general terms how to appeal the case [FORM 26].

OBSERVATION *The process of appealing a decision is really a task for a lawyer, and that is expensive. The legal fees could easily consume the maximum award ($3,000) of the small claims court. Furthermore, the appeals court refuses to hear more than two-thirds of the requests for appeal. Nevertheless, the reader should know that a Notice of Appeal must be filed within 30 days of receipt of the date noted on the judgment (the judge's decision), or the postmark on the envelope the judgment arrived in. Save the envelope; you may need it.*

I have appealed only one case and that case is in progress. I pass on to you what I have learned in Appendix J.

I have had six hearings "by the court." In one case the defendant and I were asked by the court clerk to step into a small room to try for a settlement by mediation. A student attorney, practicing her mediation techniques, tried to find some middle ground that could permit us to settle our dispute without having to go before the judge. Hard heads prevailed, and the case had to be heard by the judge.

OBSERVATION *A case settled by mediation is binding only when both parties agree to sign a document in which the terms of the settlement are stipulated.*

Whether before an arbitrator or a judge, after the defendant presents his side, you get another chance to respond and even to ask the defendant some questions that will help score points with the arbitrator or judge. The defendant also gets a final opportunity to question the plaintiff.

Your last opportunity to try for settlement comes when you take the elevator down with the defendant. Don't avoid it—think of it as another opportunity. Stay calm, be nice, and try to work out an agreement on payment: Money in your hands up front and early is worth a lot more than the hoped-for outcome of a protracted collection effort.

PRESENTING YOUR CASE BEFORE THE JUDGE OR ARBITRATOR

The presence of the debtor and the debtor's lawyer might unnerve even the boldest among us. Fortunately, only rarely does the defendant appear. Even if he does, the likelihood that the debtor will bring an attorney is even less. It has not happened to me in well over a hundred cases.

Here are some specific guidelines to help you, especially if the defendant does appear to contest your claim:

PLANNING TIP

1. *Do your best to remain calm throughout the hearing.*

2. *Keep your documents in order by date and/or exhibit number.*

3. *Have the facts of your own story prepared on a 5″ × 7″ index card. No judge will prohibit you from relating your story as long as it is brief, but be complete and coherent. See [FORM 11] for an example of the plaintiff's story on a 5″ × 7″ index card.*

4. *As the defendant is relating his side of the story try to write down in outline form each point he makes, especially the inconsistencies. Do not interrupt him except to object to the introduction of statements that are hearsay. When he has finished, ask the judge for a three-minute recess to allow you to compose your response because you are hearing the details of the defense and/or counterclaim for the first time. You will likely be permitted your request, but if you are not, take a long look at the notes you took and then respond as best you can.*

5. *Speak clearly and avoid making angry or accusatory statements. Be polite to the defendant and the judge (avoid attitude). You can refer to them as "Mr. Smith" or "the defendant" and "your honor" or "Judge Jones" respectively. I once lost a case, I believe, because I was rude and excessively outspoken.*

6. *When the judge (arbitrator) asks a question in order to clarify some point or another, a good rule to follow is to count slowly to five before responding to any question put to you.*

7. *Make certain you have made all the points you intended to make. You will regret it if you fail to deliver that key point that was sum and substance of your entire case.*

8. *The judge will usually ask you if you have anything else to add. The moment that either you or the defendant get up to leave not a single word may be added.*

At the hearing, presenting proof that the debtor owes you money can be done by persons other than the plaintiff. For example, in a doctor's office the person most often familiar with the financial elements of the case is the person at the front desk in charge of entering payments on the debtor's payment (ledger) card, and that person may be the one best suited to present the facts. However, local court rules and individual judges and arbitrators have the discretion to permit or deny such plaintiff stand-ins; see [FORM 38] for an example of such a ruling.

If you are preparing for your first encounter in court, I urge you to write down on a 5″ × 7″ index card your response to the first question the judge is going to ask you in one form or another: What is your case about? Have the card ready to read, if need be, for the hearing itself.

Finally, if the plaintiff's representative suddenly found himself at a loss for words, unable to sustain the argument or faced with issues raised unexpectedly by the defendant, he could simply say at any point in the hearing, "Mr. Arbitrator, I would like to withdraw my complaint 'without prejudice.'" As a matter of course this request would probably be granted by the arbitrator. In this manner the plaintiff is allowed to reinitiate his claim at a future date, albeit not without some loss of time and effort.

Admittedly, the plaintiff or his stand-in will feel some trepidation at the first appearance before the arbitrator, even though he is commonly an (unpaid) volunteer lawyer. It is my impression that most arbitrators are relatively sympathetic to your plight. However, they are trained to make decisions on the basis of the facts related to your case and the proof that you present to substantiate them.

TESTIMONY OFFERED IN THE FORM OF DOCUMENTS— WHAT IS NOT PERMITTED

When it's your turn to come before the arbitrator, ask for his name and write it down. Have your documents ready to present in the order you need them for clarity, conciseness, and brevity in the presentation and in support of your claim; this presentation usually will take two to five minutes. Only on one occasion did I require about eight minutes to present my case.

PLANNING TIP *If you are going to present testimony from a witness, you cannot usually present testimony in the form of a letter or document even if you went to the trouble of having the letter or other written statement notarized. (There are some exceptions to this rule, but I have never experienced them.) A notary public is a licensed person who may be a lawyer or a secretary in a lawyer's office, a bank officer, insurance or real estate agent, and even in small towns, a grocery or drug store clerk. For the sum of between $1 and $3, the notary will witness your signature, put his seal on your document, and sign a statement that the person whose statement is*

recorded in the document appeared before him. The notary has notarized the document. The document in essence represents a person's sworn statement, which in certain instances takes the place of the appearance of the actual person. Evidence of this kind is not allowed to be introduced under normal circumstances. If the defendant attempted to introduce such a document you would say, "I object," and the judge, if he agrees, would say: "Objection sustained." Testimony from persons other than the plaintiff and the defendant must in general be given in person. (The reader is encouraged to consult other sources for the exceptions.)

OBTAINING INFORMATION ABOUT THE DEBTOR'S ASSETS DURING THE HEARING

I would urge all would-be plaintiffs to go to their hearing with a copy of [FORM 23] in which one can find two amendments that allow (encourage) you to ask the judge/arbitrator to ask the defendant where he works or banks. This information could aid you in your collection efforts should you win. I tried it once with success. You say to the judge: "In the event you should find in my favor I would like you to ask the defendant to provide you with his place of employment and banking facility." You would then cite the information in the Observation below. You continue: "Please ask the defendant where he works." Then ask: "Please ask the defendant where he banks." A second approach is to request permission to cross examine the defendant. Begin by asking: "Would you please state what your occupation?" and then proceed to ask: "Where are you currently employed?"

OBSERVATION *According to §1803(b) and §1805(a), amendments passed in 1991 (see McKinney's Consolidated Laws of New York Annotated (Uniform Justice Court Act), the plaintiff (claimant) is encouraged to ask the arbitrator (judge) during the hearing to question the debtor about his assets, and to obtain information about those assets (place of employment, bank accounts, property owned, stock accounts) to facilitate and perhaps even direct the arbitrator's or judge's questioning. These amendments were enacted to address the "continuing dilemma of getting small claims judgments enforced." (See [FORM 23].)*

SENDING STAFF TO STAND IN FOR THE BOSS: CHRISTINE'S STORY

Usually I go to the hearing, but one time I sent Christine, the young manager of my office, to stand in for me. She went, but not without feeling weak in the knees and uneasy. She arrived at 6:20 P.M. and checked the calendar to find that there were 23 adjourned cases to be called first and that she was 58th among the new cases. At 7:00 P.M. my name was called; the defendant was not present and Christine was directed to go to Room 509 and wait for her name to be called again. At 7:35 P.M. her name was called again. This time she was told to go to a hearing room next to the room she was in and to address an envelope with my office address (in which the arbitrator sends his decision, or judgment). In the hearing room the arbitrator heard four cases before Christine's. At 7:55 P.M. the case was called.

She was prepared: She had the case folder containing a signed contract, the patient's ledger card, the bad check, and the notice from the bank indicating that the personal check we had accepted as final payment was not negotiable because the account was closed.

The arbitrator, upon seeing Christine, immediately said: "Where is Dr. Rothstein?" She responded: "I'm the office manager and responsible for accounts receivable. I am the only one totally aware of the facts of this case." "Okay, tell me the facts," he said. "Well, Mr. Arbitrator, Dr. Rothstein finished the work and removed the patient's braces. We accepted a personal check as final payment and it's no good—here, see for yourself." The arbitrator said: "Okay, goodnight. You'll have my decision in the mail." The arbitrator did not request to see any other document. At 7:59 P.M. Christine walked out. Three days later a Notice of Judgment in our favor arrived in the mail.

REQUESTING PAYMENT FROM THE DEBTOR AFTER YOU RECEIVE A JUDGMENT

You will receive the arbitrator's decision—the judgment, [FORM 14], by mail in three to ten days.

Having received your judgment, you should without further delay send the debtor a letter referring to the judgment as given in your favor and request that the debtor pay you now. This is a mandatory step and sets the stage for all further action.

OBSERVATION *It is a commonly held misconception by the general public that once you have obtained a judgment that awards you the amount you claimed for, the debtor must pay you or else. Not so! There is no penalty for not paying. That is why the reader must familiarize himself with the "tools" for compelling the unwilling debtor to pay the judgment. (See Chapter 8—What You Can Do With Your Judgment).*

IN-OFFICE RECORD KEEPING

1. Prepare a permanent folder entitled "Judgments."
2. When you schedule the hearing date, write down its case number and the telephone number of the small claims court and keep it handy. (See Appendix B for all the courts.)
3. Be sure to note the date of the hearing and the case number.

These three tips will spare you numerous annoying searches and facilitate obtaining calendar information. For example, on the day of your court hearing you might call the small claims court simply to confirm that your case has not been accidentally canceled by some clerical error. (The calendar is the list of cases being heard in courtroom during the court session. The cases are listed in the numerical order in which they are being announced at the calendar call. The list is posted just outside the courtroom.)

Remember well that in the small claims court clerical error is a fact of life.

CHAPTER 7 Countering the Counterclaim

COUNTERCLAIMS AND FAIRY TALES: A STORY WITHOUT A MORAL

Sometimes things don't go as expected: Only once have I been countersued, and that occurred during the writing of this book. Sensing the case would be important, I requested that it be heard before a judge (whose decision can be appealed) rather than an arbitrator. The case took almost an hour to hear, ten times the length of the usual hearing (inquest) I had previously experienced.

The judge (who later admitted that my case was among the first of his career as a small claims court judge) split his decision. In effect, my patient's counterclaim was dismissed (I didn't have to pay the patient), but the judge also decided to excuse the balance of the fee owed for the services I had rendered (the patient didn't have to pay me).

I said previously that judges seldom make errors. But when they do, and you are the party who suffers from those errors (real or imagined), you are left with two choices: withdraw from the playing field, tail between legs, angry, shocked, and dismayed, or take an appeal and try to have the decision reversed by a higher court (see Appendix J). That is exactly what I did. I filed my "Notice of Appeal" form immediately.

Taking an appeal begins with obtaining a transcript of the hearing. Unfortunately, the recording machine at the hearing had malfunctioned, and

the transcript of the proceedings of the hearing was declared "defective"—no transcript, no appeal. The judge ruled that the case was going to be "reconstructed," not reheard (as if for the first time), as I had requested. That would solve the problem of the missing transcript. He later admitted he didn't know how to do a reconstruction of a hearing. Moreover, even my lawyer admitted he had never heard the term before, and that really worried me. Yes, I hired a lawyer; the defendant acted *pro se*. I knew with certainty that I didn't know—even remotely—how to proceed to reconstruct the hearing. I would have paid him a king's ransom to move the case along because for me it was principle of the thing.

The outcome of the reconstruction was as follows. The judge wisely conceded that his thinking was flawed regarding the legal concept that was applicable—that is, *quantum meruit*, or "as much as deserved." This is a legal doctrine that allows a person (the service provider) to recover the fair value (commonly as measured by the quoted fee) for services that were effectively provided and accepted by another person (the service receiver). In essence, the receiver should not be unjustly enriched by the labor and materials of the provider. He rewrote his judgment (decision) and ruled that the defendant was obliged to pay the balance of the unpaid bill because the work was rightly provided.

Stop! I confess. I am not telling it the way it really happened. The above is a fairy tale with a happy ending for me. The judge did in fact try to reconstruct the testimony as it was given by each of the parties in the first hearing, and even allowed the defendant and the plaintiff to elaborate on their testimonies. My lawyer was uninspired, having little to add and perhaps somewhat at a disadvantage for not having been present at the first hearing, and felt constrained to remain mute for the most part. I felt almost abandoned during the rehearing, which this time took more than an hour. There would be no repeat of a technical error—his time a court stenographer took the testimony (45 pages at $4.50 per page). The judge held firm to his prior decision. Now, however, I had a useable transcript to submit for an appeal. "The Appeal Process" I followed is outlined in Appendix J. The outcome of this appeal is also described at the end of the same appendix.

The inquisitive reader will be interested in knowing that 12 months sailed by from the moment I filed the first form [FORM 27] to begin the process until the case was decided by the three justices of the appellate term court. (I was not present at the hearing.) Researching and writing the legal brief consumed almost every bit of my spare time for six weeks. The brief turned out to be 21 pages long.[6]

It remains for the reader to draw his own conclusions, morals, and lessons from this true story as to the economies of suit, counterclaim, and appeal.

THE COUNTERCLAIM IN PERSPECTIVE: THREATS, BLUFFING, AND REALITY

I will now describe for you a more typical scenario of the events that may be encountered in a counterclaim.

The usual route:

In response to the Initial Claim you filed five weeks ago, you receive notice from the court by ordinary mail and certified mail, return receipt requested [FORM 6]. Much to your dismay, you read that for the reason stated in the notice the defendant has decided to become a plaintiff—of all things, you are now being sued!

Your heart pounds. The unthinkable is happening. Get hold of yourself—it's OK—everything is going to be alright. This is the defendant's way of saying that he did no wrong—and that you wronged him and he wants compensation for it. He is telling you he is going to be present on the night of the hearing and intends to present substantiating documents to prove how you wronged him and why he should be remunerated, or at least why he should not be obliged to pay you.

Now go back to the notice and carefully read the complaint again. Remember, you thoughtfully considered the pros and cons before you initiated your litigation. You will usually see written before you a meritless reason for the counterclaim. Now ask yourself whether or not the defendant can document and substantiate his claims in a courtroom before a well-trained lawyer—who is the judge or arbitrator in your case and likely to ferret out the truth more readily than the defendant can imagine.

You may also find some comfort when you recall that the maximum the debtor can counterclaim for in small claims court is $3,000.

Other possibilities:

I would be telling only half the truth if I said no more. The reader, I hope, will not be discouraged by the other half. The debtor has another option. He may hire an attorney or act *pro se* and initiate a counterclaim in a higher court such as a civil court, where the monetary awards start at $3,000 and can go as high as $25,000. In fact he could even find a court in which to initiate a counterclaim for a substantially larger amount. The fact is that anybody can sue anybody else for whatever desired amount as long as the claim does not exceed the monetary limit of the awards allowed by that court. If this were to occur, your case would be heard at the same time as the counterclaim, but in the higher court. This is one of the reasons professionals, including

---

6 You don't need to be a lawyer to research and write a good legal brief. For assistance, see Harsen and Bourdeau, *Legal Research for Beginners*, Barron's Educational Series, Inc., Hauppauge, New York (1997).

lawyers, tend to refrain from suing clients for unpaid bills. It is for the same reason many physicians and dentists often decline to initiate even a truly legitimate claim. They have been advised repeatedly by their practice management consultants that they are inviting a counterclaim (breach of contract or malpractice) when they initiate an action to collect an unpaid bill.

A counterclaim that is initiated in civil court can rightly be viewed as more threatening because the awards can be much larger and accordingly even a "favorable" settlement can be costly in amount as well as in legal fees and expenses. Furthermore, professionals are obliged to notify their insurance carrier of claims initiated against them. Should the debtor not be bluffing and the professional have misjudged the merits and strength of the case, the insurance company will have to employ a lawyer to defend the case. Such a scenario may result in a rise in the professional's insurance premium, and add to the anxiety already engendered by the counterclaim. It is easy to understand how a professional might forgive an unpaid bill. Who needs it?

My response to this is twofold. You never would have initiated a claim in the first place if you hadn't first examined all the reasons not to initiate a claim. (See Chapter 3—Deciding Whether Small Claims Court Is the Right Approach for You). William Shakespeare wrote in *Henry IV*, Part I, "The better part of valor is discretion." My second response is perhaps based on a more personal philosophy. We should not allow the other fellow's possible responses to put such fear in us that we are deterred from action that is basically just. Shakespeare wrote in *Julius Caesar*, "Cowards die many times before their deaths; the valiant never taste of death but once."

OBSERVATION *To the above commentary I would add this second true story: I sued an accountant for breach of contract, when he failed to perform the service I contracted and paid for, in a New Jersey small claims court where the maximum award is $2,000. His lawyer requested (made a motion to the court) to remove the case to civil court on the grounds that I caused the accountant $7,000 in damages, an amount in excess of the limits of*

the small claims court. To my dismay his motion was granted. I was angry and shocked. His ploy was a bluff— maybe I would be frightened enough to withdraw my suit. He almost succeeded; I will admit it was tough going for me because I had to learn as I went along. The accountant was indeed a scoundrel, and I was the first to sue him (out of many others of his clients whom he had defrauded). I didn't recover what I paid him. He declared bankruptcy just before my hearing. I do not doubt that there are professionals who have pressed a claim in a small claims court only to drop the case because of the anxiety engendered by a counterclaim in a higher court. I am forced to draw the conclusion that a counterclaim for a frighteningly large amount of money may well cause a claimant to reconsider the merits of going forward even if the counterclaim is totally without merit.

When the debtor initiates a counterclaim, there are three possibilities:

1. He's bluffing! He has no real intention of presenting himself because he has no case. He does not appear.
2. He appears for the hearing by himself, possibly with substantiating papers.
3. He appears for the hearing with substantiating documents and his attorney.

The hearing is exactly the same as presented in scenario 9 (see Chapter 5—Twelve Scenarios After You File an Initial Claim Form).

1. You present your side of the argument in 2 to 5 minutes.
2. He or his lawyer presents his side of the dispute (i.e., the reason for the counterclaim he stated on the notice you received [FORM 6]).
3. And he has to prove his case with documents and witnesses (expert witnesses where workmanship is in question).

Here are some specific guidelines to help you:

PLANNING TIP

1. *Do your best to remain calm throughout the hearing.*

2. *Keep your documents in order by date and/or exhibit number.*

3. *Have your own story prepared on a 5" × 7" index card. No judge will prohibit you from relating your story as long as it is brief, but be complete and coherent. See [FORM 11] for an example of the plaintiff's story on a 5" × 7" index card.*

4. *As the counterclaiming defendant is relating his side of the story, try to write down in outline form each point he makes. Do not interrupt him except to "object" to the introduction of statements that are hearsay. When he has finished ask the judge for a three-minute recess to allow you to compose your response because you are hearing the details of the counterclaim for the first time. You will likely be permitted your request, but if you are not, take a long look at the notes you took and then respond as best you can.*

5. *Speak clearly and avoid angry or accusatory statements (just the facts), and be polite to the defendant and the judge. You can refer to them as "Mr. Smith" or "the defendant" and "your honor" or "Judge Jones," respectively.*

6. *When the judge or arbitrator asks a question in order to clarify a point, a good rule to follow is to count slowly to five before responding to any question put to you.*

7. *Make certain you have made all the points you intended to make. You will feel miserable if you failed to deliver that key point that was sum and substance of your case.*

8. *The judge will usually ask you if you have anything else to add. The moment that either you or the defendant get up to leave not a single word may be added.*

OBSERVATION *Here is what I have encountered insofar as the defendant being represented by a lawyer at the hearing. In over 100 cases, spread across 15 years, no defendant has ever brought a lawyer with him to court. Indeed, only one debtor out of all of them came forth to defend against my claim, and that debtor convinced the arbitrator of her position (my documentation was insufficient to prevail). A handful of other defendants have also appeared, but because they wanted to try to settle the case, or didn't realize that they were not obligated to come.*

THE OBJECTION AND OTHER USEFUL TOOLS IN OPPOSING THE COUNTERCLAIM

If the counterclaim is unfounded, the defendant cannot possibly provide the necessary documents and the witnesses. The arbitrator or judge will almost always reject written statements of a witness submitted by a party where the witness is able to appear in person. The defendant must present documents that can be verified as authentic, and testimony from available fact witnesses and expert witnesses who appear in person. (See Chapter 4—Preparing and Filing a Claim.) If, for example, the defendant claims that the dental bridge you recently made broke and it is your fault, the defendant must bring another dentist with him to testify as to the alleged defect. A letter from the dentist saying your bridge is faulty cannot be admitted as testimony. The fact that a witness has sworn a statement before a notary does not change this rule.

Be calm, but be prepared to hear a story very different from your own. Take notes with the pen and paper you brought with you just for that reason. But remember this: you do not have to respond. The allegations of the defendant may be so far-fetched that a response is unwarranted. If, in your most considered judgment, a response is deemed necessary, never offer a single word more than is sufficient to respond to a misstatement, or answer a question put to you. And be prepared to say "I object" if you think the evidence may be hearsay or otherwise inadmissible.

WARNING *Objecting is very important, primarily because it allows you to prevent the defendant from making points that may help him to win his case. And secondarily, because, even though the judge may overrule (deny) your objection, it will appear on the record, and if you appeal your case, the justices in the higher appellate court may rule that the decision of the judge in the lower court was in error.*

Most of us are very nervous and become easily flustered when immersed in an unfamiliar environment—for example when the judge or arbitrator asks a question in order to clarify a point. A good rule to follow is to count slowly to five before responding to any question put to you. And never hesitate to ask for the question to be repeated if you are in doubt as to its meaning, or need a few more moments to compose a response.

Other responses when appropriate, may include: "I rest my case" or "I have nothing further to add" or "I can't comment on that."

OBSERVATION *When you cross-examine the defendant, he gets one more opportunity to question you. The rule is: You initiated the suit, you get to make the initial presentation, but he usually gets to have the last say. If he is a counterclaimant, the roles are reversed as to his claim. Never underestimate what your adversary may be capable of saying—anticipate and be prepared as best you can with a defense or rebuttal.*

Finally, remember: The merit of your presentation will be determined largely by your supporting documents. You would not have initiated an action if you thought that you were vulnerable to a serious counterclaim.

CHAPTER 8

What You Can Do with Your Judgment

You may ask, "Why do you have to do anything with your judgment?" After all, you won—the debtor has to pay. The judgment says so—doesn't it?

What the judgment states is that the debtor "has a legal obligation to pay the judgment and must present proof to the court upon *satisfaction* (payment) of the judgment and that failure to pay the judgment may subject the debtor to any one, or combination of, the actions (a-f)," listed on the front of the judgment [FORM 14]. Most people do not realize that the judgment they receive from the small claims court does not force the debtor to pay. There is no penalty whatsoever for refusing to pay a small claims judgment. Many debtors have avoided paying their debt because the plaintiffs did not know how to proceed legally to enforce the judgment they won. Here are the details of how to enforce your judgment.

Once you have won a judgment in your favor, you are permitted to take all the legal actions listed on the front of the judgment [FORM 14]. In fact, the instructions for carrying out these actions are provided on the back of the form [FORM 14]. Unfortunately, what is omitted in these instructions is what this guide provides—simplified details.

WARNING *Once you have received your judgment, take action to begin collection without a moment's delay. People are commonly on the move, and your judgment debtor could move to a neighboring state, making collection that much more difficult. If your debtor has moved to a nearby state and you still have momentum to continue your collection efforts, you must follow a procedure that seems much like suing the debtor anew, from the very beginning. Neighboring states have reciprocal agreements to honor each other's court decisions.*

As you will see in Appendix H, the procedure for having another state recognize and enforce your judgment always begins by obtaining an "exemplified" copy of your judgment from the small claims court clerk of the court where you originally won it. An exemplified copy is one that is certified to be a true copy and bears special seals to prove it. In New York that copy costs $10, and in New Jersey and Connecticut it costs $5 and $1 respectively.

What happens depends on whether you won the judgment by default in appearance (the defendant did not show up at the hearing) or if you obtained your judgment after a trial and the defendant was present. Appendix H presents the procedures for having your judgment recognized in New York, New Jersey, and Connecticut for both alternatives.

I have never actually had to undertake such a procedure. Consequently, my knowledge of the process is based on multiple conversations with knowledgeable court clerks and is supported by other reference sources, including attorneys.

....

NOTE *Chart II, on page 47, "Putting your Judgment to Work," will help you see at a glance the three basic legal directions you can move in. Juxtaposed with Chart I, it is a schematic overview of the whole process outlined in this guide.*

....

Once you've received a judgment in your favor, you can begin to obtain payment using a few basic processes. With knowledge of only a home address you can put a lien on the debtor's personal property and mar his credit rating. With knowledge of only an employer and work address you can begin a garnishment of the debtor's salary. With knowledge of only a bank name you can freeze the debtor's account and seize the entire debt owed to you (assuming the debtor has sufficient funds in the account to begin with).

FINDING YOUR DEBTOR'S ASSETS AND STARTING TO GARNISH HIS SALARY (INCOME) OR EXECUTE AGAINST HIS PROPERTY (BANK ACCOUNT, ETC.)

In the best of all possible worlds you had the foresight to obtain and retain your debtor's place of employment, his Social Security number, a copy of the first check he gave you, and of course a copy of the first credit card payment to you. You even made a mental note of the year and make of his car and the license plate number if you used an information form at the beginning of your relationship with the debtor. Furthermore, you had the kind of staff and office policies that enabled you to keep meticulous track of your debtor's every change of work and home address. But, if you are like the rest of us mortals, your records probably could use a bit of clean up here and there.

If you have the basic information described above, you can file the Income Execution [FORMS 18,

19] and/or the Property Execution [FORM 25] with the marshal. But keep your fingers crossed because your debtor could still thwart you by declaring bankruptcy and naming you as one of his creditors. If there are not enough assets to pay all his creditors, even though you have a lien, his debt to you will be reduced or even voided. This has happened to me no less than six times in my practice, most recently during the writing of this manuscript. (See [FORM 67].)

Even if the defendant does not declare bankruptcy, he could still change jobs and residence or both, as sometimes happens. The good news is that your income execution does not have to be refiled, but it's disheartening and sometimes costly to have to start a new search to find a new place of employment or residence and advise the marshal of the change. Did you ever lose a fish that you just caught because it leaped out of your hands after you had it on deck?

All is well if your records are in order, and you have current information, but, if they are wanting and you lack the minimum basic information for your debtor, you have a problem. Do what lawyers sometimes do—pay ($75 to $125) for a good skip-trace agency to help find your debtor. They may be found by checking under "Collection Agencies" or "Skip Tracing" in the Business-to-Business Yellow Pages. A check of the New York City Yellow Pages showed multilistings for collection agencies, but you must be careful to choose one that has expertise in skip tracing. Under the heading Skip Tracing only two were listed. Skip tracers provide a variety of services, including finding your debtor's place of employment, home address, possible location of bank accounts, and in some cases even an unlisted telephone number. Agencies like these are able to access data bases that allow them to obtain information you or I could obtain only with great difficulty, or not at all. Here is the basic information they request from you to begin a "Skip and Asset" search:

Debtor's Name:[7]

Last Known Address:

City, State, and Zip Code:

....

7 These and the following items are those that are typically provided. Even if you only have the debtor's last known home address it's a starting point for an investigation.

Telephone:
Social Security Number:
Driver's License Number and State:
Plate Number and State:
Vehicle Registration:

The more information you provide, the more effective the agencies are. They may also provide collection service and indeed may even buy your judgment for 35% to 50% of the collection amount. This relieves you of the burden of trying to collect the judgment yourself, and you have the satisfaction of knowing there is a bloodhound on your debtor's trail. A collection attorney presented with little or no information about the debtor's assets or his whereabouts is likely to delegate the collection to one of these skip-trace agencies.

Another instrument you have available to you upon obtaining your small claims judgment is the Information Subpoena (see Appendix E and [FORM 22]). An Information Subpoena is a legal document, obtained at the small claims clerk's window for $2, that can help you find the location of assets of the debtor. In essence the court orders and directs a person or institution to answer certain questions about where the assets of the defendant may be found. Appendix C should be consulted for definitive information regarding this subpoena in New York, New Jersey, and Connecticut.

The Information Subpoena may be served upon the judgment debtor, (who in all likelihood will not respond to it) and upon any person or corporation or entity you believe has knowledge of the debtor's assets, or place of employment, such as the telephone company or the debtor's landlord or bank. The Information Subpoena does not have to be served in person. (See [FORM 8] under "Procedure for an Information Subpoena.")

The document recommended for service on a bank in New York is called an Information Subpoena and Restraining Notice [FORM 22]. Here is the good news: The bank or other person holding your debtor's account or other assets is prohibited from paying out or transferring funds in an amount equal to double what is owed you. And those assets will remain frozen for 12 months. This approach is

exactly how the Internal Revenue Service gets you to pay your back taxes.

CHOOSING THE RIGHT APPROACH TO COLLECT ON YOUR JUDGMENT

Choosing the right approach will depend on knowing where your debtor resides, works, and keep assets and whether he owns property. See Chart II, page 47.

A. The Easiest Approach (using just the home address):

You can open a dialogue by mail [FORM 15] or phone and try to get a commitment (an amount and date) for payment in full.

or

B. Impair Credit (using just the home address):

You can obtain a Transcript of the Judgment ($15 in New York) [FORM 17] from the small claims court window where you filed your original claim and register it in the county clerk's office ($20). (Fees may vary from time to time so call to verify the amount.) Both of these fees are required to be reimbursed by the debtor. Once you have registered your judgment it creates a lien on real property (as a rule, including shares in a co-op). The lien is a "security interest," which transforms the debtor's real property into collateral for your debt. Registering the judgment is a necessary step in the process. The judgment can also affect all further financial dealings involving your debtor's credit rating. All the major credit agencies, such as Experian (formerly TRW), Equifax, Transunion, and so on, access the documents registered in the county clerk's office, so you can place a major hurdle in your debtor's path with this action (for details see Appendix C). (When the judgment debtor pays the debt, partially or fully, to your satisfaction, you must then file a form to indicate that the debtor has satisfied the judgment. This action results in the debtor's credit report being cleared of the impact of your judgment.) Appendix I and [FORM 16] provide the reader with further guidance on how to complete a satisfaction.

or

C. Garnish Debtor's Salary (using just the work address):

You can fax or mail your judgment along with a completed Blumberg Form T 239, "Income Execution" [FORMS 18, 19] to a city marshal (see Appendix A) with a check for $45.07. An order or directive by the marshal or the sheriff to pay the plaintiff a portion of the debtor's salary or other compensation will require the employer to do so. A garnishment can be very embarrassing to the garnishee vis-à-vis his employer and may induce a settlement. If a settlement does not occur, you will receive, on a monthly basis starting about two months from the time you initiate the garnishment, what amounts to between 10% and 25% of the debtor's weekly salary until the debt is completely paid, including the $45.07 fee (for details on how to fill out one of these forms see Appendix G and [FORM 19]).

or

D. Levy the Debtor's Bank Account (using just the name of his bank):

You can initiate a proceeding against personal property of the debtor through use of an Execution against Property (Blumberg Form B320— [FORM 25] to see a completed example), such as bank and trade accounts owing the debtor. Usually you will need to find these assets and keep them from "disappearing" by use of an Information Sub-poena and Restraining Notice. [FORMS 22, 24] are actual examples of an asset search using this instrument. Appendix G provides the details of the procedure for both the income execution and the execution against property.

E. Threatening Letters to the Debtor:

You can do all the above without notifying the debtor. However, sometimes people will respond to letters that indicate your intention to begin these procedures at specific dates in the future. Notice letters will bring rewarding responses from certain individuals, but if you use this method and indicate in your letters that you are going to do something—do it! Then indicate in a brief note that you followed through. See [FORMS 7, 15].

The judgment you receive is valid for 20 years. Put it in the folder you made specifically for judgments because collections may be stalled for a variety of reasons. For instance, you may register your judgment in the county clerk's office where its effect on the debtor may be felt years later when he decides to sell his house. I have had judgments that remained in my files for three to four years until I was able to locate the debtor's new home address and place of employment. Sometimes you must be patient, but by all means be persistent.

CHAPTER 9

Questions and Answers

Q1. CAN I SEND A STAFF PERSON OR A FRIEND TO THE HEARING OR TRIAL, INSTEAD OF GOING MYSELF?

A. If moneys are being withheld for the stated reason that your work was improperly done or left unfinished, you should be present. This is true whether you are an unpaid carpenter or chiropractor. If the defendant simply is not paying you and your work was completed or in progress and done well, you could send the office manager as I have previously related in Christine's story (see Chapter 6). Every claim has different facts surrounding it. I suggest letting those facts help guide you in determining who tells the story at the hearing (especially in those cases where choice presents itself). Sometimes I enjoy going to court. At other times I am so far removed from the facts of the case, I bring the office manager along to present them. Obviously, if you are the only person with direct knowledge of the facts, you should appear in court.

OBSERVATION *Some courts may have specific rules regarding who must be present at the small claims court hearing. In White Plains, for example, in cases involving all physicians, dentists, and chiropractors the doctor's assistant, bookkeeper, or manager is not permitted to give testimony alone. The person who "rendered the services" must be present to testify—see [FORM 38].*

Q2. WHAT IF THE DEBTOR OWES ME MORE THAN THE LIMIT ALLOWED IN SMALL CLAIMS COURT?

A. Option: If the amount in excess of the limit is not more than $1,000 to $2,000, I would seriously consider claiming only for the maximum allowed in the small claims court. Above that amount you must initiate that claim in your state's trial court, which is not always an easy task. Option: Initiate the claim in the trial court, but hire an attorney if the amount at stake (or the principle) seems worth it. Option: Turn the claim over to a collection attorney specialist. Option: Hire a topnotch collection agency, which, like the attorney, will take 35% to 50% of the collection. Think of it this way: 35% of $5,000 is $1,750. That leaves you with $3,350. I "sell" only the very difficult cases (those in which I can't locate the person and the assets), and when I do, I work with a company that handles the entire gamut of procedures related to the problems of debt collection.

Q3. IF THE RESPONSIBLE PARTY (THE ONE WHO SIGNED THE CONTRACT FOR YOUR SERVICES) IS AN UNEMPLOYED SPOUSE, CAN I NAME THE SPOUSE WHO IS EMPLOYED AS THE RESPONSIBLE PARTY ON THE INITIAL CLAIM FORM? [FORM 1]

A. Yes. Spouses are responsible for each other's debts and the debts of their children who are still minors.

Q4. IF I FILE A CLAIM AND DO NOT APPEAR IN COURT THE NIGHT OF MY HEARING, CAN I REFILE MY CLAIM?

A. Yes. The next day or whenever you want to within the Statute of Limitations.

Q5. IF I AGREE TO SETTLE BEFORE THE COURT DATE AND THE DEBTOR FAILS TO LIVE UP TO HIS END OF THE AGREEMENT AND THE COURT DATE HAS PASSED, WHAT CAN I DO?

A. File another Initial Claim form as soon as possible, and don't make the same mistake. If you make an agreement to settle, make sure the settlement amount is in your hands before the hearing date. If you have not received the payment in hand, go to the hearing so that you can negotiate from a position of greater strength.

Q6. CAN I COMPEL A PERSON TO COME TO COURT TO TESTIFY?

A. Yes, in theory. You can obtain a Subpoena to Testify at the small claims court clerk's window. The clerk will prepare it for you upon request and you pay nothing for it. He requires only the index number of your case. (See [FORM 9] and Appendix C to see a completed example). The subpoena must be served in person on the party whom you want to testify. The server must give the person being served $15 and complete an Affidavit of Service, have it notarized, and then return it to the plaintiff who returns it to the small claims court clerk (see [FORM 9]. A person whom you have subpoenaed, and who does not appear the night of the trial or hearing, runs the risk of being declared in contempt of court and/or fined. The small claims court does not have the power to enforce such a subpoena, but a subpoena gives most people who are served a cause for anxiety. At least, one occasion when I used it, the person appeared in court. Outcome—although I won the case, I didn't collect because the debtor filed for bankruptcy. (See Chapter 4—Preparing and Filing a Claim and Appendix C.)

Q7. FOR HOW LONG DOES MY JUDGMENT REMAIN IN FORCE?

A. Twenty years in New York, 15 years in New Jersey, and 15 years in Connecticut. Save your judgments in your judgments folder.

Q8. DOES MY JUDGMENT ALONE COMPEL THE DEBTOR TO PAY ME?

A. No, but you now have the legal entitlement to begin getting the money.

Q9. WHAT DO I DO IF I WANT TO START AN ACTION, BUT THE DEBTOR DOES NOT LIVE, WORK, OR DO BUSINESS IN NEW YORK CITY (MANHATTAN, BROOKLYN, BRONX, QUEENS, AND STATEN ISLAND)?

A. You must initiate your action in the county court that has jurisdiction over the town or city where the debtor lives or does business. (See Appendix A for Bergen, Hudson, and Nassau County court information). If for example he lives in Jersey City, you will have your hearing at the Hudson County Court House at 595 Newark Avenue, Jersey City, NJ 07306.

Q10. CAN I INITIATE MY CLAIM FOR THESE OUT-OF-TOWN CASES BY MAIL?

A. Yes. You must send a self-addressed, stamped envelope to the court house (see Appendix A for addresses), requesting the number of small claims forms you need to initiate the action(s) and state whether you are an individual or a corporation. At the same time, you should request any written information or instructions. You can also use [FORMS 31, 32, 40, 41] provided in the forms section of this book.

WARNING *A glance at Appendix A will show you that in Nassau County (and every small claims court in New York state) the maximum you can sue for is $3,000.*

However, in New Jersey, the maximum you can sue for is $2,000, and there are no night court hearings (none in Connecticut either). Filing a claim by mail for an individual plaintiff costs $12, plus a surcharge that may vary between $1 and $7, depending on how far away from the courthouse the summons has to be served. The court clerk will send you a list of towns and the surcharges for delivery of the summons. A telephone call to the small claims court clerk regarding filing fees, to whom they can be paid, and how to make them payable is good advice.

Q11. IF MY DEBTOR HAS MOVED AND HIS TELEPHONE IS DISCONNECTED, HOW DO I LOCATE HIM?

A. If you really enjoy sleuthing and bloodhound work, here are some of the approaches you can take:

- Send a brief letter to the debtor and just below your return address put "Forwarding and Address Correction Requested." It costs $.32 more when the postman returns your letter with the correct address.
- Simplest and cheapest—call your local telephone directory assistance.
- Call the post office of your debtor's last address and request the debtor's change of address card; if need be do same by mail (service charge is $1). A search at city hall and the county clerk's office will permit you to search a citizen's public records, such as voter registration lists, deeds, marriage licenses, certain tax records, and real estate transactions.
- For debtors who have unusual last names you can use the local phone directory to call people with the same name. Sometimes they are helpful in giving you a handle on the debtor you are looking for.
- Reverse telephone directories are commonly found in libraries and used by many real estate offices. Unlike the typical telephone book, which lists people by their last names in alphabetical order, the reverse directory lists people's addresses in alphabetical order. You can then locate your debtor's neighbors, who may be willing to assist you in locating your debtor.

- Do you have CD-ROM? Invest in some high-tech software like Phone Disc USA, which allows you to access almost 85 million names, addresses, and telephone numbers. These lists are updated quarterly and the price is about $90. (Phone Disc: (800) 284-8353)
- Call the "person to contact in case of an emergency" if you took that piece of information on your new patient information sheet at the initial contact visit.
- Joseph Culligan, a licensed private investigator has published a paperback book (and a 70-minute video based on the book) entitled *You, Too, Can Find Anybody*. It is a reference manual that contains an array of devices and schemes to help you locate your debtor. Cost: $20.

Q12. I DON'T KNOW WHERE MY JUDGMENT DEBTOR WORKS OR BANKS ANY OF HIS ASSETS. WHAT DO I DO NOW?

A. If the sum of money is worth it and you are persistent, you can begin by contacting an agency that does all phases of collection. It will be able to do skip-tracing, which is an attempt to locate your debtor's new home, place of employment, bank accounts, and other personal property.

A second approach is for you to serve an Information Subpoena and Restraining Notice (a legal demand for the answer to questions regarding the debtor's home address, employer, and bank information [FORM 22] and Appendix E) on the debtor, or the debtor's bank, employer, telephone, gas or electric company, and even his credit card company. The Information Subpoena compels each of them to supply you with the information you want. The debtor of course will deny you this information, but his bank and the other companies are legally bound to supply specific information regarding what their records contain about the debtor's employer and bank accounts. In addition, upon receipt of this subpoena the bank will stop the debtor from making any withdrawals and put a hold on his account for two times the amount of his debt to you. The hold lasts for 365 days. When you have located an asset, you can contact the marshal or sheriff to proceed with a property execution [FORM 25].

A third approach is to have a specialist in locating assets do the work for you. One such specialist is Lutz Asset Research (see Appendix A and [FORM 68]). They serve a Restraining Notice and Information Subpoena [FORM 22] on every bank in two counties of your choice where the debtor works and lives, thereby freezing assets—bank accounts and/or safe deposit vaults—until the sheriff can seize them. For example, if you were to choose Brooklyn and Manhattan, Information Subpoenas would be served on between 120 and 130 banks. Furthermore, Lutz can search for assets among the various stock brokerage houses. This service is fairly expensive so you have to decide if the procedure is worth the cost. Would you spend between $150 and $300 in return for $3,000? It's a good deal when you're certain that the defendant has a bank account with enough money to cover the debt. However, one might think twice about paying a flat fee when there is doubt that your debtor even has a bank account. The motto at the house of Lutz is: "When you have your debtor by the bank account, his heart and mind will follow."

Q13. IF I DECIDE TO ACCEPT A PERSONAL CHECK CAN I DO ANYTHING TO MAKE SURE THE CHECK IS GOOD?

A. Yes. Call the bank that the check is drawn on and ask whether there are sufficient funds to cover the amount of the check. They will ask you for the account number, which can be found on the front of the check. Every bank will verify for you immediately by telephone whether there are sufficient funds to cover a check that has been drawn on it. But remember, even if the answer is yes, by the time his check clears in your bank (3 to 5 days from the time the check is deposited in your bank) the funds may well have been withdrawn to pay other bills. Better safe than sorry—ask the maker of the check to write on the back of the check "OK to cash this check" underscored by his signature. If his intentions are good he won't hesitate; if they are not, he may opt for an alternative approach to payment.

The moral of the story is: don't accept personal checks, but when you feel obligated to, and you are in doubt, first verify sufficient coverage. Then go to the nearest branch of his bank and cash the check. Better yet, ask the defendant to pay by credit card or certified bank check or bank teller's check, but not by an ordinary bank money order because your debtor can stop payment on a bank money order, although not on a U.S. Postal Money Order.

Q14. WHAT ARE SOME ROUTINE MEASURES I CAN TAKE THAT WILL ASSIST ME IN PREVENTING OR SUCCESSFULLY PURSUING A SMALL CLAIMS LITIGATION?

A. Below is a medley of suggestions that can help you—take your choice.

- Have a written contract outlining the fees for your services or goods.
- Spell out the terms of payment for your services in that contract.
- Make certain you have the signature of the responsible party on that contract.
- If insurance is involved, include a paragraph that indicates the responsible party remains responsible for all of the bill, including that part of the bill usually covered by insurance (if for some reason insurance fails to continue its payments) as well as any parts not covered by insurance.
- On your responsible party information form include a box for Social Security information and boxes for bank and checking account numbers.
- If you are too embarrassed to do the above, or even if you are not, then make it a practice to retain photocopies of the first and final personal checks you accept.
- If possible never accept as the final payment a personal check for an amount that will make you suffer if it turns out to be lost because of a stopped payment, insufficient funds, or account closed notation on a returned check. After you have been in business a while, you will have seen all of them—so much for the voice of experience.

- Make it an office policy to reserve the right to request payment at any time by certified bank check. Have this policy on a sign behind the reception desk as well as on your contract.
- On your responsible party information form, include a box that asks: How are you going to pay your bill today? check? cash? money order? credit card? How will you be paying your bill in the future?
- Look at the answers you receive to the above items.
- Indicate in your contracts that there will be an interest charge (18% annually) on accounts 30 days overdue. Even if you waive the interest in the end, you can use it as a bargaining chip in the collection settlement.
- If paid by credit card, make a record of the type of card—Visa, MasterCard, and so on—the number and the expiration date.
- On your responsible party information sheet, include a box that asks for employer's name, address, and telephone.
- Be sure to have the responsible party provide you with an emergency contact, along with the relationship, name, and telephone number.
- Don't accept clients who refuse to abide by any of your office or business policies.

Q15. HOW CAN I DETERMINE IF MY DEBTOR IS A TRUE CAREER NONPAYER AND WHAT CAN I DO ABOUT IT?

A. In New York State, Connecticut, and New Jersey, there is a special provision that requires that all unsatisfied small claims judgments to be indexed alphabetically and chronologically under the debtor's name to facilitate securing information about evasive small claims judgment debtors. To do this search you must indicate your desire to the small claims court clerk who will guide you through the procedure. I did such a search on one occasion and discovered that prior to the time that these records were computerized they were logged in cumbersome books that were tedious to look through. So depending on the court and how records are kept you might find that this search is a breeze or a tempest in a teapot. If your search reveals your debtor is an incorrigible nonpayer, here is the reward in New York: If the debtor has at least two unpaid judgments and your judgment has not been paid after 30 days from the date you received it, you are entitled to three times the amount of your judgment assuming the debtor has the ability to pay. The small claims court clerk will advise you how to proceed in collecting your bounty. The county clerk's office also keeps records, which you may freely access, of the judgments against businesses and individuals that were filed in this office.

Chart I: Schematic Overview of the Process

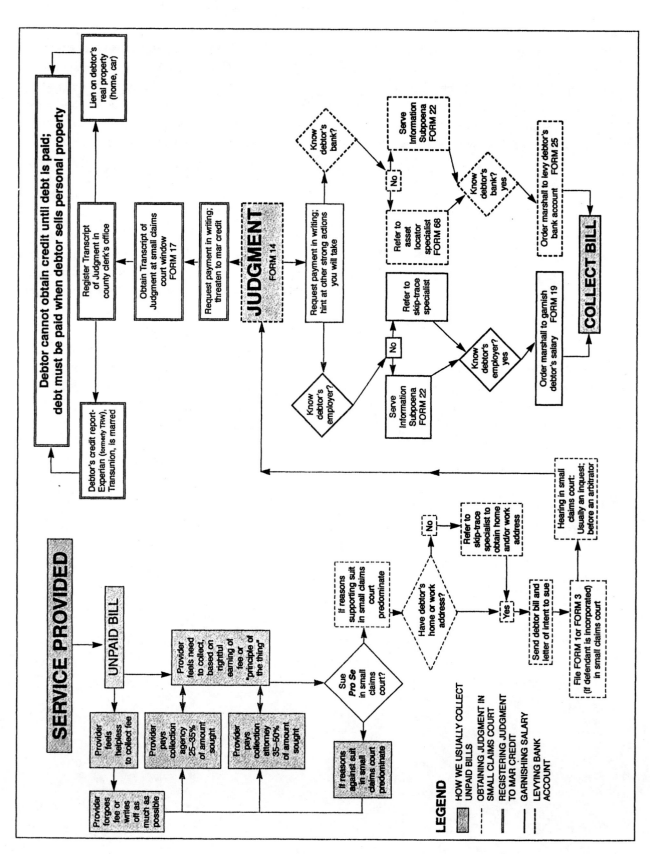

Chart II: Putting Your Judgment to Work with Minimal Effort

WITH A HOME ADDRESS
1. File Initial Claim form **(Form 1 or 3 in NYC)**
2. Obtain Judgment **(Form 14)**
3. Obtain a Transcript of Judgment **(Form 17)**
4. File transcript in County Clerk's office **(See Appendix F)**

WITH A WORK ADDRESS
1. File Initial Claim form
2. Obtain Judgment
3. Garnish debtor's salary (Income Execution) **(Forms 19 and 20)** and **(See Appendix G)**

WITH NAME OF DEBTOR'S BANK
1. File Initial Claim form
2. Obtain Judgment
3. Garnish (levy) debtor's account (Property Execution) **(Forms 20 and 25)** and **(See Appendix G)**

WHAT YOU HAVE ACHIEVED
a. Put a lien on debtor's property

b. Marred his/her credit rating

c. Made it impossible for the debtor to buy or sell a house, car, boat, real estate, etc. without first satisfying the debt owed to you

WHAT YOU HAVE ACHIEVED
a. Compelled payment of your bill over a period of time

b. Settled the matter insofar as "It's the principle of the thing"

WHAT YOU HAVE ACHIEVED
a. Prevented the debtor from closing his account

b. Stopped his/her withdrawals to pay any bills but yours

c. Compelled immediate payment of your total bill

YOUR PARTICIPATION
Attend brief hearing in defense of workmanship (if counterclaim, defendant must bring an expert witness)

YOUR PARTICIPATION
Attend brief hearing...

YOUR PARTICIPATION
Attend brief hearing...

STAFF'S ROLE
See Christine's story: shows how staff in charge of receivables may stand in at hearing for professional or owner

STAFF'S ROLE
See Christine's story

STAFF'S ROLE
See Christine's story

Addresses, Telephone Numbers, and Important Information

KINGS COUNTY

BROOKLYN SMALL CLAIMS COURT [FORM 1 or 3]

141 Livingston St. (at Jay St.)

Brooklyn, NY 11201

Subways: IND: A, C; IRT: 2, 3, 4, 5; BMT: N, R

Small Claims Court: (718) 643-7914

Civil Court: (718) 643-5069

Maximum you can sue for: $3,000

Maximum number of claims allowed per session: two

Cost per claim: $10 per individual claim not in excess of $1,000, and $15 for any claim between $1,000 and $3,000, cash only; $22.84 per corporation claim, cash only

File first paper: 2nd floor, Room 201, Mon.-Fri. 9:00 A.M.–4:30 P.M.

Defendant is notified by regular mail and certified mail.

Late night to file first paper: Thurs. until 8:30 P.M.

Courtroom location: 1st floor, Room 101

Court sessions: for day, get letter from employer stating you work steady nights

Days: Mon., Tues., Wed., and Thurs.

Nights: Mon., Tues., Wed., and Thurs.

Court session begins with the calendar call: 9:30 A.M. and 6:30 P.M.

LAW LIBRARY OF THE KINGS COUNTY SUPREME COURT (PUBLIC ACCESS)

360 Adams St. (main entrance on Court St.), 3rd floor

Brooklyn, NY 11201

(718) 643-8080

Open Mon. through Fri., 9:00 A.M.–7:00 P.M.

LAW LIBRARY OF THE BROOKLYN LAW SCHOOL

250 Joralemon St.

Brooklyn, NY 11201

(718) 780-7973

BROOKLYN BUSINESS LIBRARY

280 Cadman Plaza West

Brooklyn, NY 11210

(718) 722-3333, (718) 722-3350

BROOKLYN BAR ASSOCIATION

123 Remsen St.

Brooklyn, NY 11201

(718) 624-0675

BROOKLYN SHERIFF'S OFFICE [FORM 21]
Municipal Building
210 Joralemon St.
9th floor, Room 909
Brooklyn, NY 11201
(718) 802-3545

BROOKLYN COUNTY CLERK'S OFFICE
The Supreme Court building
360 Adams St.—basement level Room 189
Brooklyn, NY 11201
General information: (718) 643-5897
Register Transcript of Judgment: window no. 2 and
   pay $25

CITY MARSHAL'S OFFICE
(See Yellow Pages under "City Marshals")
City Marshal Marchisotto
16 Court St.
Brooklyn, NY 11201
(718) 858-9535

APPELLATE TERM OF THE SUPREME COURT
Second Judicial Department
111 Livingston St., 19th floor
Brooklyn, NY 11201
(718) 643-5730

PROCESS SERVER
(See also Yellow Pages under "Process Servers")
Service Plus
Licensed Process Servers
Nationwide Service and Investigations
32 Court St., Suite 205
Brooklyn, NY 11201
(718) 243-9317
(This listing is not to be construed as an endorsement.)

NEW YORK COUNTY
MANHATTAN SMALL CLAIMS COURT
(New York County–Downtown) [FORM 1 or 3]
111 Centre St.
(entrance at 75 Lafayette St., near City Hall)
New York, NY 10013
Small Claims Court: (212) 374-5779; recording:
   (212) 374-5776

Civil Court recording: (212) 374-8174
Maximum you can sue for: $3,000
Maximum number of claims allowed per session:
   three
Cost per claim: $10 per individual claim not in
   excess of $1,000, and $15 for any claim between
   $1,000 and $3,000, cash only; $22.84 per corpo-
   ration claim, cash only
Defendant is notified by regular mail and certified
   mail.
File first paper: 3rd floor, Room 322, Mon. through
   Fri. 9:00 A.M–5:00 P.M.
Late night to file first paper: Thurs., 1st floor, Room
   118, 9:00 A.M.–8:30 P.M.
Courtroom location: 1st floor, Room 107
Court sessions: for day, get letter from employer
   stating you work steady nights
Days: Thurs. only
Nights: Mon., Tues., Wed., and Thurs.
Court sessions begin with the calendar call: 9:30 A.M.
   and 6:15 P.M.

LAW LIBRARY (PUBLIC ACCESS)
Louis Lefkowitz State Office Building
80 Centre St., Room 468
New York, NY 10013
(212) 374-8564
Hours: Mon. through Fri., 9:30 A.M.–12:00 P.M;
   1:00 P.M.–4:30 P.M.

MANHATTAN BAR ASSOCIATION
(Association of the Bar of the City of New York)
42 West 44th St.
New York, NY 10036
(212) 382-6600

MANHATTAN SHERIFF'S OFFICE [FORM 20]
253 Broadway
8th floor, Room 800
New York, NY 10007
(212) 240-6715; (212) 240-6730
Chief Sheriff: Theresa Mason (212) 788-8731

APPELLATE TERM OF THE SUPREME COURT
First Judicial Department
Foley Square
(near the Brooklyn Bridge; Subway is IRT 4 or 5)
60 Centre St., Room 408
New York, NY 10007
(212) 374-8500

NEW YORK COUNTY CLERK'S OFFICE
Foley Square
(near the Brooklyn Bridge; subway is IRT 4 or 5)
60 Centre St.
New York, NY 10007
(212) 374-8315
File Official Transcript of Judgment in Room 109B
    (Basement), docket section
Filing fee: $25
For information regarding name of person in whose
    name a business is registered: (212) 374-8359;
    record search in Room 117B

CITY MARSHAL'S OFFICE—
(Downtown Manhattan, see also Yellow Pages
under "City Marshals")
City Marshal Moses
116 John St.
New York, NY 10003
(212) 349-4303
Fax: (212) 349-4309

PROCESS SERVER
(See also Yellow Pages under "Process Servers")
AAA Attorney Service Co. of New York, Inc.
20 Vesey St.
New York, NY 10007
(212) 233-3508
(This listing is not to be construed as an
endorsement.)

HARLEM SMALL CLAIMS COURT (New York
    County—Uptown—in preparation) [FORM 1 or 3]
Temporary Location:
Adam Clayton Powell Jr. State Office Bldg.
163 West 125th St., 8th floor
New York, NY 10027
Small Claims Court: (212) 678-6740

Subways: IND: A, C, D; IRT: 2, 3, Exit 125th St.
Permanent site under renovation may be opera-
    tional before 1998:
    121st St. (between 3rd and Lexington Ave.)
    New York, NY 10035
Subways: IND: A, C, D; IRT: 2, 3, Exit 125th St.
Maximum you can sue for: $3,000
Maximum number of claims allowed per session:
    three
Cost per claim: $10 per individual claim not in
    excess of $1,000, and $15 for any claim
    between $1,000 and $3,000, cash only; $22.84
    per corporation claim, cash only
File first paper: 2nd floor, Mon. through Wed.,
    9:00 A.M.–4:30 P.M.
Defendant is notified by regular mail and certified
    mail.
Late night to file first paper: Thurs. until 8:00 P.M.
Courtroom location: 8th floor
Court sessions: for day, get letter from employer
    stating you work steady nights
Days: Mon., Tues., and Wed.
Nights: Thurs. only.
Court session begins with the calendar call:
    9:30 A.M. and 6:30 P.M.

QUEENS COUNTY

QUEENS SMALL CLAIMS COURT [FORM 1 or 3]
120-55 Queens Blvd.
Kew Gardens, NY 11424
Small Claims Court: (718) 520-4741
Civil Court: (718) 520-4741
Maximum you can sue for: $3,000
Maximum number of claims allowed per session:
    three
Cost per claim: $10 per individual claim not in
    excess of $1,000, and $15 for any claim between
    $1,000 and $3,000, cash only; $22.84 per corpo-
    ration claim, cash only
File first paper: ground floor, Room G-20 Mon.
    through Fri. 9:00 A.M.–4:30 P.M.
Late night to file first paper: Thurs. until 8:30 P.M.
Courtroom location: 1st floor
Court sessions: for day, get letter from employer
    stating you work steady nights
Days: Mon., Tues., Wed., and Thurs.

Nights: Mon., Tues., Wed., and Thurs.
Court session begins with the calendar call: 9:30 A.M.
and 6:30 P.M.

LAW LIBRARY OF THE QUEENS COUNTY
SUPREME COURT (PUBLIC ACCESS)
88-11 Sutphin Blvd., Room 600
Jamaica, NY 11435
(718) 520-3140
Hours: Mon. through Fri., 9:00 A.M.–4:30 P.M.

QUEENS COUNTY BAR ASSOCIATION
90-35 148th St.
Jamaica, NY 11435
(718) 291-4500

QUEENS COUNTY SHERIFF'S OFFICE
4271 65th Pl.
Woodside, NY 11377
(718) 803-3091

QUEENS COUNTY CLERK'S OFFICE
88-11 Sutphin Blvd.
Room 106, section 5
Jamaica, NY 11435
(718) 520-3141

APPELLATE TERM OF THE SUPREME COURT
Second Judicial Department
111 Livingston St., 19th floor
Brooklyn, NY 11201
(718) 643-5730

PROCESS SERVER
(See also Yellow Pages under "Process Servers")
ASAP Process Serving
97-20 101 Ave.
Ozone Park, NY 11416
(718) 845-5523
(This listing not to be construed as an endorsement.)

RICHMOND COUNTY
STATEN ISLAND SMALL CLAIMS COURT
[FORM 1 or 3]
927 Castleton Ave. (at Bemont St.)
Staten Island, NY 10310

Small Claims Court: (718) 390-5421
Civil Court: (718) 390-5416
Maximum number of claims allowed per session:
five
Cost per claim: $10 per individual claim not in
excess of $1,000, and $15 for any claim between
$1,000 and $3,000, cash only; $22.84 per corpo-
rate claim, cash only
Defendant is notified by regular mail and certified
mail.
File first paper: "Downstairs Clerk's Office,"
Mon. through Fri., 9:00 A.M.–1:00 P.M.;
2:00 P.M.–5:00 P.M.
Late night to file first paper: Thurs. 5:30 P.M.–8:00 P.M.
Courtroom location: 1st floor
Court sessions: for day, get letter from employer
stating you work steady nights
Days: for senior citizens, the disabled, and night
workers
Nights: Thurs. only
Court session begins with the calendar call: 9:30 A.M.
and 6:30 P.M.

LAW LIBRARY OF THE RICHMOND COUNTY
SUPREME COURT (PUBLIC ACCESS)
18 Richmond Terr.
Staten Island, NY 10301
(718) 390-5291
Hours: Mon. through Fri., 9:00 A.M.–4:30 P.M.

RICHMOND COUNTY BAR ASSOCIATION
2012 Victory Blvd.
Staten Island, NY 10314
(718) 442-4500

STATEN ISLAND WOMEN'S BAR ASSOCIATION
1 Edgewater Pl.
Staten Island, NY 10305
(718) 273-7799

SHERIFF'S OFFICE STATEN ISLAND
350 St. Mark's Pl.
Staten Island, NY 10301
(718) 876-5307

STATEN ISLAND COUNTY CLERK'S OFFICE
18 Richmond Terr.
Room 103, "Court Desk"
Staten Island, NY 10301
(718) 390-5389

APPELLATE TERM OF THE SUPREME COURT
Second Judicial Department
111 Livingston St., 19th Fl.
Brooklyn, NY 11201
(718) 643-5730

PROCESS SERVER
(See also Yellow Pages under "Process Servers")
A Victory Process Servers
29 Hartford St.
Staten Island, NY 10308
(718) 984-5572
(This listing is not to be construed as an
endorsement.)

BRONX COUNTY
BRONX SMALL CLAIMS COURT [FORM 1 or 3]
851 Grand Concourse (at 161 St.)
Bronx, NY 10451
Small Claims Court: (718) 590-2693
Civil Court: (718) 590-3601
Maximum you can sue for: $3,000
Maximum number of claims allowed per session: three
Cost per claim: $10 per individual claim not in
    excess of $1,000, and $15 for any claim between
    $1,000 and $3,000, cash only; $22.84 per corpo-
    ration claim, cash only
File first paper: 1st floor, Room 111 Mon. through
    Fri., 9:00 A.M.–4;30 P.M.
Late night to file first paper: Wednesday,
    9:00 A.M.–8:30 P.M.
Courtroom location: basement, "Part" 18
Court sessions: for day, get letter from employer
    stating you work steady nights; also for the dis-
    abled and the elderly
Days: Friday only
Nights: Mon., Tues., and Wed.
Court session begins with the calendar call: 9:30 A.M.
    and 6:30 P.M.

LAW LIBRARY OF THE BRONX SUPREME COURT
(PUBLIC ACCESS)
851 Grand Concourse, Room 829
Bronx, NY 10451
(718) 590-3678
Hours: Mon. through Fri., 9:30 A.M.–1:00 P.M.

BRONX BAR ASSOCIATION
851 Grand Concourse
Bronx, NY 10451
(718) 293-5600

BRONX COUNTY SHERIFF'S OFFICE
332 E. 149th St., 2nd floor
Bronx, NY 10451
(718) 585-1551

BRONX COUNTY CLERK'S OFFICE
851 Grand Concourse
Room 118, main floor, "Docket Department"
Bronx, NY 10451
(718) 590-3640

APPELLATE TERM OF THE SUPREME COURT
First Judicial Department
Foley Square
60 Centre St.
New York, NY 10007
(212) 374 -8500

PROCESS SERVER
(See also Yellow Pages under "Process Servers")
All County Service Corp.
2111 White Plains Rd.
Bronx, NY 10462
(718) 792-0099
(This listing is not to be construed as an
endorsement.)

NASSAU COUNTY [FORMS 31, 32]
....
WARNING *An individual may initiate a claim against
another individual or against an incorporated entity by
filing an initial claim form in any one of Nassau
County's four district courts. However, if you are an
incorporated entity and want to sue another incorporated*

entity, you have the option to file the initial claim form in the night court of the First District Court in Hempstead; otherwise, you must file in the district court that has jurisdiction over the town or village where the corporate entity you want to sue resides.

••

DISTRICT COURT OF NASSAU COUNTY—
FIRST DISTRICT
99 Main St.
Hempstead, NY 11550
Small Claims Court: (516) 572-2261
Civil Court: (516) 572-2266
Maximum you can sue for: $3,000
Maximum number of claims allowed per session: five; for corporations five total per calendar month
File initial claim by mail: send self-addressed, stamped envelope to get form, individual or corporation, sign the initial claim form before a notary public
Cost per claim: $10 per individual claim not in excess of $1,000, and $15 for any claim between $1,000 and $3,000, cash only; $22.84 per corporation claim, cash only
File first paper: 2nd floor, civil office, Mon. through Fri., 9:00 A.M.–4:30 P.M., not between 1:00 P.M. and 2:00 P.M.
Late night to file first paper: none
Court sessions: Days: Mon. and Fri.
Nights: Tues., Wed., and Thurs., 1st floor
Court session begins with the calendar call: 9:30 A.M. and 6:00 P.M.

DISTRICT COURT OF NASSAU COUNTY—
SECOND DISTRICT
99 Main St.
Hempstead, NY 11550
Small Claims Court: (516) 572-2261 (2)
Civil Court: (516) 572-2266
Maximum you can sue for: $3,000
Maximum number of claims allowed per session: five total per calendar month
File initial claim by mail: Send self-addressed stamped envelope to get form, individual or corporation, sign the initial claim form before a notary public

Cost per claim: $10 per individual claim not in excess of $1,000, and $15 for any claim between $1,000 and $3,000, cash only; $22.84 per corporation claim, cash only
File first papers: 2nd floor, civil office, 9:00 A.M.– 1:00 P.M.; 2:00 P.M.–4:30 P.M.
Late night to file first papers: none
Court sessions: Days: Mon. and Fri., 2nd floor, Courtroom 280
Nights: Tues., Wed., and Thurs., 1st floor
Court session begins with the calendar call: 9:30 A.M. and 6:00 P.M.

DISTRICT COURT OF NASSAU COUNTY—
THIRD DISTRICT
435 Middle Neck Rd.
Great Neck, NY 11023
Small Claims Court: (516) 571-8402
Civil Court: (516) 571-8402
Maximum you can sue for: $3,000
Maximum number of claims allowed per session: five total per calendar month
File initial claim by mail: Send self-addressed stamped envelope to get form, individual or corporation, sign the initial claim form before a notary public
Cost per claim: $10 per individual claim not in excess of $1,000, and $15 for any claim between $1,000 and $3,000, cash only; $22.84 per corporation claim, cash only
File first papers: Mon. through Fri., 9:00 A.M.– 1:00 P.M.; 2:00 P.M.–4:30 P.M.
Late night to file first papers: none
Court sessions: Days: Mon. and Thurs., Courtroom 1st floor
Nights: None
Court session begins with the calendar call: 9:30 A.M.

DISTRICT COURT OF NASSAU COUNTY—
FOURTH DISTRICT
87 Bethpage Rd.
Hicksville, NY 11801
Small Claims Court: (516) 571-7089
Civil Court: (516) 571-7089
Maximum you can sue for: $3,000

Maximum number of claims allowed per session: five total per calendar month

File initial claim by mail: Send self-addressed stamped envelope to get form, individual or corporation; sign the initial claim form before a notary public.

Cost per claim: $10 per individual claim not in excess of $1,000, and $15 for any claim between $1,000 and $3,000, cash only; $22.84 per corporation claim, cash only

File first papers: 1st. floor, Mon. through Fri., 9:00 A.M.–1:00 P.M.; 2:00 P.M.–4:30 P.M.

Late night to file first papers: none

Court sessions: Days: Mon., Tues., Wed., 1st floor
Nights: None

Court session begins with the calendar call: 9:30 A.M.

NASSAU COUNTY BAR ASSOCIATION
15 and West St.
Mineola, NY 11501
(516) 747-4070

NASSAU COUNTY SHERIFF'S OFFICE
240 Old Country Rd.
Mineola, NY 11501
(516) 571-2113

NASSAU COUNTY CLERK'S OFFICE
240 Old Country Rd.
Mineola, NY 11501
(516) 571-2282 (recording); (516) 571-2666 (voice)

APPELLATE TERM OF THE SUPREME COURT
Ninth and Tenth Judicial Districts
100 Supreme Court Dr.
Mineola, NY 11501
(516) 571-2903

PROCESS SERVER
(see also Yellow Pages under "Process Servers")
Always Dependable Process Service Ltd.
44 Adams St.
East Rockaway, NY 11518
(516) 596-0004
(This listing is not to be construed as an endorsement.)

SUFFOLK COUNTY SMALL CLAIMS COURT [FORM 33]

WARNING *Exceptions for Incorporated Individuals or Entities: If you are an incorporated entity your hearing will most likely be held during the day court session and if you filed in a more outlying area such as Babylon in the Second District Court, it is likely that your hearing will be held in Hauppauge in the North County Complex, Building C, 158 Veterans Memorial Highway, (516) 853-5406.*

ISLIP TOWNSHIP
FIRST DISTRICT COURT (See Fifth District Court)
400 Carleton Ave.
Central Islip, NY 11722
Small Claims Court: (516) 853-5402
Civil Court: (516) 853-7611
Maximum you can sue for: $3,000
Maximum number of claims allowed per session: five

File initial claim by mail: 2nd floor, window 13

Cost per claim: $10 per individual claim not in excess of $1,000, and $15 for any claim between $1,000 and $3,000, cash only; $23.16 per corporation claim, cash only

File first paper: Mon. through Fri., 9:00 A.M.–1:00 P.M.; 2:00 P.M.–4:30 P.M.

Late night to file first paper: none

Court sessions: Days: only for corporations
Nights: second Wednesday night of the month (for individual claims)

Court session begins with the calendar call: 9:30 A.M. and 6:00 P.M.

Peculiarity: Individual claims must be filed with the Fifth District Court (same address for both courts).

BABYLON TOWNSHIP
Second District Court
375 Commack Rd.
Deer Park, NY 11729
Small Claims Court: (516) 854-1950
Civil Court: (516) 854-1950
Maximum you can sue for: $3,000
Maximum number of claims allowed per session: five per calendar month

File initial claim by mail: Send self-addressed stamped envelope to request form (individual or corporation)

Cost per claim: $10 exact cash only; $23.16 per corporate claim

File first papers: 2nd floor

North Fork Bank, Mon. through Fri., 9:00 A.M.–1:00 P.M. and 2:00 P.M.–4:30 P.M.

Late night to file first paper: none

Court sessions: Days: Mon. and Thurs. (only individual claims)

Nights: None

Court sessions begins with the calendar call: 9:30 A.M.

HUNTINGTON TOWNSHIP

Third District Court

1850 New York Ave.

Huntington Station, NY 11746

Small Claims Court: (516) 854-4545

Civil Court: (516) 854-4545

Maximum you can sue for: $3,000

Maximum number of claims allowed per session: five per calendar month

File initial claim by mail: Send self-addressed stamped envelope to request form (individual or corporation)

Cost per claim: $10 exact cash only; $23.16 per corporation claim

File first papers: Mon. through Fri., 9:00 A.M.–1:00 P.M. and 2:00 P.M.–4:30 P.M.

Late night to file first papers: none

Court sessions: Days: Tues. and Wed. (only individuals, not corporations)

Nights: None

Court session begins with the calendar call: 9:30 A.M.

SMITHTOWN TOWNSHIP

Fourth District Court

North County Complex, Building C

158 Veterans Memorial Highway

Hauppauge, NY 11788

Small Claims Court: (516) 853-5410

Civil Court: (516) 853-5410

Maximum you can sue for: $3,000

Maximum number of claims allowed per session: five per calendar month

File initial claim by mail: Send self-addressed stamped envelope to request form (individual or corporation)

Cost per claim: $10 per individual claim not in excess of $1,000, and $15 for any claim between $1,000 and $3,000, cash only; $23.16 per corporation claim (Beware! Call in advance for procedural variations.)

File first paper: Mon. through Fri., 9:00 A.M.–4:30 P.M. All windows closed 1:00 P.M.–2:00 P.M.

Late night to file first paper: none

Court sessions: Days: Wed. for individuals and corporations

Nights: None

Court session begins with the calendar call: 9:30 A.M.

ISLIP TOWNSHIP

Fifth District Court (See First District Court)

400 Carleton Ave.

Central Islip, NY 11722

Small Claims Court: (516) 853-5402

Civil Court: (516) 853-7611

Maximum you can sue for: $3,000

Maximum number of claims allowed per session: five per calendar month

File initial claim by mail: No

Cost per claim: $10 per individual claim not in excess of $1,000, and $15 for any claim between $1,000 and $3,000, cash only; $22.84 per corporation claim

File first papers: Mon. through Fri., 9:00 A.M.–1:00 P.M. and 2:00 P.M.–4:30 P.M.

Late night to file first papers: none

Court sessions: Days: Mon., Tues., Wed., Thurs. and Fri., Courtroom 2nd Fl. for individuals (not incorporated) only

Nights: None

Court sessions begins with the calendar call: 9:30 A.M.

BROOKHAVEN TOWNSHIP

Sixth District Court

150 W. Main St.

Patchogue, NY 11772

Small Claims Court: (516) 854-1440

Civil Court: (516) 854-1440

Maximum you can sue for: $3,000

Maximum number of claims allowed per session: five per calendar month

File initial claim by mail: Send self-addressed stamped envelope to request form (individual or corporation)

Cost per claim: $10 per individual claim not in excess of $1,000, and $15 for any claim between $1,000 and $3,000, cash only; $23.16 per corporation claim

File first paper: Mon. through Fri., 9:00 A.M.– 1:00 P.M.; 2:00 P.M.–4:30 P.M.

Late night to file first paper: none

Court sessions: Days: Thurs. and Fri., Courtroom 1st floor, for individual claims only

Nights: None

Court session begins with the calendar call: 9:30 A.M

LAW LIBRARY OF THE SUPREME COURT
(PUBLIC ACCESS)
400 Carleton Ave.
Central Islip, NY 11722
(516) 853-7865
Hours: Mon. through Fri., 9:00 A.M.–5:00 P.M.

LIBRARY OF STATE UNIVERSITY OF NEW YORK
(SUNY) AT STONY BROOK
Stony Brook, NY 11790
(516) 632-7110 (Reference library)
(516) 632-7160
Hours: Mon. through Thurs. 8:30 A.M.–12:00 A.M., and Fri. 8:30 A.M.–10:00 P.M., Sat. 8:30 A.M.–8:00 P.M., and Sun. 12:00 P.M.–12:00 A.M.

APPELLATE TERM OF THE SUPREME COURT
Ninth and Tenth Judicial Districts
100 Supreme Court Dr.
Mineola, NY 11501
(516) 571-2903

SUFFOLK COUNTY BAR ASSOCIATION
560 Wheeler Rd.
Hauppauge, NY 11788
(516) 234-5511

SUFFOLK COUNTY SHERIFF'S OFFICE
100 Center Dr.
Riverhead, NY 11901
(516) 852-2200

SUFFOLK COUNTY CLERK'S OFFICE
County Center
210 Center Drive
Riverhead, NY 11901
(516) 852-2200

SUFFOLK COUNTY CIVIL BUREAU
112 Old Country Rd.
Westhampton, NY 11977
(516) 852-8000

PROCESS SERVER
(See also Yellow Pages under "Process Servers")
Everready Process Service Inc.
129 Main St.
Stony Brook, NY 11790
(516) 751-0239
(This listing is not to be construed as an endorsement.)

WESTCHESTER COUNTY

Westchester County is composed of six cities: White Plains, Yonkers, New Rochelle, Mount Vernon, Peekskill, and Rye; 19 towns (e.g., Bedford and Cortland); and 19 villages (e.g., Pelham Manor and Elmsford). Each city, town, and village has its own small claims court for a total of 44 courts. A complete list may be found in the Westchester-Putnam County White Pages (Area Code 914)—see "Local Government Offices City, Town & Village" in the blue section in the back of the book.

WHITE PLAINS SMALL CLAIMS COURT [FORM 37]
White Plains City Court
77 S. Lexington Ave.
White Plains, NY 10601
Small Claims Court: (914) 422-6056
Civil Court: (914) 422-6056
Maximum you can sue for: $3,000
Maximum number of claims allowed per session: three per individual per month; five per corporation per month

Cost per claim: $10 per individual claim not in excess of $1,000, and $15 for any claim between $1,000 and $3,000, cash only; $22.84 per corporation claim, cash only

Hours to file initial claim: Mon. through Fri., 8:30 A.M.–4:00 P.M.

File through the mail: Send self-addressed stamped envelope and request initial claim form (individual or corporation)

Late night to file first paper: None

Courtroom location: Main floor

Court sessions: Days: Alternate Wed.

Nights: Alternate Wed.

Court session begins with the calendar call: 4:30 P.M. and 6:30 P.M.

LAW LIBRARY OF THE WESTCHESTER COUNTY COURT HOUSE (PUBLIC ACCESS)
111 Grove St., 9th floor
White Plains, NY 10601
(914) 285-3900
Hours: Mon. through Fri. 9:00 A.M.–5:00 P.M.

WESTCHESTER COUNTY BAR ASSOCIATION
300 Hamilton Ave.
White Plains, NY 10601
(914) 761-5151

WESTCHESTER COUNTY SHERIFF'S OFFICE
110 Grove St., 2nd floor
White Plains, NY 10601
(914) 285-3053

WESTCHESTER COUNTY CLERK'S OFFICE
110 Grove St., Room 330
White Plains, NY 10601
(914) 285-3080

CITY MARSHAL'S OFFICE—WHITE PLAINS
(See also Yellow Pages under "City Marshals")
City Marshal Kowalick
45 S. Broadway
Yonkers, NY 10701
(914) 476-2277

APPELLATE TERM OF THE SUPREME COURT
Second Judicial Department
111 Grove St.
White Plains, NY 10601
(914) 422-6058

PROCESS SERVER
(see also White Plains Yellow Pages under "Process Servers")
United States Process Service, Inc.
7 Central Park Ave.
Yonkers, NY 10705
(914) 968-4757
(This listing is not to be construed as an endorsement.)

PELHAM SMALL CLAIMS COURT [FORM 34]
Pelham Justice Court
34 5th Ave.
Pelham, NY 10803
(914) 738-2205
Civil Court: (914) 738-2205
Maximum you can sue for: $3,000
Maximum number of claims allowed per session: three
Cost per claim: $10 per individual claim not in excess of $1,000, and $15 for any claim between $1,000 and $3,000, cash only; no corporations, partnerships or associations may use the small claims portion of the justice court.
File first paper: Tues. and Fri. 9:00 A.M.–11:30 A.M., or by mail
Defendant is notified by regular mail and certified mail.
Late night to file first paper: none
Courtroom location: Justice Court, ground floor
Court sessions: Days: Wed.
Court session begins with the calendar call: 9:30 A.M.

NEW JERSEY
HUDSON COUNTY COURT HOUSE
SMALL CLAIMS COURT [FORM 41]
Special Civil Part, Room 711
595 Newark Ave.
Jersey City, NJ 07306
Small Claims Court: (201) 795-6672
Civil Court: (201) 795-6680

Maximum number of claims allowed per session: Unlimited

Maximum you can sue for: $2,000

Cost per claim: $14 plus $2 for distant service and $2 each extra person you want to name as defendant; $14 per corporation claim

File first paper: 7th floor, Room 711 Mon. through Fri., 8:30 A.M.–4:30 P.M.

File through the mail: See [FORM 41]. Send self-addressed stamped envelope to court house, mark it: "Attn.: Special Civil Part," and request the number of forms and the instruction booklet necessary to help you fill out the form.

Late night to file first paper: none

Courtroom location: 7th floor, Room 711

Court sessions: Days Only: Mon. and Thurs.: 8:30 A.M.–12:30 P.M.; 1:30 P.M.–4:30 P.M.

Court session begins with the calendar call: 8:30 A.M.

LAW LIBRARY OF THE HUDSON COUNTY COURT HOUSE (PUBLIC ACCESS)
595 Newark Avenue, 6th floor
Newark, NJ 07306
(201) 795-6629
Hours: Mon. through Fri., 8:30 A.M.–4:00 P.M.

HUDSON COUNTY BAR ASSOCIATION
583 Newark Ave.
Jersey City, NJ 07306
(201) 798-4708 ([201] 798-2727 for lawyer referral service)

HUDSON COUNTY CLERK'S OFFICE
583 Newark Ave., 1st floor
Jersey City, NJ 07306
(201) 795-6112

HUDSON COUNTY SHERIFF'S OFFICE
595 Newark Ave., ground floor
Jersey City, NJ 07306
(201) 795-6300

SUPERIOR COURT OF NEW JERSEY–
APPELLATE DIVISION
Richard J. Hughs Justice Complex, CN 006
Trenton, NJ 08625
(609) 292-4822
Call for *pro se* appeals forms and instruction package.

PROCESS SERVER
(See Yellow Pages under "Process Servers")
DGR Subpoena and Messenger Service, Inc.
47 Bloomfield Ave.
Caldwell, NJ 07006
(201) 403-1700
(800) 326-0404
(This listing is not to be construed as an endorsement.)

BERGEN COUNTY

BERGEN COUNTY COURT HOUSE
SMALL CLAIMS COURT [FORM 40]
10 Main St.
Special Civil Part, Room 430
Hackensack, NJ 07601
(201) 646-2236

File through the mail: Send self-addressed stamped envelope to the courthouse, mark it "Attn.: Special Civil Part," and request forms and instruction booklet necessary to file a small claims action.

Maximum you can sue for: $2,000

Maximum number of claims allowed per session: unlimited

Cost per claim $14 plus $1 to $7 depending on where the summons is to be delivered; $14 per corporation claim

Late night to file initial claim: None

Courtroom location: 1st floor, Room 122

Court sessions: Days Only: Mon. and Tue. 9:00 A.M.–12:30 P.M. and 1:30 P.M.–4:00 P.M.

Court session begins with the calendar call at 9:00 A.M. and 1:30 P.M.

LIBRARY OF THE BERGEN COUNTY
JUSTICE CENTER (PUBLIC ACCESS)
10 Main St., Room 208
Hackensack, NJ 07601
(201) 646-2056
Hours: Mon. through Fri., 8:30 A.M.–4:30 P.M.

BERGEN COUNTY BAR ASSOCIATION
61 Hudson St.
Hackensack, NJ 07601
(201) 488-0032

BERGEN COUNTY CLERK'S OFFICE
10 Main St., 1st Floor
Hackensack, NJ 07601
(201) 646-2101

BERGEN COUNTY SHERIFF'S OFFICE
10 Main St., 2nd Floor
Hackensack, NJ 07601
(201) 646-2200

SUPERIOR COURT OF NEW JERSEY–APPELLATE DIVISION
Richard J. Hughes Justice Complex, CN 006
Trenton, NJ 08625
(609) 292-4822
Call for *pro se* appeals forms and instruction package.

PROCESS SERVER
DGR Subpoena and Messenger Service, Inc.
47 Bloomfield Ave.
Caldwell, NJ 07006
(201) 403-1700
(800) 326-0404
(This listing is not to be construed as an endorsement.)

CONNECTICUT

[FORM 54] as exemplified by:
Fairfield County: Greenwich-Stamford-Norwalk
Connecticut is not judicially divided into counties. It is comprised of geographical areas. Appendix B lists all of the superior courts of Connecticut with small claims divisions by geographical area (G.A.). See also [FORM 51]

[FORM 51] is a general instruction sheet.
[FORM 54] shows how the initial claim form is completed.

SUPERIOR COURT LOCATION G.A. 1.:
The Greenwich-Stamford-Norwalk area northeast of Westchester, NY
See Appendix B for all of Connecticut's G.A. court locations.
Superior Court (G.A. 1)
123 Hoyt St.
Stamford, CT 06905
General information: (203) 965-5207
Small Claims Court: (203) 965-5236
Civil Court: (203) 965-5207
Maximum you can sue for: $2,500
Claims per session: unlimited
Cost per claim: $30 per individual claim, personal checks are acceptable (some restrictions); if you win your case the $30 fee is added to the amount of your judgment award and is collectible from the defendant; $30 per corporation claim, added to the judgment if you win
Note: If claim is against a business, find out if the business is a corporation. Call the Secretary of State's office, Commercial Recording Division (203) 566-8570, or write to Secretary of State, Corporate Information, 30 Trinity Street, Hartford, CT 06106. If the business is not a corporation, call the Town Clerk's office (203) 965-5308 (G.A. 1) and get the name(s) of the owner(s).
File first paper: 2nd floor, Mon. through Fri., 9:00 A.M.–1:00 P.M.; 2:30 P.M.–4:00 P.M.
File through the mail: yes
Defendant is notified of claim by first class mail
Late night to file first paper: None
Courtroom location: Justice Court, ground floor
Court sessions: Days Only: Tue.
Court sessions: 10:00 A.M.–11:30 P.M.; 1:30 P.M.–4:00 P.M.
Court session begins with the calendar call at 10:00 A.M. and 11:30 A.M.

HARTFORD SMALL CLAIMS COURT (G.A. 14)
Superior Court
95 Washington St.
Hartford, CT 06106
(860) 548-2751
Court sessions: Hearings on Fri. 10:00 A.M.

PLANNING TIP *All small claims forms, instruction booklets, geographic areas (22 of them), list of courts, lists of sheriffs, and instructions for using sheriff are used statewide and can be obtained in a bulk package from the above office on request with a stamped ($1.70), self-addressed 8½" × 11" envelope.*

CONNECTICUT STATE LAW LIBRARY
at STAMFORD-NORWALK SUPERIOR COURT
(PUBLIC ACCESS)
123 Hoyt St.
Stamford, CT 06905
(203) 359-1114
Mon. through Fri., 9:00 A.M.–5:00 P.M.

REGIONAL BAR ASSOCIATION
(STAMFORD-NORWALK)
970 Summer St.
Stamford, CT 06905
(203) 327-7041

LEGAL REFERRAL SERVICE
1 Lafayette Circle
Bridgeport, CT 06601
(203) 336-3851

NOTE *This service will send you a booklet on using the small claims court, which lists a variety of legal services offered in Connecticut: statewide, in Hartford County, and in the Greater New Haven area; legal consultations are specifically available to help the needy in matters of eviction, domestic problems, elder law, and special education.*

HIGH SHERIFF'S OFFICE OF FAIRFIELD COUNTY
Sheriff Edwin Mak
1061 Main St.
Bridgeport, CT 06604
(203) 579-6239

SHERIFF'S OFFICE (GREENWICH)
Sheriff Joseph Purcell (Fairfield County)
30 Grey Rock Dr.
Greenwich, CT 06831
(203) 531-8544

TOWN CLERK AT TOWN HALL (GREENWICH)
101 Field Point Rd.
Greenwich, CT 06830
(203) 622-7897

TOWN CLERK AT TOWN HALL (STAMFORD)
888 Washington Blvd.
Stamford, CT 06901
(203) 977-4054

PROCESS SERVER—Not applicable

NOTE *Connecticut does not have process servers. The work of serving papers in legal matters is done solely by sheriffs. Each geographical area (G.A., 22 in all) has many sheriffs. To locate a sheriff call the county sheriff's office (in some counties designated as the "High Sheriff") of the county in which your debtor lives.*

SECRETARIES OF STATE: NEW YORK, NEW JERSEY, AND CONNECTICUT

SECRETARY OF STATE CONNECTICUT
Commercial Recording Division
30 Trinity St.
Hartford, CT 06106
(860) 566-8570

SECRETARY OF STATE CONNECTICUT
Corporation Information
30 Trinity St.
Hartford, CT 06106
(860) 566-2764

SECRETARY OF STATE NEW YORK
Corporation Bureau
41 State St., 2nd floor
Albany, NY 12231
(518) 473-2492
(900) 835-2677 ($4.00 flat rate to get corporate
    information direct by phone)

SECRETARY OF STATE NEW YORK
Summons Unit
41 State St., 2nd floor
Albany, NY 12231
(518) 473-2492

To obtain information regarding who to name as
defendant in a suit against a corporation

SECRETARY OF STATE NEW JERSEY
820 Bear Tavern Rd.
West Trenton, NJ 08628
(609) 530-6431
To request corporate information by Federal Express
  Division of Commercial Recording

DEPARTMENT OF STATE NEW JERSEY
CN451
Trenton, NJ 08625-0451
To request information about corporations by regu-
  lar mail ($5 per request)
Request a "Corporation Status Report"

SPECIALIST IN SKIP-TRACE (NATIONWIDE)

Locating a person's home address and place of
employment, and other investigative services:

MARKLE INVESTIGATIONS
(Licensed, bonded and insured)
10 Columbus Blvd.
Hartford, CT 06106

(203) 725-6865
Fax: (203) 234-8678
(This listing is not to be construed as an endorsement.)

LAW OFFICES

HOWARD LEE SCHIFF, P.C. (ESPECIALLY
CONNECTICUT, MASSACHUSETTS, AND
RHODE ISLAND)
1205 Main St.
P.O. Box 280245
East Hartford, CT 06128-7602
(860) 528-9991
Fax: (860) 528-7602
(For collection and asset location: this listing is not
  to be construed as an endorsement.)

SPECIALIST IN ASSET LOCATION (NEW YORK)

LUTZ ASSET RESEARCH [FORM 68]
330 West 42nd St., 30th floor
New York, NY 10036-6902
Voice: (212) 760-0240 (2) (3)
Fax: (212) 760- 0241
(This listing is not to be construed as an endorsement.)

Location and Telephone Number of Small Claims Courts

THE SMALL CLAIMS COURTS OF NEW YORK

(*Indicates that this court is given special attention in Appendix A)

ALBANY COUNTY

Albany City Court—Civil Part
209 City Hall, Eagle and Maiden La.
Albany, NY 12207
(518) 434-5113

Watervliet City Court
15th and Broadway
Watervliet, NY 12189
(518) 270-3803

ALLEGHENY COUNTY

No large city small claims court; only town or village justice courts.
Inquire: (716) 268-5815

BRONX COUNTY*

Civil Court of the City of New York—
Bronx Branch
851 Grand Concourse (at 161 St.)
Bronx, NY 10451
(718) 590-3601

BROOME COUNTY

Binghamton City Court
Governmental Plaza
Binghamton, NY 13901
(607) 772-7041

CATTARAUGUS COUNTY

Olean City Court
P.O. Box 631
Olean, NY 14760
(716) 375-5620

Salamanca City Court
225 Wildwood Ave.
Municipal Center
Salamanca, NY 14779
(716) 945-4153

CAYUGA COUNTY

Auburn City Court
153 Genesee St.
Auburn, NY 13021
(315) 253-1570

CHAUTAUQUA COUNTY

Dunkirk City Court
342 Central Ave.
City Hall
Dunkirk, NY 14048
(716) 366-2055

Jamestown City Court
City Hall
Jamestown, NY 14701
(716) 483-7561 or (716) 483-7562

CHEMUNG COUNTY

Elmira Civil Court
317 E. Church St.
Elmira, NY 14901
(607) 737-5681

CHENANGO COUNTY

Norwich City Court
45 Broad St.
Norwich, NY 13815-0430
(607) 334-1224

CLINTON COUNTY

Plattsburgh City Court
41 City Hall Pl.
Plattsburgh, NY 12901
(518) 563-7870

COLUMBIA COUNTY

Hudson City Court
427 Warren St.
Hudson, NY 12534
(518) 828-3100

CORTLAND COUNTY

Cortland City Court
25 Court St.
Cortland, NY 13045
(607) 753-1811

DELAWARE COUNTY

No large city small claims court
Inquire: (607) 746-2123

DUTCHESS COUNTY

Beacon City Court
463 Main St.
Beacon, NY 12508
(914) 838-5030

Poughkeepsie City Court
Civic Center Plaza
Poughkeepsie, NY 12601
(914) 451-4091

ERIE COUNTY

Buffalo City Court
50 Delaware Ave.
Buffalo, NY 14202
(716) 847-8200

Lackawanna City Court
714 Ridge Rd., Room 225
Lackawanna, NY 14218
(716) 827-6486

Tonawanda City Court
200 Niagara St.
Tonawanda, NY 14150
(716) 693-3484

ESSEX COUNTY

No large city small claims court
Inquire: (518) 873-3600

FRANKLIN COUNTY

No large city small claims court
Inquire: (518) 483-6767

FULTON COUNTY

Gloversville City Court
City Hall, Frontage Rd.
Gloversville, NY 12078
(518) 773-4527

Johnstown City Court
City Hall
Johnstown, NY 12095
(518) 762-0007

GENESEE COUNTY
Batavia City Court
P.O. Box 385
Batavia, NY 14021
(716) 343-8180

GREENE COUNTY
No large city small claims court
Inquire: (518) 943-2050

HAMILTON COUNTY
No large city small claims court
Inquire: (518) 548-7111

HERKIMER COUNTY
Little Falls City Court
659 E. Main St.
Little Falls, NY 13365
(315) 823-1690

JEFFERSON COUNTY
Watertown City Court
Municipal Bldg.
245 Washington St.
Watertown, NY 13601
(315) 785-7785

KINGS COUNTY*
Civil Court of the City of New York—Kings Branch
141 Livingston St. (at Jay St.)
Brooklyn, NY 11201
(718) 643-6419 or (718) 643-8133

LEWIS COUNTY
No large city small claims courts
Inquire: (315) 376-5333

LIVINGSTON COUNTY
No large city small claims courts
Inquire: (716) 243-7010

MADISON COUNTY
Oneida City Court
109 N. Main St.
Oneida, NY 13421
(315) 363-1310

MONROE COUNTY
Rochester City Court
Hall of Justice
Rochester, NY 14614
(716) 428-2444

MONTGOMERY COUNTY
Amsterdam City Court
Public Safety Bldg., Room 208
Amsterdam, NY 12010
(518) 842-9510

NASSAU COUNTY
Nassau District Court #1*
99 Main St.
Hempstead, NY 11550
(516) 572-2200

Nassau District Court #2*
99 Main St.
Hempstead, NY 11550
(516) 572-2264

Nassau District Court #3*
435 Middle Neck Rd.
Great Neck, NY 11023
(516) 571-8400 or (516) 571-8402

Nassau District Court #4*
87 Bethpage Rd.
Hicksville, NY 11801
(516) 571-7090

Glen Cove City Court
13 Glen St.
Glen Cove, NY 11542
(516) 676-0109

Long Beach City Court
1 West Chester St.
Long Beach, NY 11561
(516) 431-1000

NEW YORK COUNTY*

Civil Court of the City of New York—
  New York Branch
111 Centre St.
New York, NY 10013
(212) 374-7915

NIAGARA COUNTY

Lockport City Court
Municipal Bldg., One Locks Plaza
Lockport, NY 14094
(716) 439-6660

Niagara Falls City Court
520 Hyde Park Blvd.
Niagara Falls, NY 14301
(716) 286-4505

North Tonawanda City Court
City Hall
North Tonawanda, NY 14120
(716) 693-1010

ONEIDA COUNTY

Rome City Court
301 James St.
Rome, NY 13440
(315) 339-7693

Sherril City Court
601 Sherril Rd.
Sherril, NY 13461
(315) 363-0996

Utica City Court
413 Oriskany St. West
Utica, NY 13502
(315) 724-8157

ONONDAGA COUNTY

Syracuse City Court
511 State St.
Syracuse, NY 13202
(315) 477-2782

ONTARIO COUNTY

Canandaigua City Court
2 N. Main St.
Canandaigua, NY 14424
(716) 396-5011

Geneva City Court
Castle St., City Hall
Geneva, NY 14456
(315) 781-2802

ORANGE COUNTY

Middletown City Court
2 James St.
Middletown, NY 10940
(914) 346-4050

Newburgh City Court
57 Broadway
Newburgh, NY 12550
(914) 565-3208

Port Jervis City Court
14-18 Hammond St.
Port Jervis, NY 12771
(914) 858-4034

ORLEANS COUNTY

No large city small claims court
Inquire: (607) 746-2123

OSWEGO COUNTY

Fulton City Court
141 S. 1st St.
Fulton, NY 13069
(315) 593-8400

Oswego City Court
City Hall
Oswego, NY 13126
(315) 343-0415

OTSEGO COUNTY
Otsego City Court
81 Main St.
Otsego, NY 13137
(607) 432-4480

PUTNAM COUNTY
No large city small claims court
Inquire: (914) 225-3641

QUEENS COUNTY*
Civil Court of the City of New York–
Queens Branch
120-55 Queens Blvd.
Kew Gardens, NY 11435
(718) 520-4733

RENSSELAER COUNTY
Rensselaer City Court
City Hall
Rensselaer, NY 12144
(518) 462-6751

Troy City Court
51 State St.
Troy, NY 12180
(518) 274-2816

RICHMOND COUNTY*
Civil Court of the City of New York—
Richmond County Branch
927 Castleton Ave.
Staten Island, NY 10310
(718) 390-5342 or (718) 390-5416

ROCKLAND COUNTY
No large city small claims court
Inquire: (914) 638-5070

SARATOGA COUNTY
Mechanicville City Court
36 N. Main St.
Mechanicville, NY 12118
(518) 664-9876

Saratoga Springs City Court
City Hall
474 Broadway
Saratoga Springs, NY 12866
(518) 587-3550

SCHENECTADY COUNTY
Schenectady City Court
Jay St., City Hall
Schenectady, NY 12305
(518) 382-5077

SCHOHARIE COUNTY
No large city small claims court
Inquire: (518) 295-8316

SCHUYLER COUNTY
No large city small claims court
Inquire: (607) 535-7760

SENECA COUNTY
No large city small claims court
Inquire: (315) 539-5655

ST. LAWRENCE COUNTY
Ogdensburg City Court
330 Ford St.
Ogdensburg, NY 13669
(315) 393-3941

STEUBEN COUNTY
Corning City Court
12 Civic Center Plaza
Corning, NY 14830
(607) 936-4111

Hornell City Court
108 Broadway
Hornell, NY 14843
(607) 324-7531

SUFFOLK COUNTY
Suffolk District Court #1*
400 Carleton Ave.
Central Islip, NY 11722
(516) 853-5400

Suffolk District Court #2*
72 E. Main St.
Babylon, NY 11702
(516) 669-6100

Suffolk District Court #3*
1850 New York Ave.
Huntington Station, NY 11746
(516) 854-4545

Suffolk District Court #4*
North County Complex Building C158
Hauppauge, NY 11787
(516) 853-5400

Suffolk District Court #5*
400 Carleton Ave.
Central Islip, NY 11722
(516) 853-7626

Suffolk District Court #6*
150 W. Main St.
Patchogue, NY 11772
(516) 854-1440

SULLIVAN COUNTY
No large city small claims court
Inquire: (914) 794-4066

TIOGA COUNTY
No large city small claims court
Inquire: (607) 687-0544

TOMPKINS COUNTY
Ithaca City Court
120 E. Clinton St.
Ithaca, NY 14850
(607) 274-6594

ULSTER COUNTY
Kingston City Court
1 Garraghan Dr.
Kingston, NY 12401
(914) 338-2974

WARREN COUNTY
Glen Falls City Court
42 Ridge St.
Glen Falls, NY 12801
(518) 798-4714

WASHINGTON COUNTY
No large city small claims court
Inquire: (518) 746-2520

WAYNE COUNTY
No large city small claims court
Inquire: (315) 946-5870

WESTCHESTER COUNTY
Mt. Vernon City Court
Municipal Building
Mt. Vernon, NY 10550
(914) 665-2400

Peekskill City Court
2 Nelson Ave.
Peekskill, NY 10566
(914) 737-3405

Rye City Court
21 3rd St.
Rye, NY 10580
(914) 967-1599

White Plains City Court*
77 S. Lexington Ave.
White Plains, NY 10601
(914) 422-6050

Yonkers City Court
100 S. Broadway
Yonkers, NY 10701
(914) 377-6352

WYOMING COUNTY
No large city small claims court
Inquire: (716) 786-3148

YATES COUNTY
No large city small claims court
Inquire: (315) 536-5120

....

NOTE *The small claims courts listed above are derived from the group of courts known as the city courts (79 in 61 cities), the district courts (Nassau and Suffolk counties) and the Civil Court of the City of New York, which is considered to be one court, composed of six courts in the five boroughs comprising New York City. Not included in this list are the 1,487 town and village justice courts such as those found in the eastern part of Suffolk County, Westchester County (see list under Westchester, Appendix A), and counties that are noted in the above list to have "no large city small claims court." In this guide the town court of Pelham in Westchester County is presented to exemplify this type of court.*

....

COUNTY JUSTICE CENTERS WITH SMALL CLAIMS COURTS IN NEW JERSEY
(*Indicates that this court is given special attention in Appendix A)

ATLANTIC COUNTY
Special Civil Part: Small Claims
1201 Bacharach Blvd.
Atlantic City, NJ 08401
(609) 345-6700

BERGEN COUNTY*
Special Civil Part: Small Claims
10 Main St., Room 430, Justice Center
Hackensack, NJ 07601
(201) 646-2289

BURLINGTON COUNTY
Special Civil Part: Small Claims
49 Rancocas Rd.
Mount Holly, NJ 08060
(609) 265-5075

CAMDEN COUNTY
Special Civil Part: Small Claims
Hall of Justice Complex, 101 S. 5th St.
Camden, NJ 08103
(609) 225-7433

CAPE MAY COUNTY
Special Civil Part: Small Claims
9 N. Main St., Dept. #203
Cape May Court House, NJ 08210
(609) 463-6446

CUMBERLAND COUNTY
Special Civil Part: Small Claims
Box 615
Bridgeton, NJ 08302
(609) 451-8000

ESSEX COUNTY
Special Civil Part: Small Claims
470 Martin Luther King Blvd.
Newark, NJ 07102
(201) 621-5368

GLOUCESTER COUNTY
Special Civil Part: Small Claims
Old Courthouse, 1 N. Broad St.
Woodbury, NJ 08096
(609) 853-3365

HUDSON COUNTY*
Special Civil Part: Small Claims
595 Newark Ave.
Jersey City, NJ 07306
(201) 795-6680

HUNTERDON COUNTY
Special Civil Part: Small Claims
65 Park Ave., P.O. Box 728
Flemington, NJ 08822
(908) 788-1216(9)

MERCER COUNTY
Special Civil Part: Small Claims
Box 8068
Trenton, NJ 08650
(609) 695-2540

MIDDLESEX COUNTY
Special Civil Part: Small Claims
P.O. Box 1146
New Brunswick, NJ 08903
(908) 981-2066

MONMOUTH COUNTY

Special Civil Part: Small Claims
Courthouse & Monument St.
Freehold, NJ 07728
(908) 577-6749

MORRIS COUNTY

Special Civil Part: Small Claims
Washington & Court St.
Morristown, NJ 07963
(201) 285-6150

OCEAN COUNTY

Special Civil Part: Small Claims
Box 2191
Toms River, NJ 08754
(908) 929-2016

PASSAIC COUNTY

Special Civil Part: Small Claims
71 Hamilton St.
Paterson, NJ 07505
(201) 881-4107

SALEM COUNTY

Special Civil Part: Small Claims
92 Market St.
Salem, NJ 08079
(609) 935-7510

SOMERSET COUNTY

Special Civil Part: Small Claims
Bridge & Main St., P.O. Box 3000
Somerville, NJ 08876
(908) 231-7014 or (908) 231-7015

SUSSEX COUNTY

Special Civil Part: Small Claims
43-47 High St.
Newton, NJ 07860
(201) 579-0918

UNION COUNTY

Special Civil Part: Small Claims
2 Broad St.
Elizabeth, NJ 07207
(908) 527-4319

WARREN COUNTY

Special Civil Part: Small Claims
314 2nd St.
Belvidere, NJ 07823
(908) 475-6227

THE SMALL CLAIMS COURTS OF CONNECTICUT

(by Geographic Area/G.A.)
(*Indicates that this court is given special attention
in Appendix A)

FAIRFIELD COUNTY

G.A. 1*
Stamford-Norwalk Superior Court
123 Hoyt St.
P.O. Box 3281, Ridgeway Station
Stamford, CT 06905
(203) 965-5237

G.A. 2 Superior Court
172 Golden Hill St.
Bridgeport, CT 06604
(203) 579-6562

G.A. 3 Superior Court
146 White St.
Danbury, CT 06810
(203) 797-4050

G.A. 20 Superior Court
17 Belden Ave.
P.O. Box 2225
Norwalk, CT 06850
(203) 846-4206

HARTFORD COUNTY

G.A. 17 Superior Court
Municipal Building
131 N. Main St. (P.O. Box 1400)
Bristol, CT 06010
(860) 582-8111

LITCHFIELD COUNTY
G.A. 18 Superior Court
80 Doyle Rd.
P.O. Box 667
Bantam, CT 06750
(860) 567-3942 or (860) 567-3946

MIDDLESEX COUNTY
G.A. 9 Superior Court
1 Court St., Civil Clerk's Office
2nd floor
Middletown, CT 06457-3374

NEW HAVEN COUNTY
G.A. 4 Superior Court
7 Kendrick Ave.
Waterbury, CT 06702
(203) 596-4050

G.A. 5 Superior Court
106 Elizabeth St.
Derby, CT 06418
(203) 735-9654

G.A. 6 Superior Court
121 Elm St.
New Haven, CT 06510
(203) 789-7465

G.A. 7 Superior Court
54 W. Main St.
Meriden, CT 06450
(203) 238-6128

G.A. 22 Superior Court
14 W. River St.
Milford, CT 06460
(203) 874-1116

HARTFORD COUNTY
G.A. 12 Superior Court
410 Center St.
Manchester, CT 06040
(860) 643-6517

G.A. 13 Superior Court
111 Phoenix Ave.
Enfield, CT 06082
(860) 741-3727

G.A. 14 Superior Court
101 Lafayette St.
Hartford, CT 06106
(860) 566-1680

G.A. 15 Superior Court
125 Columbus Blvd.
New Britain, CT 06051
(860) 827-7106

G.A. 16 Superior Court
105 Raymond Rd.
West Hartford, CT 06107
(860) 236-5166

NEW LONDON COUNTY
G.A. 10 Superior Court
112 Broad St.
New London, CT 06320
(860) 443-8346 or (860) 437-0747

G.A. 21 Superior Court
1 Courthouse Sq.
Norwich, CT 06360
(860) 887-3731

TOLLAND COUNTY
G.A. 19 Superior Court
55 W. Main St.
P.O. Box 980
Rockville, CT 06066
(860) 872-4548

WINDHAM COUNTY
G.A. 11 Superior Court
Municipal Building
172 Main St.
P.O. Box 688
Danielson, CT 06239
(860) 774-0078

Subpoenas in a Nutshell

SUBPOENA FOR WITNESS (to Testify)
(Obtained prior to the hearing)
(Example and Instructions New York, see [FORM 8 and 9])

Purpose: To compel a person who has information that can help you support your claim to come to the hearing and testify.

When obtainable: After the Notice of Claim (Summons) has been served on the defendant. In New York it is recommended that you serve it 5 to 10 days before the hearing date. (Do it as soon as possible.) In New Jersey, when the defendant responds to (answers) the Notice of Claim and gives notice of his intention to defend against the claim, the court issues a hearing date. As soon as the date is set a subpoena is obtainable. It must be served at least five days before the hearing. In Connecticut, it is legal to serve it a mere 18 hours before the hearing. (Why wait?)

Obtainable by mail: In New York, New Jersey, and Connecticut under some circumstances. If the plaintiff lives out of state allowances can be made upon request; in Connecticut, ask for a "civil" subpoena.

Obtainable by a friend or assistant to the plaintiff: It varies. Call the court and inquire.

Where obtained: At the small claims court window. Be ready to provide the index number of the case and the name and address of the person that you want to appear. The document consists of two sides: the subpoena, and an Affidavit of Service. In New Jersey, you can usually obtain it at the small claims court window, but in certain other New Jersey courts you must purchase it at a store that sells legal forms and bring it to the small claims court window and sign it in front of the clerk. A process server can prepare and serve a subpoena as well. In Connecticut, you can obtain it at the small claims court window.

Cost: Free in all states. The only expense is the fee the sheriff charges to serve the subpoena [in Connecticut], $25 to $30 plus a witness fee of 10 cents per mile). In New York and New Jersey a process server charges between $16 and $55.

Who to serve it on: Anyone who can give testimony that will help you prove your claim.

Where it can be served: A subpoena from the Civil Court of the City of New York can be served only within the City of New York (or in Nassau County or Westchester County); in New Jersey, anywhere in the state. In Connecticut, it can be served in the Geographic Area over which the Superior Court has jurisdiction.

Type of service: In person, by anyone over the age of 18 except you, the plaintiff. A process server or sheriff does it professionally. In New Jersey, the plaintiff may serve the subpoena or hire a process server to do it. In Connecticut, the sheriff or any person over 18 except the plaintiff may serve it.

How to serve it: Assuming you don't want a process server to do it for you, after obtaining the subpoena from the small claims court, make a copy of it. Choose a friend to serve the subpoena; then find the person for whom the subpoena is intended. Hand a copy of it to the person while you are showing them the original and give them $15. If the person refuses to take it from you and/or is hostile, place it down on the desk or the floor, and leave. (In New Jersey and Connecticut, you are required only to give the witness a mileage fee [$2 to $8, or $2 per 30 miles traveled] when you serve the subpoena; in Connecticut, a sheriff usually serves the subpoena.) Make note of the approximate height, weight, age, and gender of the person being served. Complete the form according to the instructions on the Affidavit of Service and have the affidavit notarized. Bring or mail the Affidavit of Service and the original subpoena back to the small claims court clerk. In New Jersey and Connecticut, it is optional to have a copy of the subpoena and the Affidavit of Service returned to the court (but bring it to the hearing as proof of service).

When it can be served: Every day except Sunday and national or religious holidays; in Connecticut, it can be served on Sunday.

SUBPOENA FOR RECORDS ("Duces Tecum")
(Obtained prior to the hearing)
(Example and Instructions New York, [FORM 10], Appendix D)

Purpose: To obtain documents that are held by the defendant or any person, business, or organization that can assist you in proving your claim.

When obtainable: In New York after the Notice of Claim (Summons) has been served on the defen-

dant. In New Jersey and Connecticut, when the defendant responds to (answers) the Notice of Claim and gives notice of his intention to defend against the claim, the court issues a hearing date. As soon as the date is set you can obtain a subpoena.

Obtainable by mail: In New York, New Jersey, and Connecticut under some circumstances. If the plaintiff lives out of state, allowances can be made upon request; in Connecticut, ask for a "civil" subpoena.

Obtainable by a friend or assistant to the plaintiff?: It varies. Check with the court.

Where obtained: In New York, at the small claims court window. Be ready to provide the index number of the case and the address of the person that has the records (documents) you want as well as a precise description of those documents. In New Jersey, the subpoena must be purchased at a store that sells legal forms, brought to the small claims court window, and signed by a clerk of the court. (Some courts give you the name of the clerk who signs the subpoena and you may enter it on the subpoena without going back to the small claims court clerk.) Procedures are available for you to do it by mail if you live out of state. A process server can prepare and serve a subpoena as well. In Connecticut, ask for a civil subpoena.

Cost: Free in all states. The only expense is the fee the sheriff charges to serve the subpeona [in Connecticut] or the process server [in New York and New Jersey, usually between $16 and $55] charges to serve.

Who to serve it on: The defendant or any person, business, or institution that possesses a document that can help you prove your claim. If served on an corporation, it should be served on a corporate officer or registered agent of the corporation.

Where it can be served: Same as for Subpoena for Witness above.

Type of service: In person, by anyone over the age of 18 except, you the plaintiff. A process server or sheriff does it professionally. In New Jersey, the plaintiff may serve the subpoena or hire a process server to do it. In Connecticut, it is served by the sheriff.

How to serve it: Assuming you don't want a process server to do it for you, after obtaining the subpoena from the small claims court, make a copy of it. Choose a person (a friend) to serve the subpoena; then find the person for whom the subpoena is intended. Hand a copy of it to the person while you are showing them the original and give them $15. If the person refuses to take it from you and/or is hostile, place it down on the desk or the floor and leave. (In New Jersey, you are not required to give the person served any money. In Connecticut, service of a subpoena is usually done by a sheriff whose authority is more compelling.) Make note of the approximate height, weight, age, and gender of the person being served. Complete the form as per instructions on the Affidavit of Service and have the affidavit notarized. Bring or mail the Affidavit of Service and original subpoena back to the small claims court. (In New York, New Jersey, and Connecticut, the sheriff or the process server takes care of handling the final paperwork.)

Where the subpoenaed records are sent: In New York and New Jersey, the records are returned to the court. (Give the clerk the index number of your case and ask to see the subpoenaed documents. You can copy them.) In Connecticut, you can specify on the subpoena that the records be sent to you or, if they belong to the defendant, that the defendant produce them at the hearing.

When it can be served: Every day except Sunday and national and religious holidays; in Connecticut, it can be served on Sunday.

[7]NEW YORK: SUBPOENA FOR INFORMATION AND RESTRAINING ORDER
[8]NEW JERSEY: INFORMATION SUBPOENA AND WRITTEN QUESTIONS
[9]CONNECTICUT: POST JUDGMENT REMEDIES INTERROGATORIES
(Obtained immediately after you receive your judgment)
(Example and Instructions New York, [FORM 24])

Purpose: To obtain information about a judgment debtor's residence, employer, bank, and assets (and in New York to force the debtor's bank to freeze the debtor's account for up to double the amount owed to you so that you can put a levy on it).

Description: A form consisting of two parts: Part I shows the plaintiff's and the debtor's names, the judgment amount, the case number, and the person to whom the requested information is to be sent (or you the plaintiff). Part II includes the questions that the person, employer, or bank must answer.

When obtainable: After you receive your judgment.

Obtainable by mail: No in New York; in New Jersey and Connecticut, yes.

---

7 In New York, you have no recourse if the debtor does not respond to the subpoena insofar as relates to cases heard in the small claims court.

8 In New Jersey, if the defendant refuses to answer the questions within 14 days, you may take further action: The small claims court clerk will provide you with two forms to file a motion: One is entitled "A Certificate in Support of Motion for Order Enforcing Litigant's Rights" and the other "A Notice of Motion for Order enforcing Litigant's Rights." More detailed instructions are provided on an information sheet you can request from the small claims court clerk called "Instructions for Information Subpoena."

9 In Connecticut, if the defendant refuses to answer the questions within 30 days or the sheriff is unsuccessful in finding the defendant's assets, you can obtain on request from the small claims court a form called a Petition for Examination of the Judgment Debtor (called an EJD by the clerks), which is then given to the sheriff who serves it on the defendant. (The sheriff's fee for service is between $25 and $40, which you will recover when he collects the debt for you.) The EJD is a court order for the defendant to come to the courtroom where he will be examined by the judge magistrate regarding the amount, type, and location of assets, thus enabling the sheriff to complete the job of obtaining the debtor's assets for you.

Obtainable by a friend or assistant to the plaintiff: Yes, but call the court to confirm.

Where obtained: At the small claims court window. Be ready to provide the index number of the case. In New Jersey the subpoena is called an Information Subpoena and Written Questions (one for an individual and one for a corporation); in Connecticut it is called a Postjudgment Remedies Interrogatories and can be obtained by mail.

Cost: In New York, $2 for each subpoena at the small claims court window. You can obtain two each day. Attach $.50 to each subpoena served on a person, institution, and so on. In New Jersey and Connecticut, there is no cost.

Who to serve it on: In New York, New Jersey, and Connecticut the defendant (the judgment debtor) and any person, business entity, or organization that you suspect might have the above information.

Where it can be served: Same as for Subpoena for Witness above.

Type of service: OK to mail, certified or registered, return-receipt requested in New York, New Jersey, and Connecticut. You must also provide a self-addressed stamped envelope. In Connecticut, it is best to have the sheriff serve it on the debtor because if the debtor fails to complete the form, you may then request from the clerk at the small claims court a *writ of capias,* which empowers the sheriff to arrest the debtor and bring him before the judge, who will personally ask the questions on the Postjudgment Remedies Interrogatories. (My source at the small claims court says that this writ is commonly issued.)

Where the subpoenaed information is sent: In New York, New Jersey, and Connecticut, to you the plaintiff.

When it can be served: Every day except Sunday and national and religious holidays; in Connecticut, it can be served on Sunday.

Subpoena for Records

A subpoena for records could be used in any number of cases. For example, in a case where the defendant is receiving benefits directly from the insurance carrier but neglects to pay the plaintiff's bill, saying the insurance company never paid him. The subpoena would be served on the insurance company. Another example is when the defendant transfers treatment, claiming the plaintiff's work was incorrectly done. You can obtain the other doctor's records, which might help support that your work was in order.

Introduction

When you file your initial claim, the clerk sends a summons to the defendant by regular mail and by certified, return-receipt mail. The summons tells the defendant the date and case number of the hearing (SC / # # # / 97). The clerk likewise gives you a form (see [FORM 5]), which also provides you with the same date and the case number. Within 7 to 14 days, if the summons reaches the debtor, the clerk receives the "receipt of delivery." Only when the clerk receives the green card postal receipt indicating that delivery of the summons was accomplished will you be allowed to obtain the Subpoena for Records.

Upon occasion I have filed an Initial Claim form at the clerk's window only to have the postman return it to me five weeks later marked "Undeliverable." On one occasion the problem turned out to be an incorrect address.

What to Do Now

Call the small claims office to confirm they have the return receipt showing proof that the summons was delivered to the defendant. Then return to the window where you filed the Initial Claim form and request a Subpoena for Records form. The subpoena is provided without charge.

What to Furnish the Clerk

To obtain your Subpoena for Records form, you'll need to provide the clerk with the following:
- the defendant's name and the index number of the case
- the name and address of the person who possesses the documents you need
- the document(s) you want, described in specific detail.

What You Will Receive from the Clerk

A Two-Sided Form: see [FORM 10]

Side A:
The subpoena for the document(s) you want. It will be filled in with
- the name of the plaintiff and the defendant
- the name of the person who holds the documents you want to review
- the address of the person who presently holds the documents that you want to review
- the specifics of the document(s) that you want.

Side B:

An affidavit attesting that the subpoena has been served[10] on the correct person; it is completed by the person who serves the subpoena. It will be filled in with the following information:

Who served the subpoena and when and where and to whom the subpoena was served.

The affidavit states that the person who is serving the subpoena must give $15 to the recipient of the subpoena.

It states the gender, age, race, weight, hair color, and height of the subpoena recipient.

The subpoena commands the person who possesses the documents to turn them over to the court before the hearing or trial. You may review the documents prior to that point (if they have been provided) by calling the court and stating the defendant's name and the index number of the case (SC / # # # / 97); if the documents have been received, you may go to the court and review the documents or make a copy of them.[11]

SERVING THE SUBPOENA FOR RECORDS

For detailed instructions on how to serve a Subpoena for Records, see [FORM 8] and Appendix C. Anyone over age 18 (except the plaintiff) can do it. It must be served in person, unlike the Information Subpoena, which can be sent certified mail, return receipt requested. There are many subpoena and document delivery services available to handle this service when you need it. The cost will vary according to how far the process server must travel. Typical fees range between $35 and $55.

The wisest approach to having a subpoena served is to have a professional do it. After all, they are savvy to the schemes that some debtors have to avoid being served.

Check in the Yellow Pages directory under "Process Servers" and you will find a host of such agencies. Appendix A lists several such agencies, although this list is not inclusive.

••

OBSERVATION *The judge of a small claims court does not have the power to force a person to comply with a Subpoena for Records. However, the subpoena has written on it: "If you fail to provide and produce such information, you may be deemed guilty of contempt of court and be liable to pay to the party aggrieved all loss and damages sustained and in addition, forfeit $50." The Subpoena for Records can be enforced, but only if the plaintiff is willing to refile his claim in a higher court such as Civil Court, where the rules that govern subpoenas are more strictly enforced. It costs $35 to do this.*

If you don't get the document you want, bring your copy of the proof of service with the notary's seal on it with you to the hearing. You can show the arbitrator or judge that the defendant failed to comply in providing a document that would help you to substantiate your case. Even if the missing document is not crucial to your case, to some extent noncompliance demonstrates that the defendant does not respect the court and may actually have something to hide.

••

---

10 Whoever serves the subpoena must give the recipient $15 (cash, check, or money order), complete the affidavit of service on the reverse side, and take it to a notary public for notarization. (In effect it is the server's written, sworn statement that he delivered the subpoena.)

11 It is recommended that you bring your copy of the proof of service having the notary's seal to the clerk at the small claims window and he will make the document available to you.

APPENDIX E

Information Subpoena and Restraining Notice

I n New York, New Jersey, and Connecticut, the court makes available to you the Information Subpoena and Restraining Notice [FORM 22] or the equivalent of such a document. You can obtain this form at the small claims court window immediately after obtaining your judgment. It must be served within two weeks, otherwise it is invalidated. Issued by the court clerk this document compels individuals, companies (gas, electric, credit card), schools, and organizations to provide you with answers to very specific and useful questions that can help you obtain information about the defendant's place of employment, bank accounts, and assets. When served on the defendant's bank, this subpoena requires the bank to hold money in the debtor's account sufficient to pay the judgment. This is the only subpoena that can be served by mail (certified, return receipt requested). The Subpoena for Records [FORM 10] and the Subpoena to Testify [FORM 9] must be served in person. Appendix C provides details of equivalent subpoenas in the other states.

NOTE *In Connecticut, once you have been awarded a judgment, if the defendant fails to pay you, you may serve him with a Postjudgment Remedies Interrogatories form. This form asks the defendant to disclose his place of employment, his bank, and his source of income. The form further advises you that if the defendant does not disclose the requested information you may (1) obtain a court order requiring him to comply with your interrogatory or (2) obtain an order "for production or for examination of the judgment debtor or a third person." Any such examination shall be conducted before the court.*

To illustrate how the Information Subpoena works in New York, consider the following example:

You accept a personal check for $900 (instead of cash or certified bank check) as the final payment for your services. The check is returned with a notice that the account is closed. The home telephone has been changed and the new number is unlisted. The check can supply you with the following information:
- the name and address of debtor's bank
- the checking account number
- the routing number of the bank.

On a hunch, you guess that the defendant closed that account to thwart you and other creditors. The bank identified on the check may therefore be a good start. You return to the clerk at the small claims window, pay $2 and provide the following items:
- a copy of your judgment *or* the name of the plaintiff and defendant,
- The date the judgment was awarded.
- The index number of the case (SC / # # # / 97), and
- The name of the bank (company) or organization written on the defendant's last check

The clerk fills out the entire document and gives the subpoena to you.

There are three parts to the subpoena:

A: Information Subpoena and Restraining Notice
- The names of the plaintiff and the defendant
- The name of the bank (company) you want to query
- The amount of money that is to be frozen
- The plaintiff's address
- The date and the signature of the chief clerk

B: Explanation of the law (not shown in the forms section)
- An explanation of the civil law governing the action of the subpoena
- Advice to debtor that certain kinds of money are exempt from garnishment

C: Questions to be answered
- The plaintiff's and defendant's names
- The defendant's addresses
- The questions that the bank must answer within seven days from the time the bank receives them, to be signed by the bank employee, sworn before a notary, and then returned to you

Not only will the bank give you this information, it will freeze the amount owed to you if the defendant has an account with the bank. The defendant can neither close his account nor remove from it the money he owes you. [FORM 24] shows a bank's response to an Information Subpoena in which no pertinent information was available to help the collection effort. When, however, you receive an informative positive response, you can immediately file a Property Execution (see Appendix G) form by mail with the marshal [FORM 25] or the sheriff [FORMS 20, 21] who will demand that the bank turn over the funds to him. He will then forward your hard-earned money to you!

....

OBSERVATION *There are between 120 and 130 banks in Brooklyn and Manhattan combined in which the defendant can hold accounts or other assets. The clerk at the small claims court window is permitted to issue you only two Information Subpoenas each day. The solution to this problem, although a bit costly, is to have an "Asset Locator" specialist do the job for you. (See Appendix A and [FORM 68]; and in the Question and Answer section of this guide, question 12 regarding assets).*
....

Registering Judgment in the County Clerk's Office

The major effect of registering the judgment [FORM 17] against the defendant is that you damage his credit rating. Warn him you're going to do it in 10 days, do it, and then let him know you did it. This action alone transforms your judgment into a tool that packs real clout. The county clerk's office and all its official documents are public domain. It is where major credit agencies forage for their truffles—that is, the judgments you file. The major credit agencies are Experian (formerly TRW), Equifax, and Transunion. When the defendant applies for a loan to buy a car or house, the bank will access the credit report and discover that the defendant owes you. In order to get the loan, the defendant is required to pay his debt to you.

....

WARNING *It is important to remember that, when you register the judgment, you register it in the county where it is most likely to be accessed during a credit history search. If you sued your guy in Brooklyn, but he lives and does business in Manhattan, you should register your judgment in Manhattan.*

However, you do not have to go to the Manhattan County Clerk's Office to register your judgment; you can send it there by regular mail. Even if the defendant moves to Woonsocket, SD, his credit history will follow him because the credit agencies are nationwide.

....

To register your judgment you must:

1. First obtain a Transcript of Judgment [FORM 17].
2. Go to the window where you filed your Initial Claim form and request the official Transcript of the Judgment you want.
   Be prepared to have
   • $15 in exact cash
   • The index number of your case, for example: "SC / # # # / 97"
   • The name and residential address of the defendant
      You will be given your transcript on the spot. In Brooklyn you obtain this document at the small claims court clerk's window at 141 Livingston St.
3. You can now mail in the transcript (see below) or walk four blocks to the county clerk's office in the Supreme Court Building at:
   360 Adams St.—basement level, Room 189
   At window No. 2 pay $25 in cash or money order and register the judgment.

   Here's the good news: The defendant must pay the $40 you just laid out as well as the interest on the money he owes you at the time he pays his debt.

The clerk at window No. 2 puts the official county seal on the transcript, gives it a county registration number [FORM 17], and takes it from you. I recommend you make a copy of it before he does that. Copiers are available there. Sending a copy to the defendant is a concrete reminder that you are taking steps to have the debt repaid.

The debt will now be recorded by every major credit agency.

You can also register the judgment in the county clerk's office by mail:

Buy a U.S. Postal Money Order for $25. Make it payable to "Brooklyn (New York, Bronx, for example) County Clerk's Office and send it with your official transcript to the county clerk's office. (See Appendix A for addresses of county clerks offices).

WARNING *You should also send a photocopy of the transcript along with the original official transcript and a self-addressed stamped envelope. The clerk's office will "clock" the photocopy for you and return it to you so that you will have verification that the registration was accomplished.*

WESTCHESTER COUNTY

First obtain a transcript of your judgment from the court that awarded it, and then register it in the county clerk's office (See Appendix A under Westchester.)

NASSAU COUNTY

First obtain a Transcript of Judgment [FORM 17].

Go to the window where you filed your initial claim form and buy the official transcript of your judgment.

Then take the transcript to the county clerk's office.

Cost to register a Transcript of Judgment at county clerk's window: $10.

Call (516) 571-2666 to verify any changes in procedure.

SUFFOLK COUNTY

(Same procedure as for Nassau County above)

Cost to register a Transcript of Judgment at county clerk's window: $15.

Call (516) 852-2200 to verify any changes in procedure.

HUDSON COUNTY, NEW JERSEY

Unlike New York, to register a judgment in New Jersey you must send a Statement for Docketing form to the Superior Court in Trenton. (See [FORM 44]). There it is given a docket judgment number signifying that your judgment is officially registered statewide, is part of the public record, and therefore is accessible to searches by money lenders and credit agencies such as Experian (formerly TRW). Consequently, a statewide lien is now in effect on all the defendant's property.

- Send a letter with a self-addressed, stamped envelope to the small claims court office and request a Statement for Docketing. Be sure to include a copy of the judgment.
- The small claims court clerk will prepare and send you the Statement for Docketing, which includes instructions.
- You fill in some blanks at the bottom, date and sign, and send it with a check or money order for $5 payable to Clerk of the Superior Court of New Jersey to:

Richard J. Hughes Justice Complex
Superior Court of New Jersey
CN 971
DJ Number Section
Trenton, NJ 08625
(609) 292-4481

If you send a second copy of the Statement for Docketing along with the original Statement for Docketing, you will receive it back and it will bear a docket-judgment number, which signifies that your case is now registered in the Superior Court of New Jersey.

BERGEN COUNTY, NEW JERSEY

(Same procedure as for Hudson County above)

Mail to:
Richard J. Hughes Justice Complex
Superior Court of New Jersey
CN 971
DJ Number Section
Trenton, NJ 08625
(609) 984-4202

CONNECTICUT STAMFORD-NORWALK-GREENWICH AREA

In general, informative court sources have indicated that the judgment of a small claims court is accessible to and accessed by all the credit agencies that make a business of recording the credit histories of individuals. This would mean that no further filing of papers is needed to impair a debtor's credit rating. (In New York you must file an official copy of the judgment in the county clerk's office for it to have the status of a lien.) An attorney in the legal document department at the Secretary of State's office in Connecticut suggested the following procedure to ensure a statewide lien in any transaction regarding the purchase or sale of a debtor's possessions where credit is involved:

You will need to have

1. a copy of your judgment
2. a UCC-1 (Uniform Commercial Code) form [FORM 64]
3. a check or money order payable to the Secretary of State for $25

....

OBSERVATION *The Uniform Commercial Code (U.C.C.) is one of the uniform laws drafted by the National Conference of Commissioners on Uniform State Laws and the American Law Institute governing commercial transactions (including the sale and leasing of goods, transfer of funds, commercial paper, bank deposits and collections, letters of credit, bulk transfers, warehouse receipts, bills of lading, investment securities, and secured transactions). The U.C.C. has been adopted in whole or substantially by all states.*

....

Request by telephone or mail from the Secretary of State's Office (860) 566-2764 a UCC-1 form. Enclose a self-addressed stamped envelope, business size. Complete [FORM 64] as shown in the example on [FORM 65]. It consists of an original and a carbonless copy with instructions on the back [FORM 64].

Box #1 Requesting party is left blank

Box #2 For Property Execution, leave blank (if you have no knowledge of such)

Box #3 Debtor's exact legal name and address (post office box number is not acceptable)

Box #4 Secured party, your name and address (the judgment creditor)

Box #5 Left blank

Box #6 Can be completed when you can state with specificity the identity of a property owned by the debtor; otherwise it is left blank. Such information is possible to obtain in the town hall of each town and city.

Your signature is placed in the lower right corner (secured party).

To the completed form attach one copy of your judgment, enclose the check for $25, and mail to:

State of Connecticut
Uniform Commercial Code Unit
Office of the Secretary of State
30 Trinity St.
Hartford, CT 06106

You can obtain more information about filling out the form correctly by calling their office at (860) 566-4021.

The copy of your judgment will be microfilmed and put on file throughout the state and a record of it will appear on the debtor's credit report.

Income Execution to Garnish Debtor's Salary and Property Execution

T he Income Execution [FORMS 18, 19] and Property Execution [FORM 25] are expedited by the marshal's office and the county sheriff's office (each of the five boroughs of New York City has one or more marshals, but only one sheriff. Every county throughout New York City and state has a sheriff, but only big cities may have marshals as well. (See Appendix A for addresses and telephone numbers.) One may also locate a marshal's office by checking the Yellow Pages under the heading of "City Marshals." A marshal holds a charter from the city, which gives him the right, for a fee of $45.07, to initiate actions that end with your getting 10% of the defendant's weekly salary until the debt is totally paid. The marshal may also enforce the taking or sale of the defendant's personal property to satisfy your judgment; the marshal also takes 5% more (not your 5%).

Now that you have the judgment, here are the procedures that will permit you to collect the money that your debtor owes you.

BROOKLYN, BRONX, MANHATTAN, QUEENS, STATEN ISLAND

1A. Income Execution Using the Marshal:

1. Complete form T 239, Income Execution (see [FORMS 18, 19] for an example of a completed form). This form, along with many other commonly used legal forms, is available in legal stationery stores and the Blumberg stationery store in Manhattan. You sign your name followed by *pro se* (see [FORM 19]), which means you are acting as your own attorney.

2. Make a check payable to the City Marshal of your choice for $45.07.

3. Send a copy of your Notice of Judgment [FORM 14], the check, and four copies of the T 239, Income Execution, to the city marshal.

Upon receipt of your papers the marshal's office assigns the debtor an identification number and sends you a notice acknowledging receipt of your papers along with their identification number for the defendant. You use this number when you want to reference information about payment status; note it in your records.

4. The marshal first notifies the debtor as to the amount due. If no response is forthcoming in 21 days, the marshal's office notifies the debtor's employer, who upon service of the proper papers must deduct 10% of the debtor's weekly salary and turn it over to the marshal's office. The marshal in turn sends you monthly the amount collected until the entire debt is paid—including the $45.07 you paid to initiate the garnishment.

5. It takes between six and eight weeks before you receive a check from the marshal.

The Income Execution can also be expedited by the sheriff's office. Each borough (county) has a sheriff's office (see Appendix A). Not all sheriffs' offices are responsible for both the Income Execution (salary garnishment) and the Property Execution (property garnishment, i.e., money in a bank account).

1B. Income Execution Using the Sheriff:

The sheriff's office in Manhattan is the central sheriff's office for Income Execution. The sheriff's office in Brooklyn does not handle this matter.

To initiate an Income Execution using the sheriff's office requires you to submit Requisition Request for a Small Claims Execution form [FORM 20].

Make your check or money order for $20 payable to the New York City Sheriff's Office, and send the completed form and the check along with a copy of your debtor's judgment to the sheriff's office.

You can use either a sheriff or a marshal for the executions. The difference between the two is that the sheriff's powers extend to all counties of New York State. However, in New York City there is only one sheriff for each borough and many marshals. In Nassau and Suffolk counties you must use the sheriff because there are no marshals.

2A. Property Execution Using the Marshal:

1. Complete form B 320, Execution against Property, (see [FORM 25] for an example of a com-

pleted form). This form bears the more visible title of "Execution with Notice to Garnishee." This form along with many other commonly used legal forms is available in some stationery stores and the Blumberg stationery store in Manhattan. You sign your name followed by *pro se* (see [FORM 25]), which means you are acting as your own attorney. You do not need an attorney sign this document.

2. Make a check payable to the City Marshal of your choice for $20.

3. Send a copy of the Notice of Judgment [FORM 14], the check, and three copies of the B 320, Execution against Property form to the City Marshal.

2B. Property Execution Using the Sheriff:

1. You will need to complete a Requisition Request for Small Claims Execution [FORM 21], providing accurate and complete information about debtor's business, bank, and ownership of property.

2. A copy of your judgment

3. A certified check or money order for $15, payable to "Sheriff's Office of the County" carrying out the property execution for you. (See Appendix A for addresses of the sheriffs).

The sheriff's office in Manhattan handles both income and property executions on judgments obtained in any of the five boroughs. They require you to send them Requisition Request for Small Claims Execution (see [FORM 20]), copy of the judgment, and a check or money order for $20 for an Income Execution and $15 for a Property Execution.

WESTCHESTER COUNTY

1A. Income on Property Execution Using the City Marshal in a Large City Court outside N.Y.C., e.g., Yonkers:

1. After winning a judgment in your favor, immediately request payment in writing from the debtor.

2. If you are not paid after 30 days, send a letter to the Yonkers Small Claims Court office, 100 S. Broadway, Yonkers, NY 10701, (914) 377-6352,

providing the index number of the case and the names of the plaintiff and defendant(s). State that you have not been paid and that you are now requesting the small claims court to provide you with an Income (or property, i.e., bank account, etc.) Execution. Be sure to provide specific details regarding the debtor's place of employment or bank account information and have the letter notarized. This letter is known to the court as an Affidavit of Nonpayment. You do not need to file any forms or pay any fees to the small claims court.

3. The small claims court clerk prepares the execution of your choice and forwards it to one of the six City Marshals in Yonkers.

4. The City Marshal will contact you to commence proceedings. You will have to pay a fee (certified check or money order) payable to "Name, city marshal" of $10 that you will receive upon collection. No further action on your part is required.

1B. Income Execution Using the Sheriff, e.g., White Plains:

1. Mail or bring in the transcript of your judgment (which you can purchase for $5 at the small claims court) to the County Clerk's Office at 110 Grove St., White Plains, NY 10601, (914) 285-3080.

2. Request the clerk to prepare an Income Execution. You do not have to provide the clerk with any form except the transcript of the judgment and precise information regarding employment of the debtor.

3. Include a certified check or money order for $15, payable to the Westchester County Clerk's Office. The clerk will register your judgment and give you the Income Execution prepared for you.

4. If you are proceeding by mail, also request the clerk to forward the papers to the sheriff's office, same location as above, and include a certified check or money order payable to the Westchester Sheriff's Office for $23 OR

5. Bring the Income Execution papers the court clerk gives you to the sheriff's office at 110 Grove St.

6. All fees paid are recovered when the sheriff collects.

2A. Property Execution:

All steps same as above. Request the county clerk to prepare a Property Execution, also include a certified check or money order for $15. If proceeding by mail, you will need to call the sheriff in advance to find out the fee payable to the Westchester County Sheriff. The fee varies between $10.46 and $22.88 with the distance the sheriff must travel to serve the execution. All fees paid are recovered when the sheriff collects.

NASSAU COUNTY

(There are no City Marshals in Nassau County.)
1A. Income Execution:

1. Mail or bring a transcript of your judgment (which you can purchase by mail for $10 at the small claims court) to the County Clerk's Office at 240 Old Country Rd. in Mineola, (516) 571-2666.

2. Request the clerk to prepare an Income Execution. You do not have to provide the clerk with any form, except the transcript of the judgment, and precise information regarding the employment of the debtor.

3. A fee of $15, certified check or money order, is required, made payable to the Nassau County Clerk's Office. The clerk will register your judgment and give you the Income Execution prepared for you.

4. If you are preceeding by mail, request the clerk to forward the papers to the sheriff's office, same location as above. Include a certified check or money order for $23.09, payable to the Nassau County Sheriff's Office OR

5. Take the papers the county clerk gives you at the county clerk's office and bring them to the sheriff's office in Room 201 of the same building.

6. All fees paid are recovered when the sheriff collects.

1B. Property Execution:

1. Mail or bring a transcript of your judgment (which you can purchase for $10 by mail at

the small claims court) to the County Clerk's Office at 240 Old Country Rd. in Mineola, (516) 571-2666.

2. Request the clerk to prepare a Property Execution. You do not have to provide the clerk with any form except the transcript of the judgment. You must provide the clerk with precise information regarding the debtor's bank account on property.

3. You must pay a fee of $15, certified check or money order, payable to the Nassau County Clerk's Office.

4. If you are proceeding by mail, request the clerk to forward the papers to the sheriff's office in the same building and include a certified check or money order payable to the Nassau County Sheriff's Office for an amount that varied depending on the distance the sheriff must travel to serve the execution (the mileage fee) OR

5. Take the papers the county clerk gives you to Room 201, the sheriff's office, in the same building.

6. Remember the sheriff gets a "poundage" fee of 5% of what he collects for you.

7. All fees paid are recovered when the sheriff collects.

SUFFOLK COUNTY

(There are no City Marshals in Suffolk County.)

1A. Income Execution Using the Sheriff:

1. Mail or bring a transcript of your judgment to the County Clerk's Office in Riverhead, NY, (516) 852-2041.

2. Include a completed (front side) Blumberg T 439 form, but do not sign it. (The T 439 is the preferred form and is very similar to the T 239 [FORM 18] shown in this book.)

3. Tell the clerk you want to file the transcript and that you want an Income Execution.

4. The clerk will stamp and seal the transcript of your judgment and sign and seal the T 439 form and return it to you.

5. Pay the fee, $15, with a money order or certified check payable to the Suffolk County Clerk's Office.

6. Make seven copies, front and back of the T 439 form.

7. Send the signed and sealed transcript of judgment, the original T 439 and seven copies (front and back) and a certified check or money order payable to Suffolk County Clerk's Office for $45.86, to: Suffolk County Sheriff's Department (Civil Bureau), 112 Old Country Rd., Westhampton, NY 11977, (516) 852-8000.

1B. Property Execution Using the Sheriff:

1. Mail or bring a transcript of your judgment to the County Clerk's Office in Riverhead, NY, (516) 852-2041.

2. Include a certified check or money order payable to Suffolk County Clerk's Office for $5.

3. Request that the clerk prepare an "Execution 199" form (not shown in this book).

4. Provide the clerk with exact information regarding the defendant's bank account or property owned.

5. The clerk will return to you a registered transcript and the completed Execution 199 form.

6. Make six copies of the Execution 199 form.

7. Send the registered transcript, six copies of the Execution 199 form and a certified check or money order payable to the Suffolk County Sheriff's Office for an amount that will vary depending on how far the sheriff must travel to serve the execution (the mileage fee), to: Suffolk County Sheriff's Department (Civil Bureau), 112 Old Country Rd., Westhampton, NY 11977.

8. Call the Civil Bureau, (516) 852-8000, to obtain the correct fee to serve the Property Execution. The fee will vary between $.46 and $25.30.

HUDSON COUNTY, NEW JERSEY

1A. Income Execution:

1. When you receive a judgment in your favor, you must buy Blumberg Forms T 839, Notice of Application for Wage Execution, and T 847, Order, Certification, and Execution against Earnings [FORM 46]. You can buy them at any stationery store that sells legal forms, such as Silvers on Newark Avenue in Jersey City, (201) 963-1700.

   • Fill out two copies of New Jersey Blumberg Form T 839.

- Fill out two copies of New Jersey Blumberg Form T 847.
- Make two copies of your small claims court judgment.
- Mail one copy of your judgment and one copy of Form T 839 to the defendant by certified return-receipt mail.

2. Then mail one copy of your judgment and one copy of Form T 839 with the certified mail receipt along with two copies of Form T 847 to:
   Hudson County Court House
   Special Civil Part, Room 711
   595 Newark Ave.
   Jersey City, NJ 07306
   (201) 795-6672

3. Wait 10 days (the time permitted during which the defendant can object to the garnishment). The court will send you a postcard with a hearing date if the defendant objects to the garnishment. If you do not receive an objection from the defendant, complete Form T 847 and mail all three copies (one T 839 and two Form T 847 with the proper fee), to the same address as above.

   The fee is $5 plus a surcharge between $1 and $10, depending on how many miles the constable (the equivalent of a sheriff with fewer powers and a smaller jurisdiction) has to travel to deliver the order to the debtor's employer.

   Call the Hudson County Small Claims Court at (201) 795-6672 for correct fees.

4. If there is an objection to your Notice of Application for Wage Execution you will be notified by the court of a hearing date. Keep in mind that you must appear at that hearing.

5. You will be contacted by a constable when you are about to receive a payment.

1B. Bank Levy (Property Execution):

   When you receive a judgment in your favor, you must:

1. Send a letter to small claims court, special civil part, and make the following request: "Please

issue a writ[12] of execution on the address and property listed below":

- Citibank
- 66-66 Main St.
- Jersey City, NJ 03060
- Account name—John Smith
- Checking (savings) account number—333-666-999
- Social Security number—110-10-1100 (If available, this is proof-positive identification.)

2. Enclose a copy of your judgment or provide the following information:
   - Date of the judgment
   - Docket (case) number
   - Names of the plaintiff and the defendant
   - Amount of the award written on the judgment

3. Enclose a check or money order payable to "Clerk of the Superior Court of New Jersey" The fee is $5 (plus a surcharge between $1 and $10, depending on how many miles the constable has to travel to deliver the writ to the debtor's bank).
   Call the Hudson County Small Claims Court (201) 795-6672 for correct fees.

4. Send all of the above to
   Hudson County Court House
   Special Civil Part, Room 711
   595 Newark Ave.
   Jersey City, NJ 07306
   (201) 795-6672
   Call 3 to 4 weeks later to find out to which constable your case was assigned.

   Assuming the debtor's account contained sufficient funds to cover your award, you would receive the amount awarded to you on the judgment.

BERGEN COUNTY, NEW JERSEY

1A. Income Execution:

1. When you receive a judgment in your favor, send a self-addressed stamped envelope to the small claims court (special civil part) requesting an Application for Wage Execution: Notice and Order.

----

12 A writ is a written order from the court directing that a sheriff, constable, or other judicial officer do what is commanded by the writ.

You will receive:

a. two copies of the form

Notice of Motion for Wage Execution [FORM 45]

b. two copies of the form

Order, Certification, and Execution against Earnings, Pursuant to 15 U.S.C. 1673 & N.J.S.A. 2A:17-56 [FORM 45]

c. A set of instructions as follows:

- Fill out two copies of Notice of Motion for Wage Execution [FORM 45]
- Mail one copy to the defendant by certified mail, return receipt requested (the post office will give you a certified mail receipt).
- Have the second copy notarized and attach a copy of the certified mail receipt and mail to:
  Bergen County Justice Center
  Special Civil Part, Room 430
  10 Main St.
  Hackensack, NJ 07601
  (201) 646-2236

2. Follow the above instructions and wait 10 days. If you do not receive an objection from the defendant, complete the Order, Certification, and Execution against Earnings and mail all three copies (one Notice of Motion and two Order, Certification, and Execution against Earnings with the proper fee), to the same address as above.

    The fee is $5 (plus a surcharge between $1 and $10, depending on how many miles the constable has to travel to deliver the order to the debtor's employer).

    Call the Bergen County Small Claims Court at (201) 646 2236 for correct fees.

    Special Civil: (201) 646-2083

3. If there is an objection to your Notice of Motion, you will be notified by the court of a hearing date. Keep in mind that you must appear at that hearing.

4. You will be contacted by a constable when you are about to receive a payment.

1B. Property Execution:

(Same as for Hudson County, New Jersey [see above])
    Mail to:
        Bergen County Justice Center
        Special Civil Part, Room 430

10 Main St.
Hackensack, NJ 07601
(201) 646-2236

1C. Bank Levy:

    (Same as for Hudson County, New Jersey [see above].

    Mail to Bergen County Justice Center [see above for the address].)

CONNECTICUT

as exemplified by

THE JUDICIAL DISTRICT OF STAMFORD-NORWALK (Greenwich, Stamford, New Canaan, Darien, Wilton, Norwalk, Weston, Westport)

G.A. 1

(There are 22 geographical areas (G.A.) total.)

1A. Income Execution Using the Sheriff:

    You will need the following to initiate an income execution:

1. Your original judgment and three copies of it.
2. $10 payable to the small claims court.
3. A wage execution form.

PLANNING TIP *If the debtor is a "natural person"—that is, an individual who is not incorporated—you must also obtain and complete an Exemption and Modification Claim Form Wage Execution [FORM 58].*

4. The correct name of your debtor, the name and address of the debtor's employer, and the employer's business name and address.
5. The name and address of the sheriff who you want to accomplish the procedures necessary to complete the income execution. See [FORM 55] for a list of sheriffs in this geographic area.

    Request from the clerk at the small claims court window a Wage Execution form and a Wage Exemption form. (The cost is $10.) The clerk will mail both forms to you if you provide a self-addressed stamped business envelope.

    The clerk will give you the Wage Execution form shown on [FORM 56]—Wage Execution Proceedings Application Order, Execution and the Exemption and Modification Claim Form Wage Execution [FORM 59]. You must now complete the forms and prepare copies of them according to the instructions the upper left-hand corner of the form. (See [FORM 57] and [FORM 59] for examples of these prepared forms.

1. Prepare an original and four copies each of the wage execution and wage exemption forms.

2. Attach one copy of the judgment and one copy of the Wage Exemption form to each of three Wage Execution forms you have and return all three sets to the small claims court clerk in person or by mail. (The fee is $10.)

3. The small claims court clerk will verify the accuracy of your preparation, and then give or mail you a copy, bearing the proper court seal and the official signature.

4. Bring or mail this copy of the papers to a sheriff [FORM 55].

5. Be prepared to provide the sheriff with the details of your debtor's place of employment.

   The sheriff arranges a pay plan with the employer (weekly, monthly, and so on) and sends the payments to you on a regular basis. The sheriff takes his fee from debtor's other funds.

NOTE *Prior to the time the employer is compelled to give part of the debtor's wages to the sheriff, the debtor is given sufficient time to file the Wage Exemption form. If the debtor requests to be exempted from the garnishment, and his reasons meet the state's requirements, his wages may be totally exempt.*

1B. Bank Execution using the Sheriff:

You will need the following to do a bank execution:

1. Your judgment.
2. No fee is required at the small claims court window.
3. A Bank Execution Proceedings Application and Execution form [FORM 60].
4. And if the debtor is not an incorporated entity a form entitled Exemption Claim Form Bank Execution [FORM 62].
5. The name and address of the sheriff who you want to accomplish the procedures necessary to complete the Bank Execution. (See [FORM 55]

for a complete list of the sheriffs in this geographic area.)

6. The name of the bank where your debtor banks and the branch address if you have it.
7. A check for $8, payable to that bank.

If you do not know the debtor's bank you may ask the sheriff to search for your debtor's assets in the banks you suspect your debtor may have assets. For example, you could ask the sheriff to do the bank execution on Fleet, First County, First Union, Webster, and Bank of Boston-Connecticut, which are five of the largest and most well-known banks. This will cost $8 per bank, or $40. If the bank does not find any assets belonging to your debtor, it will refund your $8.

PLANNING TIP *You will be required to provide the sheriff with a check for $8, payable to each bank on which you want the sheriff to do an execution.*

Request the clerk at the small claims court window to provide you with a Bank Execution Proceedings Application and Execution and an Exemption Claim Form Bank Execution (both are free). The clerk will mail these forms to you if you provide a self-addressed stamped envelope.

The clerk will give you the bank execution form shown on [FORM 60], which you must complete and prepare copies of, according to the instructions at the upper left-hand corner of the form. An example of a prepared form is shown on [FORM 61]. The Exemption Claim Form Bank Execution is shown on [FORM 62]; a prepared example is shown on [FORM 63].

1. Prepare an original and four copies of the bank execution form [FORM 60].

PLANNING TIP *If the debtor is a "natural person"—that is, an individual who is not incorporated—you must indicate that with an X in the box marked, "If the Judgment Debtor Is a Natural Person" on the bank execution form.*

And then:

2. Prepare an original and four copies of the exemption form [FORM 62].

3. Submit or mail all the forms to the small claims court clerk, who will review them for accuracy and give or mail you back official signed copies of each form.

4. Make a copy of the bank execution form and the exemption form for each bank on which you want the sheriff to execute it.

5. Bring or mail your copies to a sheriff [FORM 55] with a check for $8.00 payable to each bank on which you want the sheriff to do an execution and a set of forms for each.

The sheriff may freeze bank assets and withdraw the money the debtor owes you, sending you the amount you are owed and taking his fee from the debtor's funds.

NOTE *The debtor is given at least 15 days before the bank will release assets to the sheriff. This reprieve allows him time to file the exemption form and claim exemption status, if he meets the state's requirements. If he does qualify, his assets may be seized only in part or not at all.*

Collecting on Your Judgment When the Debtor Has Moved Out of State

Among lawyers, the procedure by which you obtain recognition of an out-of-state judgment is known as domesticating a foreign judgment. If you have a judgment and the energy to continue with the collection process even though your debtor has moved to another state, you will have to know a few more legal details. Assuming that your judgment is for a substantial amount of money and you know or can easily find out your debtor's new residence (and better yet where he is employed), it may be worth your while to takes steps to have the new state recognize your judgment so that you can have it enforced in that state. The Constitution provides that "full faith and credit" shall be given to the judgments of each state in the courts of the others, but not under all conditions.

When you had your hearing in court, the defendant may or may not have been present. If you won your judgment and the defendant was present, you won a judgment after trial. If the defendant was not present at the hearing (in New York City it is called an inquest), you won a default judgment. Your request for judgment recognition has a much better chance of success if you won a judgment after trial, although it can be attacked on grounds like fraud or newly discovered evidence. If you have a default judgment it cannot be accepted for registration. However, in New York, for example, it has evidentiary weight at a new hearing. If the debtor does appear, you must stand ready to win again on the merits of your proof.

In every case you will need to purchase an "exemplified" copy of your judgment from the small claims court clerk at the court where you won your judgment. Such a copy bears the court seal and an attestation from the justice that the judgment is a true copy (see [FORM 69]). In New York City the cost is $10. Call to see if you can make the purchase by mail; in Brooklyn you cannot. In New Jersey the cost is $5, and you may purchase it by mail. In Connecticut, the cost is $1 per page. Usually the judgment is one page long and purchase by mail is accepted. Do not forget to include the index number of your judgment and a self-addressed stamped envelope.

If Debtor Has Moved to New York (New York City, the borough of Manhattan, in this example):

1. Purchase an exemplified copy of your judgment from the small claims court clerk's office where your judgment was obtained.

2. Prepare an affidavit to support your motion or request for recognition, such as the one shown in [FORM 30]. Don't forget to have the affidavit notarized. (The cost is between $1 and $3).

OBSERVATION *On the affidavit you must declare that you have a judgment after trial pursuant to Section 5402, Filing and Status of Foreign Judgment, of the Civil Procedure Law and Rules. The affidavit must state: "The judgment was not obtained by default in appearance or by confession of judgment, that it is unsatisfied in whole or in part, the amount remaining unpaid, and that the enforcement of the judgment has not been stayed." Then you must add the debtor's name and his new and last known address. Remember that you cannot file a default judgment obtained in another state.*

3. The fee for filing your judgment in the county clerk's office is $170, but you can buy a money order from the post office for less than $1. Make it payable to County Clerk's Office, New York County.

4. Bring your exemplified judgment, the affidavit, and your money order to the county clerk's office in Manhattan at 60 Centre St., Room 141B, (212) 374-8591 or (212) 374-8586. See the chief clerk or the "judgment" clerk.

5. The clerk will stamp your judgment with an official registration seal so that you can forward it to a marshal or sheriff for execution.

6. Within 30 days of filing your judgment in the county clerk's office, you must mail notice of the filing to the debtor at his last known address.

NOTE *You can file your papers in any one of the five county clerk's offices in the five counties of New York City. It is not essential to file in the county where the debtor now lives.*

If you won your judgment by default, you can also file a new initial claim form in any one of the five county courts of New York City, provided that your debtor lives, works, or transacts business in one of them. Where it asks you to briefly state your claim on the Initial Claim form, see [FORM 1], you would write "I want to have the judgment I obtained from _____ recognized and enforced by the state of New York. See attached copy of exemplified judgment." Then you would have to write the reason you sued the debtor initially. Be prepared to prove your case. (You could bring a "Motion for Summary Judgment in lieu of complaint," but it is probably easier to prepare the initial claim form).

If Debtor Has Moved to New Jersey:

1. Purchase an exemplified copy of the out-of-state judgment from the small claims court clerk's office where your judgment was obtained.

2. File an Initial Claim form (Summons and Complaint) in the small claims court of the county where the debtor lives, works, or transacts business.

3. In the area on the Initial Claim form where it says "Complaint," see [FORMS 40 and 41], you should explain: "I want to have the judgment I obtained from _____ recognized and enforced by the state of New Jersey. See attached copy of exemplified judgment." If you have a judgment after trial, it is advisable to attach an affidavit saying that the judgment was obtained after trial. If not, you can still submit your claim, but you may have to prove your case anew.

4. Mail or file in person at the small claims court clerk's office your Initial Claim form, with the exemplified copy of judgment attached, an affidavit such as the one shown on [FORM 49] (only if you won your judgment after trail), and the filing fee (the cost varies depending on the distance the summons travels to be served. Between $13 and $18 is common).

5. If the defendant does not respond by the end of 10 days to the summons and complaint that is served on him, a default judgment is issued and no court hearing is required.

6. If the defendant responds to the summons and complaint, a hearing date is set.

7. You can now request that the small claims court clerk send you a form called a Notice of Motion for Summary Judgment [FORM 48], which you must complete (see example [FORM 50] and mail back to the small claims court clerk.

OBSERVATION *The Notice of Motion for Summary Judgment in effect asks the judge to rule in your favor, without going through all the steps of an actual hearing. When you have a judgment after a trial in the other state, there is nothing left to have a new trial about, unless the defendant raises issues of fact, challenging that the prior judgment was, for example, obtained by fraud on the court or the other court lacked jurisdiction or the complaint is not directed to the defendant of your prior judgment.*

8. At the hearing, which you must attend, the judge will make his decision. If you won your judgment originally by default, and the debtor appears for the hearing, be prepared to prove your case.

9. If the judge rules in your favor you will receive a judgment, which can be enforced in New Jersey.

If Debtor Has Moved to Connecticut:

If you have a default judgment:

1. Purchase an exemplified copy of the out-of-state judgment from the small claims court clerk's office where your judgment was obtained.

2. File a Small Claim and Notice of Suit (analogous to the Initial Claim form, or Summons and Complaint) in the Geographic Area Superior Court where the debtor lives, works, or transacts business. (See [FORM 52] for a list of towns and the court that has jurisdiction over them.)

3. On the form where is stated, "The above plaintiff(s) claims you owe _____ plus costs, for the following reasons," see [FORMS 53, 54], you write, "I want to have the judgment I obtained from _____ recognized and enforced by the state of Connecticut. See attached copy of exemplified judgment."

Mail in or file in person at the small claims court clerk's office the initial claim form, the affidavit, and the filing fee, which is $30.

4. If the defendant does not answer the summons and complaint, depending on the circumstances surrounding your case, either you will be awarded a default judgment enforceable in Connecticut or you will be asked to attend a hearing where the facts of your case will be presented to the judge or magistrate. If the defendant answers the summons and complaint (he has 30 days to do so), he may request a hearing and you will have to prove your case in court again. Having a judgment, however, will give you some additional support for your case.

5. A hearing date will be set. If the defendant does not appear in court, it is likely the judgment will be granted to you. Be prepared to prove your case if the defendant shows.

If you have a "judgment after trial":

1. Purchase an exemplified copy of the out-of state judgment from the small claims court clerk's office where your judgment was obtained.

2. Add to it an affidavit according to Connecticut General Statutes 52-605, which states:

"I have obtained a judgment in the county of _____, from the state of _____ which is a judgment granted after trial (not by default and not by confession of judgment). This judgment is unsatisfied in whole or part. The unpaid amount $_____. The enforcement of the judgment has not been stayed. The defendant's name and address in Connecticut is _____." (See [FORM 49] for a sample affidavit.)

3. Obtain an Initial Claim form. Where it states "The above plaintiff claims you owe _____ plus costs, for the following reasons" you write: "I want to have the judgment I obtained from _____ recognized and enforced by the state of Connecticut. See attached copy of exemplified judgment."

4. Mail or file in person at the small claims court clerk's office the Initial Claim form, the Affidavit, and the filing fee, which is $30.

5. A hearing date will be set.

6. If the defendant does not respond in 30 days, you must mail, certified return receipt requested, to the defendant a letter indicating that you have filed papers with the court to have the judgment you obtained in the previous court recognized and enforced by the new court.
7. You will be granted a judgment enforceable in Connecticut.
8. If the defendant requests a hearing, it will probably be granted. Your judgment after trial will probaly prevail, however, and you will be granted an enforceable judgment.

....

OBSERVATION *A judgment may be "stayed" when the debtor has declared bankruptcy or been declared bankrupt involuntarily. It means that you no longer have a legal right to have your judgment enforced. Consequently, you may not collect on your judgment.*

....

Procedures That Release the Debtor After You Collect

THE SATISFACTION OF JUDGMENT

One thing you can do to force a debtor to pay you after you win a judgment in your favor is file that judgment in the county clerk's office. As a result, you cause the debtor to have entered on his credit report a record of the judgment showing that you are legally entitled to be paid a specific amount. You mar the debtor's credit rating, which means that he will be considered a poor credit risk when it comes to any future financial dealings. For example, should he want to purchase a car or a home and require credit (loan, mortgage), the institutions that lend money and sell mortgages will search for such judgments in the courts and in the credit reports that are kept in the files of credit agencies such as Experian (formerly TRW).

To avoid having their credit impaired, most debtors are inclined eventually to pay their debts and when they do, they are legally entitled to have that black mark removed from their credit report. You are therefore obliged to file the Satisfaction of Judgment form [FORM 16] in the county clerk's office. This form announces to the world that your debtor has discharged his debt to you.

It is not mandatory to use a form such as the one shown in [FORM 16]. You need only to write a letter and include the following (refer to the form):

1. The current date
2. The name the plaintiff and the defendant
3. The index (case, docket) number
4. The full name of the court
5. A statement indicating that "the judgment and all obligations of the defendant(s) is the case whose index number is (same as above) has been fully satisfied"
6. Your signature
7. Your printed signature followed by *pro se*
8. Another statement indicating that "a copy of the Satisfaction of Judgment has been sent to the defendant"
9. The signature and seal of the notary public

You should mail the original to the county clerk's office and a copy to the small claims court where you won the judgment, and a copy to the debtor.

New Jersey:
You need only send a letter as outlined above to the small claims court and the debtor. Alternatively you may purchase (for a $2 fee) a form to do the same job—a Warrant of Satisfaction, form # 954—from Silver's Stationery, 578 Newark Avenue, Jersey City, NJ 07306, (201) 963-1700.

Connecticut:

Send the letter as outlined above to the appropriate small claims court and the debtor.

THE GENERAL RELEASE

It is fitting and proper upon request to provide a general release in exchange for settlement and payment; the instrument to use is the Blumberg B 110, General Release, for use by an individual [FORM 13]. In it you stipulate the sum of money agreed upon by the parties to release the defendant from all further obligations. You should not, however, give the defendant the general release and "discontinuance" referred to below, until you have the cash in hand or know that the defendant's check has cleared in the bank. Usually it is preferable to have the defendant provide a money order or certified bank teller's check if cash is not forthcoming. If a settlement provides for installment payments, the release and discontinuance are not given until the last payment has cleared.

If an attorney for the defendant completes the General Release and you sign it, you can be assured that payment is forthcoming, but the release must be notarized. It is usually accompanied by a Stipulation Discontinuing Action form (Blumberg B 493) [FORM 12]. Your signature on this form means you are willing to discontinue the litigation you initiated because the matter has been settled. Additional terms are sometimes added.

Appealing a Decision Rendered by a Judge in Small Claims Court

So you had a hearing before a judge (not an arbitrator whose decision is final) and you are shocked and infuriated by the lack of "substantial justice" in the judgment (verdict, decision, order) you just received in the mail. Here's what you can do to appeal the decision to the Appellate Term of the Supreme Court. In Brooklyn this court is located at 111 Livingston Street, 19th floor, (718) 643-5730.

This court reviews cases only after they have been decided by a lower court. It hears these cases to revise or correct decisions that may have been decided in error for one reason or another. In the majority of cases, however, its decisions uphold, or affirm, the judgments of the lower court. The appellate court is in session (term) from the first Monday in September until the last week in July, unlike small claims court, which has sessions year-round including July and August.

The appeals court in Brooklyn (second judicial department) hears cases arising from the small claims courts in Brooklyn, Queens, and Staten Island. It has sessions two days out of each month (about every 15 days) for such cases, and each day it is in session it disposes of between 30 and 40 cases. Three judges (called justices) sit on a panel to render the decisions of this court. To win an appeal you must convince two of the three that your case has legal merit.

To convince them, you must prepare and submit a legal brief, a short but concise and very formal written statement or argument explaining why and/or how the small claims court decided incorrectly. Aside from at least 4 pages of standard, preliminary information that you are asked to provide, it may generally require that you prepare between 2 and 20 pages more of double-spaced explanatory text. It typically contains a statement of the legal issues presented for review, the facts of the case and an argument supported by references to statutes or case law. Supporting exhibits, such as documents submitted to and accepted in evidence by the lower court, may also be included. The brief concludes by stating the precise remedy that the appellant desires. For instance, one might ask for a higher monetary award or even a reversal of the decision of the lower court.

An appeal is not a new trial. It is a review of the relevant portions of the case file and transcript of the minutes of the hearing (all the spoken words of the judge, the plaintiff, the defendant, and any other witnesses, in written form). The transcript and the legal brief, once compiled, are submitted to the justices of the appellate court for review.

You can submit this appeal file for review or submit your file and present your case in person before the justices of this court. You will be allowed not more than 15 minutes to present your argument at the time set for consideration of your case by the court. The defendant will have the same allowance.

A lawyer is likely to charge you between $2,000 and $3,000 to research the law and prepare the brief and file for submission, and between $200 and $300 per hour (waiting around time included) to argue the case before the appellate court. The legal research and writing of an effective brief are formidable tasks and few are the persons who are sufficiently disciplined and capable of preparing a persuasive appeal. Even more discouraging is that in two-thirds of the cases heard by this court, the lower court's decision is upheld.

If you understand at the start that the odds are against you—even more so because you are a novice in terms of legal skills—you will carefully deliberate before you consider taking on an appeal. On the other hand, here are some interesting statistics I obtained that seem to prove that many persons are willing to take on the work with few or no misgivings: In 1996 out of 2,344 small claims court cases heard by a judge, throughout the five counties of New York City, 265 resulted in appeals filed with the appellate term court. Surprisingly, more than 75% of the small claims cases are submitted *pro se*.

How many *pro se* appellants win their appeals as compared to the number of attorney-appellants who win their cases? Unfortunately, these statistics are not available.

The strength of a legal brief lies in the appellant's ability to identify the pertinent legal issues of the case at hand and to state how those issues relate to the appellant's position. The appellant must make a compelling legal argument supported by references to statute and/or case law to support the underlying question the justices will ask: "Why do you say that?"

Now, if you are still up for the challenge, here are some guidelines for obtaining legal and procedural information:

In Brooklyn, (see Appendix A for other public access libraries) there are two law libraries available to the public:

- the law library on the 3rd floor of the Supreme Court building at 360 Adams Street (main entrance on Court Street). It is open Monday

through Friday, 9:00 A.M. until 7:00 P.M. Call (718) 643-8080.
- the library of the Brooklyn Law School at 250 Joralemon Street with far more extensive hours, including the weekend. Call (718) 780-7973.

These libraries are within one block of each other. To gain access to the law school, request a Metro pass at the Brooklyn Business Library at 280 Cadman Plaza West, (718) 722-3333 or (718) 722-3350. Be prepared to tell the librarian the reason in detail that you need to use the law school library. The pass allows you access to the library for the next 24 hours and then must be renewed. The chief librarians are veterans experienced in helping you to get the information you need.

Still another place to get information about the appeal procedure (not substantive law itself) is the appeals clerk at the small claims court or at the appellate court. At the small claims court you can also obtain a brief pamphlet [FORM 26] that will guide you toward your destination. The title of the pamphlet is *Information Regarding an Appeal of an Order or Judgment*. The appeals clerk at the appellate court on Livingston Street also has a practical eight-page *pro se* guide to get you started, which includes some useful forms with instructions.

The appeals clerks of either the small claims court or the appeals court can be helpful. But if you ask them any question that even remotely sounds as if you are asking for legal advice, they will quickly and patiently suggest that you refer your question to a lawyer. It is frustrating when this happens to you, but remember, it is the burden you shouldered when you elected to do the appeal *pro se*.

The citizens of New Jersey should be pleased to know their court system has gone the extra mile to serve them. A would-be *pro se* appellant has only to call the court at (609) 292-4822 and request a *pro se* appeal kit. They will receive 32 pages of material including all the forms required and explicit instructions on preparing a legal brief. The writing is clear and the subject is thoroughly covered, including instructions on how to complete the forms. Moreover, a form is provided for those who are very poor, which excuses them from having to make any payment if they meet the court's standards for indigence. The bad news is that unlike New York whose fee to file a Notice of Appeal is $25, New Jersey charges a stiff $175. (See [FORM 47] for additional information on NJ appeals.)

The residents of Connecticut, on the other hand, may or may not be pleased to know (depending on whether they won or lost in small claims court) that they may not appeal their case to a higher court because the small claims court judgment is final.

LEGAL NOTE *Connecticut does allow up to four months to make a motion to reopen a case where a judgment has been awarded. Such a reopening is based upon the finding of relevant new evidence and or new witnesses. A Motion To Open Judgment form is available on request from the small claims court clerk. Cases are rarely reopened.*

I also recommend two books that are found in the law school library: *Practitioners Handbook for Appeals* and *New York Appellate Practice: How to Take a Civil Appeal in New York State* (see bibliography). The first book is relatively short but very thorough. I managed to comprehend a moderate amount of what I was reading. It also offered a foreword by the former chief judge of the New York State Appeals Court, Sol Wachtler. The second book is a compendium of articles—some very basic but others rather far-reaching for the layperson. Finally, any guidance you can obtain from an attorney friend may also be helpful.

I have avoided sending you to the primary source of information on the procedural aspects of civil litigation in New York, namely New York's *Civil Practice Law and Rules* (CPLR) (See bibliography.) Speaking as a layperson, I found the CPLR to be tough sledding and not easily digested. What it lacks in comprehensibility it compensates for by its thoroughness of coverage. In New Jersey these laws are entitled *Civil Practice and Court Rules of New Jersey,*

published by Gould Publications, Binghamton, New York.

THE APPEAL PROCESS

OBSERVATION *You are allowed 30 days (New Jersey permits 45), from the date written on the decision you received in the mail, to file a Notice of Appeal—the first document you must prepare to secure your right to appeal. It is prudent to save the envelope in which the decision was mailed to you because it bears the postmark date. These precautionary moves will help you validate a request for an extension of the 30-day period. Beside receiving the decision late, other valid reasons, such as illness or absence from the state or country, may warrant making a request for an extension. Such a request must be submitted on a specific form, which is available from the appeals clerk's window in the appellate term court.*

A. Filing the Notice of Appeal [FORM 27] in New York and [FORM 47] in New Jersey:

To appeal a decision of the small claims court in Brooklyn (Kings County), Queens, or Staten Island (Richmond County), you must appeal to the Appellate Term of the Supreme Court (Second Judicial Department) in Brooklyn, at (718) 643-5730.

To appeal a decision of the small claims court in New York or the Bronx, you must appeal to the Appellate Term of the Supreme Court (First Judicial District) in Manhattan, at (212) 374-8500.

These are the courts to which your papers may be sent from the small claims court office, and where your case will most likely be heard.

The Notice of Appeal is the Blumberg Form T471. A completed one is shown on [FORM 27]. You can obtain this form at a good stationery store for $1. Notice that you, the original suing party, are now called the plaintiff (claimant)-appellant and the other party is called the defendant-respondent. The Notice of Appeal form for New Jersey is shown on [FORM 47].

You will need to have an original and two copies:

The first copy is for your records.

The second copy must be served on the defendant. This is accomplished by having someone over age 18 mail it to him by certified return-receipt mail. (The receipt is your proof of service.) Another way of serving a Notice of Appeal is to have a process server do it for you. The process server makes a living by delivering important documents in person, especially court documents. [FORM 27] shows the Affidavit of Service the process server gives you after serving the Notice of Appeal in person. This method of service is an optional and more expensive way to ensure the Notice was delivered, but it removes even the slightest doubt that the document reached its destination. It is served accompanied by a copy of the judge's decision in the small claims court. Moreover, the Notice of Appeal provides the defendant an opportunity to appear, file an answering brief, and make an appearance, *pro se* or with counsel, at the appellate hearing.

The original Notice of Appeal [FORM 27] should now be taken back to the small claims court window (of the court that awarded you the judgment) with the completed Affidavit of Service that you had notarized and a certified mail receipt, which shows the name and address of the defendant to whom you mailed the second copy; or (optional) with the Affidavit of Service that is notarized by the person who served it [FORM 27]. You pay the clerk a $25 fee in cash or with a U.S. postal money order. This initiates the next step.

B. Obtaining the transcript (minutes) of the hearing:

Upon payment of $25, the clerk will give you two blank forms—(1) a Notice of Settlement of Transcript form [FORM 28] and (2) an Affidavit of Service of Notice of Settlement form [FORM 28] for later use along with a receipt slip bearing the plaintiff's and defendant's names and case number, a one-page instruction sheet, and the identification numbers that specify the exact tape cassette on which your hearing was recorded (and the numbers that describe where on that tape your hearing begins and ends). The clerk will direct you to the office of the court reporter with your papers (Room 716 in Brooklyn Small Claims Court), which will prepare the tape of your hearing for delivery to a court-appointed tran-

scription company, experienced in taking recorded testimony and converting it into the written word.

At the court reporter's office your identification numbers will be recorded on still another form—referred to as the CIV-LT-90 request form. Only your address and signature are required on this form. It serves to request that the court reporter provide the tape of your hearing to the transcription company of your choice. The court reporter will give you a list of court-appointed transcription companies from which you must choose one. Call the company you choose and speak to an officer. Let that person know that your case is about to arrive at the office and that you want to be apprised of its progress.

The tape of the hearing is now released to the transcription company that will complete the transcription within 10 working days for $2.50 to $3.50 per page (minimum charge $25.00). If your hearing was recorded by a court stenographer, the transcription of tape will cost between $4.50 and $5.50 per page. The transcription company will likely send the completed work to the appellant by messenger service. The transcript is also sent to the small claims court clerk's office.

C. "Perfecting" the minutes of the hearing:

LEGAL NOTE *New York's Civil Practice Law and Rules indicates that from the time you receive the transcript you are permitted 15 days to correct or amend it and serve it on the defendant, who is likewise allowed 15 days to make objections, corrections, and amendments. "At any time thereafter and on at least four days' notice to the adverse party, the transcript...shall be submitted to the judge or referee before whom the proceedings were had if the parties cannot agree on the amendments to the transcript" (Article 55, Rule 5525 [c].)*

Now you must "perfect" the minutes by correcting any errors or omissions. Note any errors you find in the transcript on the "list of errors" page (the last page of the transcript); then make two more copies of the corrected transcript.

Keep the first copy for your records.

Telephone the office of the judge who originally heard your case (The small claims court clerk will give you the judge's telephone number.) and request an appointment to "settle the minutes" (transcript). The judge's law clerk will arrange a date and time for the judge to review the corrected transcript with you and the defendant.

The second corrected copy must be served (mailed certified return-receipt requested) by any person over age 18, except the plaintiff, to the defendant along with a form called the Notice of Settlement of Transcript (see above). This tells the defendant the date and time of the appointment with the judge to settle the minutes. (See [FORM 28] and note[13].) The person who serves this notice must fill out the Affidavit of Service of Notice of Settlement [FORM 28] and have it notarized. It is important to keep the affidavit because it proves to the judge, who is going to settle the transcript of the case, that you sent the transcript and the Notice of Settlement of Transcript to the defendant.

The original transcript with corrections, original Notice of Settlement of Transcript, and an original Affidavit of Service of Notice of Settlement must be given to the appeals clerk at the small claims court. The appeals clerk will prepare, file, and make it available for the judge to have on the day the judge settles the minutes.

D. "Settling" the minutes:

You and the defendant meet before the judge on the appointed day and time to correct the minutes. In the end, both of you must agree that they are accurate. This is called settling the minutes.

E. Submitting your legal brief and settled minutes for examination by the appeals court:

The judge sends your corrected minutes back to the small claims court clerk who sends them, along with your Notice of Appeal and all other court records and papers related to your case, to the appeals clerk at the Appellate Court, 111 Livingston Street in Brooklyn. This bundle of papers is called the clerk's return on appeal.

Between three and six weeks after the appeals court clerk receives the clerk's return on appeal from the small claims court, you will receive a postcard indicating that your papers have been officially filed in the appellate term court's office. The postcard will also bear the appellate term's court case number assigned to your case. When you prepare your brief your case number must be placed on the title page.

OBSERVATION *The Brooklyn Appellate Term Court receives the clerk's return on appeal from the small claims courts of Westchester County (10th Judicial Department) and Nassau and Suffolk Counties (9th Judicial Department) as well as the boroughs of Queens (11th Judicial Department) and Brooklyn and Staten Island, which comprise the 2nd Judicial District. The totality of these districts constitute the Second Judicial Department of the Appellate Division of the Supreme Court. Manhattan and the Bronx (1st Judicial Department) have their own appellate term court in Manhattan.*

You now have 90 days to compile your legal brief and file it along with the settled minutes of the hearing at the appeals clerk's window at 111 Livingston Street. An eight-page guide for *pro se* appellants is available at the appeals clerk's window. It's easy-to-read and quite instructive regarding how to put the brief together. (From this guide I learned that the four parts of a brief could be condensed into a document with as few as four pages.) The guide instructs you that on page three of your brief you should tell your story; however, it does not tell you substantively how to prepare a brief: to identify the relevant legal principles, marshal your arguments, and specify the error made by the lower court as to the applicable legal rule or its application in your case. You must now send a complete copy of the brief to the defendant and file three copies of it, along with an affidavit that you sent it to the defendant, with the appeals clerk. Your brief and transcript will be read by each of three appellate term court justices. The appeals clerk will assign your case

---

13 The Notice of Settlement of Transcript is essentially a letter to the defendant telling the date, the time, and the room number where the judge is going to review the accuracy of any corrections you or the defendant have made to the transcript.

a court date (put your case on the calendar of appeals) to one of a number of possible appellate term courts including

- Brooklyn on Livingston Street
- Queens on Sutphin Boulevard
- Mineola on Supreme Court Drive in Nassau
- White Plains on Grove Street in Westchester.

The appeals court will notify you by post-card, two to four weeks before the date your case is to be heard, of the date, time, and court location of your hearing. The *New York Law Journal*[14] publishes the court calendars of the majority of the state and federal courts, for as many as 30 days in advance of the hearing date.

You will have your hearing generally between three and nine months after filing your brief and you will be notified by mail well in advance of the hearing date. Never be reluctant to telephone the appeals office to check on the status of your case (date, time, and location of your hearing).

....

WARNING *You must note on the title page of your legal brief whether you will appear in person to present your argument. Even if you do not appear, your brief will still be read and you will not be prejudiced merely by failing to appear. It should not come as a surprise if you receive a response from the defendant. You may wish to be present in court to reply to any arguments presented by the defendant or questions asked by the court. However, it will say on the postcard you receive to notify you of the date of your hearing that "It is not necessary for you to be present unless you wish to argue. You will not be permitted to argue unless you have filed a brief."*
....

The Result of an Appeal

As was noted above, in the majority of cases, the appeals court agrees with the lower court's decision. However, other possibilities include reversing or modifying the lower court's decision wholly or in part, to the benefit or detriment of either the plaintiff or the defendant. In some cases the appeals court may even refer the case back to another court for further hearing to resolve some related issues of the case. In such cases where the appeals court modifies or reverses a lower court's decision, it will also provide the reasoning for its position.

GOOD LUCK
The Ruling of the Justices of the Appellate Term Court With Regard to the Case Cited in Chapter 7— Countering the Counterclaim:

The decision came in the mail 15 days after the three justices rendered their decision on February 5, 1997. See [FORM 29]. The plaintiff was present at the appellate term hearing, even though his presence was optional. (He had previously elected to submit his legal brief in advance and to forego the 15 minutes he was permitted to defend and support his case with oral argument before the justices of the court.) The defendant was not present. Even if he had been present he would not have been permitted to argue his case because he had not responded to the plaintiff's brief with an answering brief.

....

OBSERVATION *On February 5 the court was scheduled to hear 17 cases. Of those cases, 7 were submitted to be read only. Of the 10 other cases, the parties for which were present, 5 had originated in the small claims court and were argued orally by either the plaintiff or the defendant, but in no case by both. To be candid, their arguments were not impressive. On the other hand, in the remaining 5 cases, both the plaintiff's and the defendant's attorneys presented arguments that seemed to be well prepared and thoughtfully presented. The justices were attentive and pleasant and asked pointed questions when appropriate. The presiding judge at times would abruptly terminate the argument, when he was certain that further presentation would not be helpful.*

....

14 The *New York Law Journal* is a daily newspaper for lawyers that is published at 345 Park Ave. South, New York, NY 10010, (212) 779-9200. It lists the upcoming court cases by index number, followed by plaintiff's and defendant's names. Thus, you would look in the section of the paper called "Court Calendars" under the heading "Second Department," the subheading "Appellate Term Court," and the sub-subheading "2nd and 11th Judicial District," if your case was being heard in the Brooklyn Appellate Term Court.

This newspaper publishes each court's list of cases for as many as 30 consecutive days prior to the day the case is scheduled to be heard. It also publishes full summaries of a select number of appellate cases after decision has been rendered.

The plaintiff had requested: (1) monetary damages for the unpaid balance of the payment due for professional services he rendered; (2) statutory (legal) interest on the unpaid balance up to the time of the appellate court decision, which is presently 9% in New York, 5.6% in New Jersey, and 10% per annum in Connecticut; and (3) court costs (i.e. filing fees, cost of producing a transcript).

OBSERVATION *Legal interest is a rate of interest fixed by the legislature of each state as either the maximum rate of interest permitted to be charged by law or a rate of interest to be applied when the parties to a contract intend an interest to be paid but do not fix that rate in their contract. If a judge adds interest to an award, it is computed as simple interest over the time from the date of occurrence of the transaction (see [FORM 1]) until the date of the judge's decision.*

The justices of the appellate term court affirmed the decision rendered by the judge in the small claims court. Their decision reflected their belief that "substantial justice" had been rendered at the lower court level and the plaintiff was not entitled to collect the unpaid part of his bill from his former patient.

The process of the above appeal extended over a period of almost 13 months from the time the Notice of Appeal [FORM 27] was first served on the defendant. The case might have been completed in its entirety in 9 months. Unfortunately, the case had to be heard two times at the small claims court level: A recording machine failed to function properly at the first hearing; a rehearing was necessary so that a transcript could be produced.

I would like to point out to the reader that the author strove to be diligent and thorough in the presentation of the facts and law in his legal brief. Indeed, even a few of his attorney friends confided that the brief was well done (for a lay person). He steadfastly believed his arguments would prevail. They didn't. The satisfaction comes from doing the best you can when you believe in the "principle of the thing."

My mom used to say: "Nothing ventured, nothing gained—but you must always act on the courage of your convictions," so here's to you, Mom.

List of Forms

(Note: All forms for New York City are applicable in the five boroughs.)

Form 1
New York City Statement of Claim (Initial Claim form for a non-incorporated person)

Form 2
Letter of Demand an incorporated plaintiff must send the debtor before filing an Initial Claim form (commercial)

Form 3
New York City Statement of Claim (Initial Claim form for a corporation)

Form 4
Completed sample of New York City Statement of Claim (Form 1—Initial Claim form for a non-incorporated person)

Form 5
New York City Instructions to Claimant (given to plaintiff when the Initial Claim form is filed)

Form 6
New York City Notice of Claim and Summons to Appear (sent to defendant when the claim is filed)

Form 7
Compilation of New York City Notices to small claims defendant

Form 8
New York City Instructions for Service of Subpoena

Form 9
Sample completed New York City Subpoena to Testify and Affidavit of Service of Subpoena

Form 10
Sample completed New York City Subpoena for Records and Affidavit of Service of Subpoena

Form 11
Sample completed index card relating facts of plaintiff's claim for use when appearing in court

Form 12
Sample completed New York City Stipulation Discontinuing Action (Blumberg—B 493)

Form 13
Sample completed New York City General Release (Blumberg—B 110) (form sent to plaintiff to which plaintiff signs his name to acknowledge agreement to settle dispute for the amount noted in the document)

Form 14
Sample completed New York City Notice of Judgment (sent by the court to plaintiff and defendant stating judge or arbitrator's decision)

Form 15
Sample letter to defendant immediately upon receipt of judgment

Form 16
Sample completed New York City Satisfaction of Judgment (Blumberg—B 242) (when judgment debtor has paid the debt to the plaintiff's satisfaction, plaintiff must file this form in the county clerk's office if plaintiff has registered his judgment with the county clerk)

Form 17
Sample completed New York City Transcript of Judgment (with county clerk's registration stamps on reverse)

Form 18
New York City Income Execution form (Blumberg—T 239) (form to be sent to marshal or sheriff)

Form 19
Sample completed New York City Income Execution form (Blumberg—T 239)

Form 20
Manhattan Requisition Request for Small Claims Execution form (required by Manhattan sheriff's office to initiate either an income or property execution)

Form 21
Brooklyn Requisition Request for Small Claims Execution form (required by Brooklyn sheriff's office to initiate property execution)

Form 22
Sample completed New York City Information Subpoena and Restraining Notice (in this sample, information is being requested from a bank—the form to be completed by bank personnel is on the reverse)

Form 23
Excerpt from *McKinney's Consolidated Laws of New York Annotated* (1991 amendment to law providing for judgment creditor's right to obtain information about location of debtor's assets and debtor's employer)

Form 24
Sample completed New York City Response to Subpoena from a bank (alternative sample response on reverse)

Form 25
Sample completed New York City Execution of Income (or against Property) with Notice to Garnishee (Blumberg—B 320)—form sent to marshal or sheriff after an asset such as a bank account, car, or house, has been located

Form 26
New York City informational pamphlet regarding taking an appeal from a judicial order or judgment

Form 27
Sample completed New York City Notice of Appeal (Blumberg—T 471) (sample completed Affidavit of Service of Notice of Appeal on reverse)

Form 28
Sample completed New York City Notice of Settlement of Transcript (sample completed Affidavit of Service of Notice of Settlement of Transcript on reverse)

Form 29
Sample New York City written decision of Appellate Term Court

Form 30
Sample New York City Affidavit in Support of Plaintiff's Motion for Civil Court of City of New York to recognize out-of-state judgment and attesting to fact that plaintiff received judgment after trial

Form 31
Nassau County Statement of Claim (Initial Claim form for a non-incorporated person)

Form 32

Nassau County Statement of Claim (Initial Claim form for a corporation to file)

Form 33

Suffolk County Statement of Claim (Initial Claim form for a non-incorporated person, with instructions on reverse)

Form 34

Westchester County Statement of Claim (Initial Claim form for a non-incorporated person for use in Pelham Justice Court, a town court)

Form 35

Westchester County Statement of Claim (Initial Claim form for a non-incorporated person for use in Mount Kisco Justice Court, a village court)

Form 36

Westchester County Statement of Claim (Initial Claim form for a non-incorporated person for use in White Plains City Court)

Form 37

Westchester County Statement of Claim (Initial Claim form for a corporation for use in White Plains City Court)

Form 38

Westchester County Notice from City of White Plains ruling that professional corporations must bring small claims as corporations and professionals (e.g., physicians, chiropractors, must be present to give testimony when they are claimants)

Form 39

New Jersey instructions for filing a small claim, accompanies Initial Claim form

Form 40

Bergen County Statement of Claim (Initial Claim form)

Form 41

Hudson County Statement of Claim (Initial Claim form, Summons to defendant on reverse)

Form 42

New Jersey sample completed Affidavit certifying to court that process cannot be served on defendant

Form 43

New Jersey list of mileage charge for service of summons

Form 44

Hudson County Statement of Docketing form, available on request after case has been heard. When registered in Superior Court in Trenton, the Statement permanently registers the judgment state-wide for the purposes of property execution

Form 45

Bergen County Income Execution form, Notice of Motion for Wage Execution (Order on reverse)

Form 46

New Jersey Notice of Application for Wage Execution (Blumberg—T 839), (Order, Certification and Execution against Earnings on reverse—Blumberg—T 847)

Form 47

New Jersey Notice of Appeal form

Form 48

Sample completed New Jersey Notice of Motion for Summary Judgment seeking recognition for out-of-state judgment

Form 49

Sample completed New Jersey Affidavit in Support of Motion for Summary Judgment stating that out-of-state judgment was rendered

Form 50

Sample New Jersey Order recognizing out-of-state judgment

Form 51

Connecticut instructions to plaintiff bringing a small claim (location of all geographical area court locations in state on reverse)

Form 52

Connecticut list of towns indicating geographic area court having jurisdiction

Form 53

Connecticut Statement of Claim (Initial Claim form)

Form 54

Sample completed Connecticut Statement of Claim (Initial Claim form)

Form 55

Connecticut list of sheriffs for each county

Form 56

Connecticut Wage Execution Proceedings Application (used to initiate garnishment of debtor's salary)

Form 57

Sample completed Connecticut Wage Execution Proceedings Application

Form 58

Connecticut Exemption and Modification Claim Form Wage Execution form that must accompany Wage Execution Proceedings Application when debtor is non-incorporated person

Form 59

Sample completed Connecticut Exemption and Modification Claim Form Wage Execution

Form 60

Connecticut Bank Execution Proceedings Application and Execution used to place a lien on debtor's bank account

Form 61

Sample completed Connecticut Bank Execution Proceedings Application and Execution

Form 62

Connecticut Exemption Claim Form Bank Execution, form that must accompany Bank Execution Proceedings Application when debtor is a non-incorporated person

Form 63

Sample completed Connecticut Exemption Claim Form Bank Execution

Form 64

Connecticut Form UCC-1 (form used to register a judgment on a person's credit report and put a lien on debtor's property state-wide, instructions on reverse)

Form 65

Sample completed Connecticut Form UCC-1

Form 66

Notice from United States Bankruptcy Court of final meeting of creditors of debtor who has filed for bankruptcy

Form 67

Notice from United States Bankruptcy Court that debtor is released from all debts

Form 68

Lutz Asset Research form (reverse side, letter reporting progress)

Form 69

A Judgment (reverse side, exemplified copy)

Form 70

A Judgment where the plaintiff lost

INSTRUCTIONS:
Place only ONE letter or number in each space and leave a blank space between words.

CIVIL COURT OF THE CITY OF NEW YORK
SMALL CLAIMS PART
STATEMENT OF CLAIM

(FOR OFFICE USE ONLY)

(Your)   **I CLAIMANT'S INFORMATION**

LAST NAME

FIRST NAME   MIDDLE INITIAL

ADDRESS

BOROUGH, CITY, TOWN OR VILL.   STATE   ZIP

OTHER INFO (Doing Business As or In Care Of)

PHONE NO. ( )

CERT'D #

(Their)   **II DEFENDANT'S INFORMATION***

LAST NAME (or Business Name)

FIRST NAME   MIDDLE INITIAL

ADDRESS

BOROUGH, CITY, TOWN OR VILL.   STATE N Y   ZIP

OTHER INFO (Doing Business As or In Care Of)

PHONE NO. ( )

COA CODE

CLAIM AMT.
$

FEE
STANDARD FEE PLUS POSTAGE
☐ CLAIMANT V. DEFENDANT
NO FEE; POSTAGE ONLY
☐ DEFENDANT V. THIRD PARTY
☐ CLAIMANT V. ADD'L DEFENDANT
☐ WAGE CLAIM TO $300

III CLAIM

Amount Claimed: $_____ (Maximum $3,000)   Date of Occurrence or Transaction:_____

LANGUAGE

REASON FOR CLAIM:

Damaged caused to:	☐ automobile	☐ other personal property	☐ real property
Failure to provide:	☐ repairs	☐ proper services	☐ goods ordered
Failure to return:	☐ security	☐ property	☐ deposit ☐ money
Failure to pay for:	☐ wages	☐ services rendered	☐ insurance claim ☐ money loaned
	☐ rent	☐ commissions	☐ goods sold and delivered
Breach of:	☐ contract	☐ lease	☐ warranty ☐ agreement
Loss of:	☐ luggage	☐ property	☐ time from work ☐ use of property
Returned:	☐ check (bounced/stopped)		☐ merchandise (not reimbursed)

Other: (Be brief)

_____

Identifying Numbers(s) - (Receipt #, Claim #, Account #, Policy #, Ticket #, License #) _____

_____

Today's Date   Signature of Claimant or Agent

DATE DATA ENTERED

DATE NOTICES MAILED

CASE TYPE:

MULTI DFT ☐   CTR/CLM ☐

3 PARTY ☐   CRS/CMPLT ☐

FIRST DATE

DAY COURT
☐ STATUTORY   ☐ OTHER

*DEFENDANT'S: (The full legal name and street address (no box number) of the party you are suing. Indicate whether you are suing this party as a person or a business.)

CIV-SC-50 (Revised 2/95)   [NOTE: If you are suing a business, indicate whether it is a partnership, a corporation or an individual with a business certificate. This information can be obtained in the County Clerk's Office in the county in which the business is located. Failure to check this information may result in a judgment which cannot be collected.]

FORM 1

DC 292

UCS-124 (Rev. 11/90)

Commercial Claim Arising Out of a Consumer Transaction
DEMAND LETTER

TO: _____   Date:

    Name of Defendant

_____

_____

    Address

    You have not paid a debt owed to _____ , which you incurred on _____ , 199 _____ . The amount remaining unpaid on the debt is $ _____ . Demand is hereby made that this money be paid. Unless payment of this amount is received by the undersigned no later than _____ , 199 _____ , a lawsuit will be brought against you in the Commercial Claims Part of the Court.

    If a lawsuit is brought, you will be notified of the hearing date, and you will be entitled to appear at the hearing and present any defense you may have to this claim.

    (If applicable) Our records show that you have made the following payment in partial satisfaction of this debt (fill in dates and amounts paid) _____ .

    A copy of the original debt instrument - your agreement to pay - is attached. [The names and addresses of the parties to that original debt agreement are _____

_____

_____

(to be completed if claimant was not a party to the original transaction)].

_____

_____

_____

       Typed or Printed Name and Address
            of Claimant

16-193..1/91cb

FORM 2

(FOR OFFICE USE ONLY)

INSTRUCTIONS:
Place only ONE letter or number in each space and leave a blank space between words.

CIVIL COURT OF THE CITY OF NEW YORK
COMMERCIAL CLAIMS PART
STATEMENT OF CLAIM

Example: Business Name: Ted Rothstein DDS PC
Other Info (In Care Of): Ted Rothstein

(Your)   I. CLAIMANT'S INFORMATION

BUSINESS NAME

OTHER INFO
(Doing Business As or In Care Of)

PRINCIPAL OFFICE ADDRESS

BOROUGH, CITY, TOWN OR VILL.   STATE   ZIP

PHONE NO. (   )

CERT'D #

(Their)   II. DEFENDANT'S INFORMATION

COA CODE

LAST NAME
(or business name)

FIRST NAME   MIDDLE INITIAL

CLAIM AMT.
$

ADDRESS
(of Residence or Place of Business or Employment)

BOROUGH, CITY, TOWN OR VILL.   STATE [N|Y]   ZIP

OTHER INFO
(Doing Business As or In Care Of)

PHONE NO. (   )

FEE

STANDARD FEE PLUS POSTAGE
☐ CLAIMANT V. DEFENDANT

NO FEE; POSTAGE ONLY
☐ DEFENDANT V. THIRD PARTY
☐ CLAIMANT V. ADD'L DEFENDANT
☐ WAGE CLAIM TO $300

III. CLAIM

Amount Claimed: $_____ (Maximum $3,000)   Date of Occurrence or Transaction: _____

Briefly state your claim here: (Include Indentifying Number(s) — Receipt #, Claim #, Account #, Policy #, Ticket #, License #)

LANGUAGE

DATE DATA ENTERED

DATE NOTICES MAILED

CASE TYPE:

MULTI DFT ☐   CTR/CLM ☐

3 PARTY ☐   CRS/CMPLT ☐

FIRST DATE

_____   _____
Today's Date   Signature of Claimant or Agent

YOU MUST COMPLETE ONE OF THE CERTIFICATIONS ON THE REVERSE SIDE

DAY COURT
☐ STATUTORY   ☐ OTHER

(FOR OFFICE USE ONLY)

CIV-SC-70 (Revised 1/95)

☐ CONSUMER TRANSACTION
☐ OTHER COMMERCIAL CLAIMS

FORM 3 SIDE 1

COMPLETE THIS SECTION FOR A COMMERCIAL CLAIM

*CERTIFICATION: (NYCCCA 1803-A)

I hereby certify that no more than five (5) actions or proceedings (including the instant action or proceeding) pursuant to the commercial claims procedure have been initiated in the courts of this State during the present calendar month.

_____

Signature of Claimant

_____

~~Signature of Notary~~/Clerk/~~Judge~~

*NOTE: The Commercial Claims Part will dismiss any case where this certification is not made.

COMPLETE THIS SECTION FOR A COMMERCIAL CLAIM
ARISING OUT OF A CONSUMER TRANSACTION

†CERTIFICATION: (NYCCCA 1803-A)

I hereby certify that I have mailed a demand letter by ordinary first class mail to the party complained against, no less than ten (10) days and no more than one hundred eighty (180) days before I commenced this claim.

I hereby certify, based upon information and belief, that no more than five (5) actions or proceedings (including the instant action or proceeding) pursuant to the commercial claims procedure have been initiated in the courts of this State during the present calendar month.

_____

Signature of Claimant

_____

~~Signature of Notary~~/Clerk/~~Judge~~

†NOTE: The Commercial Claims Part will not allow your action to
proceed if this certification is not made and properly completed.

FORM 3 SIDE 2

CIVIL COURT OF THE CITY OF NEW YORK
SMALL CLAIMS PART
STATEMENT OF CLAIM

INSTRUCTIONS: Place only ONE letter or number in each space and leave a blank space between words.

(FOR OFFICE USE ONLY)

SC#

CERT'D #

TODAY'S DATE

COA CODE

CLAIM AMT.
$

(Your) **I CLAIMANT'S INFORMATION**
LAST NAME: ROTHSTEIN
FIRST NAME: TED MIDDLE INITIAL:
ADDRESS: 35 REMSEN ST
BOROUGH, CITY, TOWN OR VILL.: BROOKLYN STATE: NY ZIP: 11201
OTHER INFO (Doing Business As or In Care Of):
PHONE NO. (718) 852 1551

(Their) **II DEFENDANT'S INFORMATION**
LAST NAME: LAPOM
FIRST NAME: PAUL MIDDLE INITIAL:
ADDRESS: 108 E 88 ST #12
BOROUGH, CITY, TOWN OR VILL.: NEW YORK STATE: NY ZIP: 10011
OTHER INFO (Doing Business As or In Care Of):
PHONE NO. (212) 777-0180

FEE
STANDARD FEE PLUS POSTAGE
☐ CLAIMANT V. DEFENDANT
NO FEE; POSTAGE ONLY
☐ DEFENDANT V. THIRD PARTY
☐ CLAIMANT V. ADD'L DEFENDANT
☐ WAGE CLAIM TO $300
RECEIPT #

LANGUAGE

III CLAIM
Amount Claimed: $ 941.40 (Maximum $3,000) Date of Occurrence or Transaction: 6/5/95

Briefly state your claim here: (Include Indentifying Number(s) — Receipt #, Claim #, Account #, Policy #, Ticket #, License #)

Unpaid balance for completed professional services

DATE DATA ENTERED

DATE NOTICES MAILED

CASE TYPE:
MULTI DFT ☐   CTR/CLM ☐
3 PARTY ☐   CRS/CMPLT ☐

If Automobile Accident (Note: Claim must be Owner against Owner.)
License Plate Number of Defendant's Car: _____ State: _____
Place of Occurrence of Accident: _____

FIRST DATE

TRIAL DATE

6/7/95
Today's Date

Ted Rothstein
Signature of Claimant or Agent

DAY COURT
☐ STATUTORY
☐ OTHER

(FOR OFFICE USE ONLY)

CIV-SC-50 (Revised 7/94)

FORM 4

Civil Court Of The City Of New York

Small Claims/Commercial Claims Part
County of Kings
141 Livingston Street
Brooklyn, New York .   .

Index Number: SCK

10918 KSC 94

INSTRUCTIONS TO CLAIMANT

The Hearing of your claim against _____ Almodo _____

has been set for _____ DEC 1 5 1994 _____ at 6:30 P.M. in the Courtroom, Ground Floor, Room 101.

Only the Judge presiding at the Hearing can grant an adjournment.
The Clerk cannot grant any change in the scheduled date or time.

HEARING

You must be present, with any witness(es) and/or other proof of your claim, at the time and place indicated above.

If your claim .s for property damage, in order to prove your claim you must produce, at the time of trial, either:

(1) An Expert Witness (for example, a Mechanic)
(2) A Paid Receipt (itemized, marked "Paid," and signed), or
(3) Two Estimates for services or repairs (itemized and signed)

Once service of the Notice of Claim is complete, you may request the Clerk to issue a Subpoena for Records and/or a Subpoena to Testify, to compel someone to appear. Such Subpoenas are issued by the Court without any fee, but you will be required to pay a fee to the person on whom the Subpoena is served. Your request for such Subpoena must be made of the Clerk before the date of the Hearing.

If you have not received a copy of the booklet "A Guide to Small Claims" or "A Guide to Commercial Claims", please request one.

JUDGES AND ARBITRATORS

The Judge can only hear a limited number of cases at each session of Court. Most Hearings are held before volunteer Arbitrators who are attorneys with at least five years of experience and thoroughly knowledgable in the law.

The decision of a Judge is subject to appeal but no appeal of an Arbitrator's decision is permitted since there is no official court transcipt of Hearings held before Arbitrators.

Either party may choose to have the case heard **only** by the Judge, by responding "by the Court," at the time of the calendar call. If you request your case "by the Court" it is quite possible that you will have to return for trial at another time.

INSTRUCTIONS FOR ANSWERING THE CALENDAR CALL

If you are ready for trial and you are willing to have your case heard by an Arbitrator . . . . **Answer: (Your Name/Claimant), Ready**

If you wish: to request a postponement of your case,
to change the amount of the claim, or
to add an additional party . . . . **Answer: Your Name, Application**

If you are ready for trial but you are not willing to have your case heard by
an Arbitrator and you are requesting that the case be heard **only** by the Judge . . . . **Answer: Your Name, Ready By the Court**

RESULT OF NON-APPEARANCE (DEFAULT)

If the Defendant (the person you are suing) fails to answer or appear for trial an Inquest may be held. In an Inquest, you (the Claimant) must prove your case to the satisfaction of the Arbitrator even though the Defendant is not present. In almost all instances the Inquest will result in a **Judgment** in favor of the Claimant.

If you (the Claimant who is suing) fail to appear, the case will generally be **Dismissed**.

SETTLEMENT

If you and the Defendant are able to work out a settlement, the written agreement (Stipulation of Settlement) should be filed with the Court. This should be done on or before the date set for the Hearing. The document provided to the Court must include the SC Number of your case and the year.

If the Defendant admits the claim but desires more time to pay, and you are not willing to accept the plan for payment, you must both appear personally on the date set for the Hearing. At that time, with the aid of the Court, you may be able to reach agreement on the terms of payment.

AVISO: ESTA INFORMACIÓN ESTÁ DISPONIBLE EN ESPAÑOL BAJO PEDIDO.

— BRING THIS SHEET WITH YOU AT ALL TIMES —

CIV-SC-67   (Revised 12/90) (Incorporates former SC-1)

FORM 5

CIVIL COURT OF THE CITY OF NEW YORK
Small Claims Part
141 Livingston Street
Brooklyn, New York 11201

CERTIFIED

MAIL

NOTICE OF CLAIM and
SUMMONS TO APPEAR

NOTICE TO DEFENDANT
This Notice of Claim and Summons to Appear is the start of a lawsuit against you. It should not be ignored. Your default may have serious consequences.
YOU MUST BRING THIS NOTICE WITH YOU EACH TIME YOU APPEAR IN COURT ON THIS CASE.

NOTICE OF CLAIM

The Claimant asks Judgment in this court for **$ 565 . 00**
together with interest and disbursements, on the following claim:

ACTION TO RECOVER PAYMENT DUE ARISING OUT OF
PROFESSIONAL SERVICES RENDERED
DATE OF OCCURRENCE: 07-12-95

SUMMONS TO APPEAR

This claim is scheduled for a Hearing to be held in the Courtroom:
141 Livingston Street (Room 101)
Brooklyn, New York 11201
On Thursday, October 12, 1995 at 6:30 PM
You, or someone authorized to represent you, must appear and present
your defense at the Hearing. If you wish, you may retain the services of
an attorney to represent you at your own expense.

**IF YOU FAIL TO APPEAR, JUDGMENT WILL BE ENTERED AGAINST YOU
BY DEFAULT, EVEN THOUGH YOU MAY HAVE A VALID DEFENSE.**
Only the Judge presiding at the Hearing can grant an adjournment.
The Clerk cannot grant any change in the scheduled date or time.

Dated   **August 18, 1995**   Chief Clerk   **Jack Baer**

CIV-SC-55 Face (12/90)

INDEX NUMBER: **SCK 6254 / 95**
PARTIES TO THIS ACTION
CLAIMANT

(Dr.) Ivan Demonet
11 Rodeo Drive
Brooklyn, NY, 11201

— against —

DEFENDANT

Dinah Paedebil
12 Meechum Street
Brooklyn, NY 11215

ESTA INFORMACIÓN ESTÁ DISPONIBLE EN ESPAÑOL EN LA CORTE

CIVIL COURT OF THE CITY OF NEW YORK

CERTIFIED

MAIL

RETURN RECEIPT REQUESTED

TO

Dinah Paedebil
12 Meechum Street
Brooklyn, NY 11215

FORM 6 SIDE 1

INFORMATION FOR THE DEFENDANT

DEMAND LETTER

If you are being sued as a result of a "Consumer Transaction," you should have received a letter from the Claimant demanding payment before you received this Notice of Claim. If you did not get such a letter, notify the Court at the time of your appearance.

SETTLEMENT

If you admit the claim:

a) and you are able to work out a settlement with the Claimant, a written agreement (Stipulation of Settlement) should be filed with the Court. This may be done on or before the date set for the Hearing. The document provided to the Court must include the SC number of your case, and the year.

b) but desire more time to pay and the Claimant is not willing to accept your plan for payment, you must appear personally on the date set for the Hearing, tell the Court that you desire time to pay, and provide your reason(s) for desiring time to pay. At that time, with the aid of the Court, you may be able to reach agreement with the Claimant and enter into a written Stipulation of Settlement.

If neither side appears in court on the date scheduled for the Hearing, the case will be marked "DISMISSED, No Appearance Either Side."

BEFORE THE HEARING

If this case involves damage to an automobile or other property covered by insurance, you might want to notify your insurance company of this Hearing. The insurance companies will often assign an attorney representative to be present at the Hearing at no cost to you if they are made aware of the case by the policy-holder.

COUNTERCLAIM AND THIRD-PARTY CLAIMS

If you have a claim against the Claimant, you may bring a "counterclaim" as part of this lawsuit, for money only, up to $3,000. You must inform the Court of your counterclaim, by either a) notifying the Claimant in writing of the amount of your claim, providing an explanation of the nature of the claim, and also delivering a copy of the writing to the Clerk before the scheduled date of the Hearing or, b) at the time of the Hearing, by asking the Judge to allow such a counterclaim. In either event you must be prepared to prove your counterclaim on the day you come to Court for the Hearing.

If you believe that a third party bears full or partial responsibility for the claim, you may be able to bring that party into the lawsuit as a "Third Party Defendant." Contact the Clerk promptly for information about filing a "third-party action."

JURY TRIAL

If you desire a jury, you must, at least one day before the day upon which you have been notified to appear, file with the Clerk of the court a written demand for a trial by jury. At that time, you will have to make an affidavit specifying the **issues of fact** which you desire to have tried by a jury and stating that such trial is desired and demanded **in good faith**. You will have to pay a jury fee and also file an undertaking (a deposit in cash) to secure the payment of any costs that may be awarded against you. Under the law the court may award additional costs to the Claimant if you demand a jury trial and a verdict is rendered against you.

CIV-SC-55 Reverse (Revised 1/93)

Side 2

FORM 6 SIDE 2

CIVIL COURT OF THE CITY OF NEW YORK
SMALL CLAIMS PART
NOTICE TO SMALL CLAIMS DEFENDANT

The enclosed Notice of Claim is the start of a lawsuit against you. It should not be ignored. Your default may have serious consequences to you.

If a judgment is recovered against you, the law gives the claimant certain rights to collect the judgment. If you do not pay the judgment within 10 days, the Sheriff may execute against your property. This means that he can seize certain of your property and sell it to satisfy the judgment. If you work and earn more than $85.00 per week, the Sheriff can take 10% of your salary and turn it over to the claimant until the judgment is paid.

The claimant can also compel you to come into court and be examined under oath as to your property, bank account and other assets. He may obtain a restraining order tying up your bank account.

Should you be licensed by any City or State agency, complaint may be lodged against you for such non-payment of the judgment and your license may be revoked or suspended.

Israel Rubin
Administrative Judge
Civil Court
City of New York

INFORMATION FOR THE JUDGMENT CREDITOR
(the party in whose favor a money judgment has been entered)

3. In addition to these rights a judgment creditor may also be entitled to utilize the following:
   a) the issuance by the Small Claims Clerk, upon request and at nominal cost, of information subpoenas where a judgment remains unsatisfied for 30 days;
   b) an action against the judgment debtor where that debtor is a business, for three times the amount of an unsatisfied judgment and attorney's fees where there are two other unsatisfied small claims judgments against that judgment debtor;
   c) an action to recover an unpaid judgment through the sale of the judgment debtor's real or personal property;
   d) an action to recover an unpaid judgment through suspension of the judgment debtor's motor vehicle license and registration if the underlying claim is based on the debtor's ownership or operation of a motor vehicle;
   e) notification of the appropriate state or local licensing authority of an unsatisfied judgment as a basis for possible revocation, suspension, or denial of renewal of a business license; and
   f) notification of the State Attorney General if the judgment debtor is a business and appears to be engaged in fraudulent or illegal business practices.

* To locate a City Marshal or a Sheriff, see reverse side.

THE JUDGMENT IS VALID FOR A PERIOD OF 20 YEARS. IF THE JUDGMENT IS NOT COLLECTED UPON THE FIRST ATTEMPT, FURTHER ATTEMPTS TO COLLECT MAY BE MADE AT A LATER DATE.

FORM # 92 (REV. 9/87)

INFORMATION FOR THE JUDGMENT DEBTOR
(the party against whom a money judgment has been entered)

Your failure to pay the judgment may subject you to any one or a combination of the following:

   a) garnishment of wage;
   b) garnishment of bank account(s);
   c) a lien on real and/or personal property;
   d) seizure and sale of real property;
   e) seizure and sale of personal property, including automobiles;
   f) suspension of motor vehicle license and registration, if claim is based on judgment debtor's ownership or operation of a motor vehicle;
   g) revocation, suspension, or denial of renewal of any applicable business license or permit;
   h) investigation and prosecution by the State Attorney General for fraudulent or illegal business practices; and
   i) a penalty equal to three times the amount of the unsatisfied judgment plus attorney's fees, if there are other unpaid claims.

FORM 7

CIVIL COURT OF THE CITY OF NEW YORK

INSTRUCTIONS FOR
SERVICE OF SUBPOENA

Subpoenae available

There are three kinds of Subpoena,

      I. Subpoena To Testify. (Ad Testificandum)
      Requires **a person** to come the Court to testify as a witness.

      II. Subpoena For Records. (Duces Tecum)
      Requires **documents, papers, writings, etc.** to be brought to the Court.

      III. Information Subpoena.
      Requires that **information** to be given to the Court.

Who May Serve a Subpoena

Anyone NOT A PARTY to the action, who is over the age of 18 and not a Police Officer, may serve the subpoena.

Methods of Service

A Subpoena to Testify or a Subpoena for Records is generally served on an individual* by personal (in hand) delivery. [*For service on a corporation or on a partnership, see the clerk.]

For service on an individual, under the circumstances it may be appropriate to use an alternate method of service such as "Substituted Service" or "Conspicuous Service."

"Substituted Service" is the personal service of the subpoena on someone other than the person who is being subpoenaed (the witness) at the actual place of business or place of residence of the witness. The server must then mail a copy of the subpoena to the witness by first class mail to the actual place of business or place of residence of the witness.

"Conspicious Service" is the service of the subpoena by leaving it at the residence or place of business of the witness. Prior to leaving the subpoena, the server must make at least two attempts. If no one is found on either attempt, on the third try the subpoena may be affixed to the door with adhesive tape, and a copy must them be mailed to the residence of the witness by first class mail.

An Information Subpoena may be served by Registered or by Certified Mail, Return Receipt Requested.

CIV-GP-63 FACE 5/90

Proof of Service

The person who serves the Subpoena to Testify or the Subpoena for Records must fill out the Affidavit of Service and have it notarized.

Procedure

The person who is going to serve the subpoena must:
1) Find the person to be served.
2) Show that person the original subpoena.
3) Give that person a copy of the subpoena.
4) Fill out the Affidavit of Service on back of the original.
5) Retain the Affidavit of Service for further procedures if the person fails to comply with the subpoena.

For an information Subpoena follow the above procedure or
1) Place a copy of the subpoena, together with the questions to be answered and $.50 in an envelope addressed to the witness.
2) Mail the envelope to the witness by Certified or Registered mail, Return Receipt Requested.

NOTE: It is suggested that you include a self-addressed, stamped envelope for the convenience of the witness. Although this is not required by law, it makes the process less burdensome on the party from whom you are requesting the information.

Fee for Service

When served with a Subpoena to Testify or a Subpoena for Records, the witness must be paid a witness fee, effective 1/1/89, of $15.00 per day. The fee must be paid a reasonable amount of time before the scheduled date. Nonpayment of the witness fee voids the duty to appear.

A person served with an Information Subpoena must be paid a fee of fifty cents ($0.50). However, no fee need be paid to a judgment debtor for responding to an Information Subpoena.

Location

A subpoena from the Civil Court of the City of New York may be served only within the City of New York or in Nassau County or Westchester County. Service anywhere else may only be done if permitted by a Judge.

Restrictions

General

A subpoena may not be served on a Sunday.
A City or State agency or a public library may be subpoenaed only by order of the court.

Time

Any witness must be served a "reasonable" amount of time prior to the date of appearance. It is suggested that service be at least 5 days before the date of the hearing.

A City or State agency or a public library must be served at least 24 hours prior to the time of appearance.

In the process of the enforcement of a money judgment, a subpoena for the purpose of taking a deposition on oral or written questions, or for an examination of books or papers requires 10 days notice.

CIV-GP-63 REVERSE (REVISED 5/90)

FORM 8 SIDE 2

Civil Court of the City of New York

COUNTY OF __KINGS__

Part

Index No. ___2403/96___

Ted Rothstein

Claimant(s)/Plaintiff(s)/Petitioner(s),

against

Bell Ramo

Defendant(s)/Respondent(s),

SUBPOENA TO TESTIFY

(SUBPOENA AD TESTIFICANDUM)

THE PEOPLE OF THE STATE OF NEW YORK

To: __Christine Collazo__ :

We Command that you lay aside all business and excuses and appear and attend

before Hon. ___LAURA _____ JUDGE, CIVIL COURT___, in Part __S.C.__, Room __101__.

at __6:30__ AM/PM, on the __16TH__ day of __May__, 19__96__,

at __141 Livingston St., Brooklyn, N.Y. 11201__,
(Address of Court)

to testify and give evidence in the action now pending in this Court, to be tried between the parties indicated above, on the

part of __Claimant__.

If you fail to attend you may be deemed guilty of Contempt of Court, and be liable to pay to the party aggrieved ALL LOSS AND DAMAGES SUSTAINED and, in addition, FORFEIT FIFTY DOLLARS.

Jack Baer
Chief Clerk, Civil Court

If required, So Ordered:

_____
Judge, Civil/Housing Court

CIV-GP-71 (3/91) (Replaces 43-2047)

FORM 9 SIDE 1

125

Civil Court of the City of New York

COUNTY OF ___Kings___

___Small Claims___ Part

Ted Rothstein

*Claimant(s)/Plaintiff(s)/Petitioner(s),
against*

Bell Ramo

Defendant(s)/Respondent(s),

Index No. ___2403/96___

**AFFIDAVIT OF SERVICE
OF
SUBPOENA TO TESTIFY**

State of New York, County of ___Kings___ ss.:

___Sid Leone___
(Name of Deponent), being duly sworn, deposes and says:

I am over 18 years of age and not a party to this action. At ___3:00___ AM/**PM**, on ___April 18, 1996___
(Time) *(Date)*

at ___35 Remsen Street, B'Klyn 11201___
(Address)

in the County of ___Kings___, City of New York, I served the within Subpoena to Testify *(Subpoena Ad*

Testificandum) in this matter on: ___Christine Collazo___
(Name of Person Served)

known to me to be the Witness named herein by delivering and leaving with him/her personally a true copy thereof, and at the same time and place showing the original to him/her, and paying to him/her the sum of $ ___15.00___, as fees for travelling to and from the place where s/he was required by the said Subpoena to attend, and for one day's attendance.

Description of Individual Served in Person:

Sex: __F__	Color of Skin: __W__	Color of Hair: __Brown__
Approximate Age: __21__	Approximate Weight: __135__	Approximate Height: __5'9"__

Sworn to before me this __19__ day of ___April___, 19 __96__.

___Notary's Signature___
(Signature of Notary Public)

___Sid Leone___
(Signature of Deponent)

GENERAL INSTRUCTIONS

Anyone NOT A PARTY to the action, who is over the age of 18 and not a Police Officer, may serve the Subpoena.

1. Find the person to be served.
2. Show that person the **original** Subpoena.
3. Give that person a copy of the Subpoena.
4. Fill out the above Affidavit of Service and have it notarized.
5. Retain this Affidavit of Service for further procedures if the person fails to comply with the Subpoena.

CIV-GP-71 (Reverse 3/91)

FORM 9 SIDE 2

Civil Court of the City of New York

COUNTY OF _KINGS_

S_____ Part

Index No. _SCK 0001/95_

TED ROTHSTEIN

DBA DR. TED ROTHSTEIN
Claimant(s)/Plaintiff(s)/Petitioner(s),

ORAH CART

Defendant(s)/Respondent(s),

SUBPOENA FOR RECORDS

(SUBPOENA DUCES TECUM)

THE PEOPLE OF THE STATE OF NEW YORK

To: _DR ELI_ :

We Command that you or someone on your behalf provide and produce the following item(s):

Copy of all _____ contracts bearing Dr. Rothstein's signature From inception to present.

Reproduction of original copy of correspondence (on union stationery) or other between ___ Cart and ___ or Dr. Eli___ acting as agent for the ___ Welfare fund concerning Dr. Rothstein and litigation SCK 00001/95

at _6:30PM_ AM/PM, on the _27_ day of _April_, 19_95_,

at _141 Livingston St._
Brooklyn, N.Y. 11201   (Address of Court)

☑ to the Records Section of this Court, located in Room _201_,

☐ to the attention of Hon. Naimuh Puhrsin _____ in Part_____, Room_____.

If you fail to provide and produce such information you may be deemed guilty of **Contempt of Court,** and be liable to pay to the party aggrieved ALL LOSS AND DAMAGES SUSTAINED and, in addition, FORFEIT FIFTY DOLLARS.

Jack Baer

Chief Clerk, Civil Court

If required by law for governmental agencies, So Ordered:

_____

Judge, Civil/Housing Court

CIV-GP-70 (3/91) (Replaces 43-2046)

FORM 10 SIDE 1

127

Civil Court of the City of New York

COUNTY OF _____

_____ Part

TED ROTHSTEIN

DBA DR. TED ROTHSTEIN
Claimant(s)/Plaintiff(s)/Petitioner(s),
against

ORAH CART
Defendant(s)/Respondent(s),

Index No. __SCK 0001 / 95__

**AFFIDAVIT OF SERVICE
OF
SUBPOENA FOR RECORDS**

State of New York, County of __KINGS__ ss.:

__JON ROTHSTEIN__
(Name of Deponent), being duly sworn, deposes and says:

I am over 18 years of age and not a party to this action. At __10:05__ AM/PM, on __3/9/95__
(Time) (Date)

at __71 Notaname Road__
(Address)

in the County of _____, City of New York, I served the within Subpoena for Records (Subpoena

Duces Tecum) in this matter on: __DR. ELI__
(Name of Person Served),

known to me to be the Witness named herein by delivering and leaving with him/her personally a true copy thereof, and at the same time and place showing the original to him/her, and paying him/her the sum of $ __15.00__, as fees for travelling to and from the place where s/he was required by the said Subpoena to attend, and for one day's attendance.

Description of Individual Served in Person:		
Sex: __M__	Color of Skin: __WHITE__	Color of Hair: __White__
Approximate Age: __58__	Approximate Weight: __160__	Approximate Height: __5'10__

Sworn to before me this __9th__ day of __MARCH__, 19 __95__.

_____
(Signature of Notary Public)

ALTUHRD NAHME
Notary Public, State of New York
No. 10-10101010
Qualified in Kings County
Commission Expires Jan. 31, 1996

__Jon Rothstein__
(Signature of Deponent)

GENERAL INSTRUCTIONS

Anyone NOT A PARTY to the action, who is over the age of 18 and not a Police Officer, may serve the Subpoena.

1. Find the person to be served.
2. Show that person the **original** Subpoena.
3. Give that person **a copy** of the Subpoena.
4. Fill out the above Affidavit of Service and have it notarized.
5. Retain this Affidavit of Service for further procedures if the person fails to comply with the Subpoena.

CIV-GP-70 (Reverse 3/91)

Part of the Preparation for Your Court Hearing:
Your Story on a 5x7 Index Card
Ready to be Read at the Start of Your Hearing in
Small Claims Court

Judge Smith:

My name is Ted Rothstein. I'm an orthodontist practicing here in Brooklyn Heights. Eighteen months ago I contracted with Mr. Jones to treat his daughter's dental (bite, orthodontic) problem. <u>Here is the contract he signed</u> showing his agreement to pay me $2.500. My work was completed (or "substantially performed," i.e. between 95% and 99% completed)*. He has paid me $1,900 leaving a balance due of $600. <u>Here is the payment card</u> showing all the payments he made. I have written two letters to him and called him once requesting that he pay me. He has not paid the balance. I was available and willing to take care of any complaints or problems that Mr. Jones had about my work. I want to recover the amount he owes for the professional services I provided his daughter.

Legal note:
Substantial performance refers to a legal doctrine which recognizes that a service or work performed which does not <u>exactly</u> meet the terms of the agreement (there is some slight deviation) will nevertheless be looked upon as fulfillment of service or work (less the damages, if any, which result from the deviation from the agreed upon service).

This doctrine is intended to prevent one person from being unjustly enriched by the services of another just because there was a minor deviation in the service performed.

FORM 11

B 493—Stipulation discontinuing action, blank court. 12-88

JULIUS BLUMBERG, INC.,
PUBLISHER, NYC 10013

CIVIL **COURT** OF THE CITY OF NEW YORK

COUNTY OF NEW YORK: SMALL CLAIMS PART

Index No. SCK 1010/95

TED ROTHSTEIN,

Plaintiff(s)

against

ORAH CART

Defendant(s)

Calendar No.

STIPULATION
DISCONTINUING ACTION

IT IS HEREBY STIPULATED AND AGREED, by and between the undersigned, the attorneys of record for all the parties to the above entitled action, that whereas no party hereto is an infant, incompetent person for whom a committee has been appointed or conservatee and no person not a party has an interest in the subject matter of the action, the above entitled action be and the same hereby is discontinued, without costs to either party as against the other. This stipulation may be filed without further notice with the clerk of the Court. FOR PURPOSES OF THIS SETTLEMENT EACH PARTY RETRACTS THE STATEMENTS WHICH THE OTHER PARTY ASSERTS ARE DISPARAGING.

Dated: APRIL 26, 1995

Don Cach
The name signed must be printed beneath
DON CACH
ANY AND EVERY LAWFIRM, PC

Attorney(s) for Defendant(s)

Ted Rothstein
The name signed must be printed beneath
TED ROTHSTEIN

Attorney(s) for ~~Plaintiff(s)~~ Plaintiff(s)

ORAH CART
Defendant
241 MISTREET ROAD
Address
EVERY CITY, NY 21010

TED ROTHSTEIN
Plaintiff
35 REMSEN STREET
Address
BROOKLYN, NEW YORK 11201

FORM 12 SIDE 1

131

Index No. SCK 1035/95

CIVIL   COURT OF THE CITY OF NEW YORK
COUNTY OF NEW YORK: SMALL CLAIMS PART

TED ROTHSTEIN,

                                        Plaintiff(s)

                    against
     ORAH CART

                                        Defendant(s)

𝔖𝔱𝔦𝔭𝔲𝔩𝔞𝔱𝔦𝔬𝔫

Discontinuing Action

     ANY AND EVERY LAWFIRM, PC

Attorney(s) for DEFENDANT

     Office and Post Office Address
     ANY AND ALL LAWFIRM P.C.
     666 DEVILS WAY
     ALL CITY, NEW YORK 10001
     (212) 666 - 7711

FORM 12 SIDE 2

B 110—General Release—Individual: 6-76   JULIUS BLUMBERG, INC., LAW BLANK PUBLISHERS

To all to whom these Presents shall come or may Concern,

Know That   TED ROTHSTEIN

as RELEASOR,

in consideration of the sum of   FOUR HUNDRED FIFTY DOLLARS

($ 450.00   ),

received . ON BEHALF OF   .ORAH CART . IN THE KINGS COUNTY SMALL CLAIMS COURT MATTER, TED ROTHSTEIN, D.D.S. V. CART, INDEX NO. 1010/95

as RELEASEE,

receipt whereof is hereby acknowledged, releases and discharges   ORAH CART   AND THE UNITED FEDERATION OF TEACHERS WELFARE FUND

the RELEASEE, RELEASEE'S heirs, executors, administrators, successors and assigns from all actions, causes of action, suits, debts, dues, sums of money, accounts, reckonings, bonds, bills, specialties, covenants, contracts, controversies, agreements, promises, variances, trespasses, damages, judgments, extents, executions, claims, and demands whatsoever, in law, admiralty or equity, which against the RELEASEE, the RELEASOR, RELEASOR'S heirs, executors, administrators, successors and assigns ever had, now have or hereafter can, shall or may, have for, upon, or by reason of any matter, cause or thing whatsoever from the beginning of the world to the day of the date of this RELEASE.

Whenever the text hereof requires, the use of singular number shall include the appropriate plural number as the text of the within instrument may require.

This RELEASE may not be changed orally.

In Witness Whereof, the RELEASOR has hereunto set RELEASOR'S hand and seal on the day of   19 95

In presence of

Ted Rothtein   ...L.S.
TED ROTHSTEIN

STATE OF   NEW YORK   *COUNTY OF*   *ss.:*
   On   19 95 before me
personally came   TED ROTHSTEIN

to me known, and known to me to be the individual(s) described in, and who executed the foregoing RELEASE, and duly acknowledged to me that   he   executed the same.

If the party making payment is not the same as the party released, delete words "as RELEASEE" and add names of parties released after the word "discharges."

FORM 13 SIDE 1

STATE OF

COUNTY OF   } ss.:

        On   19   before me

personally came

to me known, and known to me to be the individual(s) described in and who executed the foregoing RELEASE, and duly acknowledged to me that   he   executed the same.

....

CIVIL COURT OF THE CITY OF NEW YORK
COUNTY OF NEW YORK: SMALL CLAIMS PART

TED ROTHSTEIN,   *RELEASOR*

DRAH CART   *RELEASEE*

𝔊𝔢𝔫𝔢𝔯𝔞𝔩 𝔕𝔢𝔩𝔢𝔞𝔰𝔢

Dated   APRIL 26   1995

LAW OFFICES OF

ANY AND ALL LAWFIRM P.C.
666 DEVILS WAY
ALL CITY, NEW YORK 10001
(212) 666 - 7711

FORM 13 SIDE 2

Civil Court of the City of New York

Index No. S.C. _5 3 ~ : / ~_

COUNTY OF _ ~ ~ ~ ~ J_

Small Claims/Commercial Claims Part

TED RUTNYTGN

Claimant(s),

against

PAUL LAPEN

Defendant(s),

NOTICE OF JUDGMENT

DECISION: After Trial/Inquest, the decision in the above action is as follows:

A. ☐ Judgment and Award in favor of _____

Ted Rutherti _____

_____

Award amount ....$ _941 4 ~_

Interest ....$ _____

Disbursements...............$ _5.84_

TOTAL JUDGMENT ....$ _947.24_

(Information below and on the reverse side applies to all parties when an award has been granted.)

B. ☐ Judgment in favor of Defendant, dismissing claim. No monetary award.

_____

_____

_____

(Information below and on the other side is not applicable.)

Date: _7/2/85_   By: _____

J.H.C./Arbitrator

INFORMATION FOR THE JUDGMENT DEBTOR

(the party against whom a money judgement has been entered)

YOU HAVE A LEGAL OBLIGATION TO PAY THIS JUDGMENT.

YOU MUST PRESENT PROOF TO THE COURT UPON SATISFACTION OF THE JUDGMENT.

Your failure to pay the judgment may subject you to any one or any combination of the following:

a) garnishment of wage(s) and/or bank account(s);

b) lien, seizure and/or sale of real property and/or personal property, including automobile(s);

c) suspension of motor vehicle registration, and/or drivers license, if the underlying claim is based on judgment debtor's ownership or operation of a motor vehicle;

d) revocation, suspension, or denial of renewal of any applicable business license or permit;

e) investigation and prosecution by the State Attorney General for fradulent or illegal business practices;

f) a penalty equal to three times the amount of the unsatisfied judgment plus attorney's fees if there are unpaid claims.

If you did not appear in court on the day the Hearing was held, you are a defaulting party. A judgment may have been taken against you even though you were not in court. If that is so, you may apply to the court in writing and ask to have the default judgment opened. You must give the judge a reasonable excuse for your failure to appear in court and show that you have a meritorious defense. The Judge may open your default judgment and give you another chance to go to court.

("Information for the Judgment Creditor" is on the reverse side.)

THE JUDGMENT IS VALID FOR A PERIOD OF 20 YEARS. IF THE JUDGMENT IS NOT COLLECTED UPON THE FIRST ATTEMPT, FURTHER ATTEMPTS TO COLLECT MAY BE MADE AT A LATER DATE.

C1V-SC-92 (Revised 5/92)

FORM 14 SIDE 1

INFORMATION FOR THE JUDGMENT CREDITOR
(the party in whose favor a money judgment award has been entered)

1. Contact the judgment debtor (the party who owes you the money) either directly or through that party's attorney if the party was represented by an attorney, and request payment. You have the right to payment within 30 days. Upon satisfying the judgment, in accordance CCA §1811(c). the judgment debtor shall present appropriate proof to the court.

2. a) If the judgment debtor fails to pay **within 30 days,** contact (by phone or in person either a New York City Marshal or the Sheriff in the County where the judgment debtor *has property* . If you do not know where the judgment debtor has property, then contact a New York City Marshal or the Sheriff in the county where the judgment debtor *resides.*

   b) Be prepared to provide the City Marshal or the Sheriff with the following information:
   1) The SC# of your case, including the year, which appears at the top of the reverse side.
   2) The county in which the case was tried.
   3) Your name, address and telephone number.
   4) The name and address of the judgment debtor.
   5) The name and address of the judgment debtor's employer and the location of the judgment debtor's real property and/or personal property, including automobile(s). *Information regarding employment or assets of the judgment debtor can be obtained through the use of an information Subpoena. See 3b)*
   c) Fees paid by you, the judgment creditor, to the City Marshal or to the Sheriff in an attempt to collect the judgment will be added to the total judgment.

3. A judgment creditor is also entitled:
   a) to the issuance by the Clerk of a Restraining Notice. Proper service of the Restraining Notice will prohibit the receiving party from and assets or interest belonging to the judgment debtor until the Sheriff or Marshal executes (collects) on the judgment.
   b) to the issuance by the Clerk, upon request and at a nominal cost, of Information Subpoenas where a judgment remains unsatisfied.
   c) to place a lien against the judgment debtor's real property.

4. In addition to any other rights, a judgment creditor may also be entitled:
   a) to recover an unpaid judgment through garnishment of wage(s) and/or bank account(s) and/or the sale of judgment debtor's real property and/or personal property;
   b) to notify the Department of Motor Vehicles of the unsatisfied judgment as a basic for the suspension of the judgment debtor's motor vehicle registration and/or driver's license if the underlying claim is based on the debtor's ownership or operation of a motor vehicle;
   c) to notify the appropriate state or local licensing authority of an unsatisfied judgment as a basis for possible revocation, suspension, for denial of renewal of a business license;
   d) to notify the State Attorney General if the judgment debtor is a business and appears to be engaged in fraudulent or illegal business practices; and;
   c) to begin an action against the judgment debtor for a penalty equal to three times the amount of the unsatisfied judgment and attorney fees where the judgment debtor is a business and there are two or more unsatisfied small claims judgments against the judgment debtor.

To contact a City Marshal:
   Look in the Yellow Pages under City Marshal.

To contact a County Sheriff:

County	Address	Borough	Zip Code	Phone Number
Bronx	880 River Avenue,	Bronx, N.Y.	10452	(718) 293 - 3900
Kings	Municipal Building,	Brooklyn, N.Y.	11201	(718) 802 - 3545
New York	253 Broadway,	New York, N.Y.	10007	(718) 240 - 6715
Queens	County Court House,	L.I. City, N.Y.	11101	(718) 392 - 4950
Richmond	350 St. Mark's Place,	Staten Island, N.Y.	10301	(718) 447 - 0041

("Information for the Judgment Debtor" is on the reverse side.)

CIV-SC-92 Reverse (Revised 9/92)

FORM 14 SIDE 2

TED ROTHSTEIN, D.D.S., PH.D.

February 15, 1995

Mr. and Mrs. Barry Almodo
351 77th Street
Brooklyn, NY 11220

Dear Mr. and Mrs. Almodo,*

On Wednesday evening February 26, the presiding Small Claims Court judge found in favor of me regarding my claim against you and Mrs. Almodo. He awarded me $385.00, and I am requesting payment in full from you at this time.

Please be advised that should you not pay me within one week, I will turn the judgment over to the City Marshal's office to begin a garnishment of your salary. In addition to my award, they will charge you a Marshal's and for all attorney's fees (approximately $50).

You have indicated that you may be moving out-of-state and accordingly, I will register the judgment in the King's County Clerk's Office should you not pay within one week. The registration will result in an additional cost to you of $45. A registered judgment will effect your credit history and credit standing irrespective of where you live in this country. Moreover, you will have to pay interest on the judgment for the time in which you delayed paying me.

I respectfully request immediate payment of the $385 that you owe me. Should you wish to discuss this matter with me, please feel free to call at (212) 555-1234.

Sincerely,
Ted Rothstein
Dr. Ted Rothstein

* This model letter is a sample post-judgment follow-up letter and the message is stated in a mild, (non-threatening) manner. The real-life letter which served as the model for the above was more threatening because the circumstances warranted such language. Indeed, in the actual case, the letter proved to be *ineffective* and the debtor paid the fee only when his wages were on the verge of being garnished. (See **[FORM 12]**). Feel free to modify the language of your letter in tenor and strength as *circumstances warrant*. The adage "you catch more bees with honey" may be true, however sometimes you can't tell if your dealing with a wasp.

35 REMSEN STREET   BROOKLYN, NEW YORK 11201-4148
TELEPHONE (718) 852-1551   FAX (718) 852-1554
5 WORLD TRADE CENTER, SUITE 367A   NEW YORK, NEW YORK 10048-0205
TELEPHONE (212) 422-2070

FORM 15

B 242—Whole or Partial Satisfaction of Judgment.
Blank Court. 8-87

Blumbergs Law Products

© 1973 BY JULIUS BLUMBERG, INC.,
PUBLISHER, NYC 10013

Civil COURT of the City of New York
COUNTY OF Kings

Index No. SCK 010107/97

Ivannah Demonet
Plaintiff(s)

against

Dinah Padebil
Defendant(s)

SATISFACTION OF
JUDGMENT

WHEREAS, a judgment was entered in the above entitled action on July 15 19 95
in the Civil Court of New York County of Kings
in judgment book 45 page No. 5 in favor of Plaintiff

Ivannah Demonet
and against Defendant, Dinah Padebil

for the sum of $ 2583 50 which judgment was docketed on July 25, 19 95
in the office of the Clerk of the County of Kings in judgment book 42 page No. 2

Plaintiff certifies that a
copy of this notice has been
sent to the defendant.

and said judgment has been fully paid and the sum of $ Ⓧ remains unpaid.
AND it is certified that there are no outstanding executions with any Sheriff or Marshal within the State
of New York,
THEREFORE, Plaintiff's satisfaction of said judgment is hereby acknowledged, and the said
Clerks are hereby authorized and directed to make an entry of full satisfaction on the docket of
said judgment.

Dated: March 5, 1997

Ivannah Demonet
The name signed must be printed beneath

Ivannah Demonet, Pro Se

STATE OF NEW YORK, COUNTY OF Kings ss.:

On the 7 day of March 1997, before me personally came

Ivannah Demonet
to me known and known to me to be the Plaintiff
in the above entitled action, and to be the same person
of judgment and acknowledged to me that (S)he

Notary's Seal

described in and who executed the within satisfaction
executed the same.

State of

County of } ss.:

On the   day of   , nineteen hundred and
before me personally came
to me known, who, being by me duly sworn, did depose and say that   he resides at No.

that   he is the   of

the corporation described in, and which executed, the foregoing instrument; that   he knows the seal of
said corporation; that the seal affixed to said instrument is such corporate seal; that it was so affixed
by order of the board of   of said corporation; and that   he signed h
name thereto by like order.

State of

County of } ss.:

On the   day of   , nineteen hundred and
before me personally came
personally known to me and to me known to be a member of the firm of

and to me known to be the person described in and who executed the foregoing satisfaction of judgment
in the firm name of
        and   he acknowledged
that   he executed same as the act and deed of said firm for the uses and purposes therein mentioned.

Index No.

COUNTY OF   COURT

Plaintiff(s)

against

Defendant(s)

Satisfaction of Judgment

Attorney(s) for

Office and Post Office Address

FORM 16 SIDE 2

Civil Court of The City of New York
TRANSCRIPT OF JUDGMENT

Index Number ___1122___ Year

SCK

JUDGMENT DEBTOR(S)

Name(s) [Surname & First Name) and Address(es)	Trade or Profession
LAPOM, PAUL 108 E. 88 St. #12 New York, N.Y. 10011	

JUDGMENT CREDITOR(S)

Name(s) & Address(es)	Attorney(s) Name(s) & Address(es
TED ROTHSTEIN 35 REMSEN St. Brooklyn, N.Y. 11201	FILED 1995 AUG -4 PM 3:23 KINGS COUNTY CLERKS OFFICE FEE 102342

AMOUNT OF JUDGMENT	JUDGMENT RENDERED	JUDGMENT DOCKETED	EXECUTION			REMARKS Date & Manner of Change of Status of Judgment Include: Assignment, Reversal, Modification, Discharge
			Returned Unsatisfied	SATISFIED		
				When	How and To What Extent	
Damages: $763.58	CIVIL Court					
Costs: $ —	KINGS County					
Prospective Fees: $40.00	Date: 3-17-94	Date: 3-17-94				
TOTAL $803.58	Time: __:__ __ M.	Time: __:__ __ M.				

STATE OF NEW YORK
County of KINGS } SS:

I, __JACK BAER__, Chief Clerk of the Civil Court of the City of the New York, __SMALL CLAIMS__ Cour hereby certify that the above is a true and correct Transcript of Judgment from the docket of judgments in my office.

I further certify that the above judgment has been _____

In testimony whereof, I have hereunto set my name and affixed my official seal this __4th__ day of __AUGUST__, 19 __95__

__Jack Baer__
Chief Clerk

CIV-GP-20 (2/91) (Replaces 43-4077)

(RECEIPT MUST BE ATTACHED TO THIS FORM)

FORM 17 SIDE 1

141

1023̧42

FILED

1995 AUG -4 PM 3: 23

KINGS COUNTY CLERK'S OFFICE
FEE _____

FORM 17 SIDE 2

Blumbergs Law Products

T 239—Income Execution; CPLR § 5231.
Civil Court, 8-87

6 blanks suggested: original; office copy; 2 copies each for debtor
and garnishee if officer cannot serve personally.

© 1980 BY JULIUS BLUMBERG, INC.,
PUBLISHER, NYC 10013

CIVIL COURT OF THE CITY OF NEW YORK, COUNTY OF   Index No.

Judgment Creditor(s)

Income Execution

Judgment Debtor(s) (name and last known address)

⌐   ¬

The People of the State of New York

TO THE ENFORCEMENT OFFICER, GREETING:

*The Enforcement Officer is the Sheriff, Marshal of the City or Constable of the
Town or Village authorized by law to enforce income executions.*

∟   ⌟

A judgment was entered in the within court in favor of the Judgment Creditor(s) and the particulars are as follows:

Entry Date	Original Amount	Amount Due	Plus Interest From

This execution is issued against
whose last known address is
whose social security number is   and who is receiving or will receive $
for each   pay period from the Employer. The Employer's name and address is

You are directed to satisfy the judgment with interest together with your fees and expenses, out of all monies now and hereafter due and owing to the Judgment Debtor from the Employer pursuant to CPLR § 5231.

Directions to Judgment Debtor: You are notified and commanded within 20 days to start paying to the Enforcement Officer serving a copy of this Income Execution on you: installments amounting to 10% but no more than the Federal limits set forth in **I. Limitations on the amount that can be withheld** below) of any and all salary, wages or other income, including any and all overtime earnings, commissions or other irregular compensation received or hereafter to be received from your Employer and to continue paying such installments until the judgment with interest and the fees and expenses of this Income Execution are fully paid and satisfied, and if you fail to do so this Income Execution will be served upon the Employer by the Enforcement Officer.

Directions to the Employer: You are commanded to withhold and pay over to the Enforcement Officer serving a copy of this Income Execution on you: installments amounting to 10% (but no more than the Federal limits set forth in **I. Limitations on the amount that can be withheld,** below) of any and all salary, wages or other income, including any and all overtime earnings, commissions or other irregular compensation now or hereafter becoming due to Judgment Debtor until the judgment with interest and the fees and expenses of this Income Execution are fully paid and satisfied.

Dated   ....The name signed must be printed beneath

Attorney(s) for Judgment Creditor(s)
Office and Post Office Address

Important Statement

This income execution directs the withholding of up to 10 percent of the judgment debtor's *gross income.* In certain cases, however, state and federal law does not permit the withholding of that much of the judgment debtor's *gross income.* The judgment debtor is referred to the New York Civil Practice Law and Rules § 5231 and 15 United States Code § 1671 *et seq.*

I. Limitations on the amount that can be withheld

A. An income execution for installments from a judgment debtor's *gross income* cannot exceed ten percent (10%) of the judgment debtor's *gross income.*

B. If judgment debtor's *weekly disposable earnings* are less than thirty (30) times the current federal minimum wage ($3.35*   per hour), or $100.50*   no deduction can be made under this income execution.

C. A judgment debtor's *weekly disposable earnings* cannot be reduced below the amount arrived at by multiplying thirty (30) times the current federal minimum wage ($3.35*   per hour), or $100.50*   under this income execution.

D. If deductions are being made from a judgment debtor's *gross income* under any orders for alimony support or maintenance for family members or former spouses and those deductions equal or exceed twenty-five percent (25%) of the judgment debtor's *disposable earnings,* no deduction can be made under this income execution.

FORM 18 SIDE 1

E. If deductions are being made from a judgment debtor's *gross income* under any orders for alimony, support or maintenance for family members or former spouses, and those deductions are less than twenty-five percent (25%) of the judgment debtor's *disposable earnings,* deductions may be made under the income execution. However, the amount arrived at by adding the deductions made under this execution to the deductions made under any orders for alimony, support or maintenance for family members or former spouses cannot exceed twenty-five percent (25%) of the judgment debtor's *disposable earnings.*

NOTE: Nothing in this notice limits the proportion or amount which may be deducted under any order for alimony, support or maintenance for family members or former spouses.

II. Explanation of limitations
Definitions

Disposable Earnings — Disposable earnings are that part of an individual's earnings left after deducting those amounts that are required by law to be withheld (for example, taxes, social security and unemployment insurance, but not deductions for union dues, insurance plans, etc.).

Gross Income — Gross income is salary, wages or other income including any and all overtime earnings, commissions and income from trusts, before any deductions are made from such income.

Illustrations

If disposable earnings is:	Amount to pay or deduct under this income execution is:
(a) 30 times federal minimum wage ($100.50*) or less	No payment or deduction allowed.
(b) more than 30 times federal minimum wage ($100.50*) and less than 40 times federal minimum wage ($134.00*)	The lesser of: the excess over 30 times the federal minimum wage ($100.50*) in disposable earnings, or 10% of gross income.
(c) 40 times the federal minimum wage ($134.00*) or more	The lesser of: 25% of disposable earnings or 10% of gross income.

III. Notice: You may be able to challenge this income execution through the procedures provided in CPLR § 5231(g) and CPLR § 5240.

If you think that the amount of your earnings being deducted under this income execution exceeds the amount permitted by state and federal law, you should act promptly because the money will be applied to the judgment. If you claim that the amount of your earnings being deducted under this income execution exceeds the amount permitted by state and federal law, you should contact your employer or other person paying your earnings. Further, YOU MAY CONSULT AN ATTORNEY, INCLUDING LEGAL AID IF YOU QUALIFY. New York State law provides two procedures through which an income execution can be challenged.

CPLR § 5231(g) Modification. At any time, the judgment debtor may make a motion to a court for an order modifying an income execution.

CPLR § 5240 Modification or protective order; supervision of enforcement. At any time, the judgment debtor may make a motion to a court for an order denying, limiting, conditioning, regulating, extending or modifying the use of any post-judgment enforcement procedure including the use of income executions.

*Based upon $3.35 minimum hourly wage. Recalculate and insert correct figures if the minimum hourly wage changes.

Return (for Sheriff's or Marshal's use only)

☐ Fully satisfied... 19.........   ☐ Unsatisfied

☐ Partially satisfied ....19......, $..

☐ Because I was unable to find the Garnishee (the Employer) within my jurisdication I returned this Income Execution to Judgment Creditor's Attorney on .... 19.........

Date and time received:

☐ Marshal, City of New York
☐ Sheriff, County of...
☐ Constable of the ☐ Town ☐ Village of...................................

FORM 18 SIDE 2

T 239—Income Execution: CPLR § 5231.
Civil Court, 4-91

5 blanks suggested: original: office copy; two copies for debtor and one for garnishee if officer cannot serve personally.

© 1980 BY JULIUS BLUMBERG, INC., PUBLISHER, NYC 10013

Blumbergs Law Products

CIVIL COURT OF THE CITY OF NEW YORK, COUNTY OF KINGS   Index No. 109118/94

Judgment Creditor(s)

TED ROTHSTEIN
35 REMSEN ST.
BROOKLYN, NY 11201

Judgment Debtor(s) (name and last known address)

BARRY ALMODO
351 77th St.
BROOKLYN, NY 11220

Income Execution

The People of the State of New York

TO THE ENFORCEMENT OFFICER, GREETING:

The Enforcement Officer is the Sheriff, Marshal of the City or Constable of the Town or Village authorized by law to enforce income executions.

A judgment was entered in the within court in favor of the Judgment Creditor(s) and the particulars are as follows:

Entry Date	Original Amount	Amount Due	Plus Interest From
2/15/95	382.58	382.58	

This execution is issued against BARRY ALMODO
whose last known address is 351 77th St. BROOKLYN, NY 11220
whose social security number is 11 -4 -7986   and who is receiving or will receive $
for each   pay period from the Employer. "Employer," herein, includes any payor of money to Judgment Debtor. The Employer's name and address is

Macy's Department Store
4462 28th St,
Long Island City, NY 11106

You are directed to satisfy the judgment with interest together with your fees and expenses, out of all monies now and hereafter due and owing to the Judgment Debtor from the Employer pursuant to CPLR § 5231.

Directions to Judgment Debtor: You are notified and commanded within 20 days to start paying to the Enforcement Officer serving a copy of this Income Execution on you: installments amounting to 10% (but no more than the Federal limits set forth in I. Limitations on the amount that can be withheld, below) of any and all salary, wages or other income, including any and all overtime earnings, commissions or other irregular compensation received or hereafter to be received from your Employer and to continue paying such installments until the judgment with interest and the fees and expenses of this Income Execution are fully paid and satisfied, and if you fail to do so this Income Execution will be served upon the Employer by the Enforcement Officer.

Directions to the Employer: You are commanded to withhold and pay over to the Enforcement Officer serving a copy of this Income Execution on you: installments amounting to 10% (but no more than the Federal limits set forth in I. Limitations on the amount that can be withheld, below) of any and all salary, wages or other income, including any and all overtime earnings, commissions or other irregular compensation now or hereafter becoming due to Judgment Debtor until the judgment with interest and the fees and expenses of this Income Execution are fully paid and satisfied.

Dated 3/7/95

.....................The name signed must be printed beneath

TED ROTHSTEIN, PRO SE

Attorney(s) for Judgment Creditor(s)

Office and Post Office Address

35 REMSEN ST.
BROOKLYN NY 11201

Important Statement

This income execution directs the withholding of up to 10 percent of the judgment debtor's gross income. In certain cases, however, state or federal law does not permit the withholding of that much of the judgment debtor's gross income. The judgment debtor is referred to New York Civil Practice Law and Rules § 5231 and 15 United States Code § 1671 et seq.

I. Limitations on the amount that can be withheld

A. An income execution for installments from a judgment debtor's gross income cannot exceed ten percent (10%) of the judgment debtor's gross income.

B. If a judgment debtor's weekly disposable earnings are less than thirty (30) times the current federal minimum wage ($4.25* per hour), or $127.50* no deduction can be made from the judgment debtor's earnings under this income execution.

C. A judgment debtor's weekly disposable earnings cannot be reduced below the amount arrived at by multiplying thirty (30) times the current federal minimum wage ($4.25* per hour), or $127.50* under this income execution.

FORM 19 SIDE 1

D. If deductions are being made from a judgment debtor's earnings under any orders for alimony, support or maintenance for family members or former spouses, and those deductions equal or exceed twenty-five percent (25%) of the judgment-debtor's disposable earnings, no deduction can be made from the judgment debtor's earnings under this income execution.

E. If deductions are being made from a judgment debtor's earnings under any orders for alimony, support or maintenance for family members or former spouses, and those deductions are less than twenty-five percent (25%) of the judgment debtor's disposable earnings, deductions may be made from the judgment debtor's earnings under this income execution. However, the amount arrived at by adding the deductions from earnings made under this execution to the deductions made from earnings under any orders for alimony, support or maintenance for family members or former spouses cannot exceed twenty-five percent (25%) of the judgment debtor's disposable earnings.

NOTE: Nothing in this notice limits the proportion or amount which may be deducted under any order for alimony, support or maintenance for family members or former spouses.

II. Explanation of limitations

Definitions

Disposable Earnings — Disposable earnings are that part of an individual's earnings left after deducting those amounts that are required by law to be withheld (for example, taxes, social security and unemployment insurance, but not deductions for union dues, insurance plans, etc.).

Gross Income — Gross income is salary, wages or other income, including any and all overtime earnings, commissions, and income from trusts, before any deductions are made from such income.

Illustrations regarding earnings:

If disposable earnings is:	Amount to pay or deduct from earnings under this income execution is:
(a) 30 times federal minimum wage ($127.50*) or less	No payment or deduction allowed.
(b) more than 30 times federal minimum wage ($127.50*) and less than 40 times federal minimum wage ($170.00*)	The lesser of: the excess over 30 times the federal minimum wage ($127.50*) in disposable earnings, or 10% of gross earnings.
(c) 40 times the federal minimum wage ($170.00*) or more	The lesser of: 25% of disposable earnings or 10% of gross earnings.

III. Notice: You may be able to challenge this income execution through the procedures provided in CPLR § 5231(i) and CPLR § 5240.

If you think that the amount of your income being deducted under this income execution exceeds the amount permitted by state or federal law, you should act promptly because the money will be applied to the judgment. If you claim that the amount of your income being deducted under this income execution exceeds the amount permitted by state or federal law, you should contact your employer or other person paying your income. Further, YOU MAY CONSULT AN ATTORNEY, INCLUDING LEGAL AID IF YOU QUALIFY. New York State law provides two procedures through which an income execution can be challenged.

CPLR § 5231 (i) Modification. At any time, the judgment debtor may make a motion to a court for an order modifying an income execution.

CPLR § 5240 Modification or protective order: supervision of enforcement. At any time, the judgment debtor may make a motion to a court for an order denying, limiting, conditioning, regulating, extending or modifying the use of any post-judgment enforcement procedure, including the use of income executions.

*Based upon $4.25 minimum hourly wage. Recalculate and insert correct figures if the minimum hourly wage changes.

Return (for Sheriff's or Marshal's use only)

☐ Fully satisfied.. 19........   ☐ Unsatisfied

☐ Partially satisfied ....19........, $...

☐ Because I was unable to find the Garnishee (the Employer) within my jurisdication I returned this Income Execution to Judgment Creditor's Attorney on .... 19........ ....

Date and time received:

☐ Marshal, City of New York
☐ Sheriff, County of..
☐ Constable of the ☐ Town ☐ Village of....................................

City of New York - Office of the Sheriff

RAUL RUSSI

Manhattan Sheriff

Requisition Request for Small Claims Execution

Read instructions on back of this page before filling out this form.

Plaintiff/Creditor_____DayPhone(   )_____

Address_____City/Zip_____

The judgement was obtained in the following Court:
□ Civil Court   □ Small Claims Part   □CourtIndexNumber_____

Date of Judgement_____Amount of Judgement_____

Court's Address_____City/Zip_____

Defendant/Debtor_____Soc. Sec. No._____

Address_____City/Zip_____

Attach a copy of your Court Judgement to this application

A. Property Execution

Debtor's Bank_____Address_____

Debtor's Business_____Address_____

I hereby direct the Sheriff to place neither custodians in charge nor to remove the property levied upon pursuant to a Property Execution in the above action. It is further understood that the Sheriff is relieved from all liability by reason thereof.

Plaintiff's/Creditor's Signature_____Date_____

B. Income Execution

Debtor's Employer:
Name_____

Address_____City/Zip_____

Do not write below this Line.

Interviewed by_____Mail Reviewed by_____Date_____

Case Nr._____Deputy_____

Date(s) Requisition(s) sent to Court:
1. Requisition _____2.Requisition_____

Application returned to Creditor_____

Form103 6/95

FORM 20 SIDE 1

Instructions

1. Why do you need to fill out this form?

After you, the Plaintiff, won a Judgement against the Defendant, the Sheriff can help you collect the money owed to you. However, in order to do so, the Sheriff needs an Execution from the Court. Only an Execution allows the Sheriff to seize the Debtor's property or wages. With the information on this form, the Sheriff can request an Execution from the Court. Please be advised that it may take up to several months until the Court sends the Execution to the Sheriff. Therefore, please wait at least 45 days before calling the Sheriff's office for an update on the status of your case.

If, despite repeated requests, the Court fails to send the Sheriff the Execution, the Sheriff will return this form to you. You may file with the Sheriff at 253 Broadway, Room 800, New York, N.Y. 10007, for a partial refund ($5) of the fee you had paid. If you wish to pursue your matter further, you may have to go to the Court to inquire why they did not provide the Sheriff with the Execution.

2. Will you get the money owed to you?

Once the Court sends the Sheriff your Execution, and, for example, there is no money in the Debtor's bank account for the Sheriff to seize, or the Debtor's business no longer exists, or if the Debtor is no longer employed, you may not collect anything. It is your responsibility to provide the Sheriff with information about the Debtor's assets. Without asset information we may not be able to collect money for you.

3. Should you complete Section A to receive Property Execution?

You should file for a Property Execution if you know that the Debtor has a bank account or an ongoing business. You need to know the Bank's name and address. If you want us to levy on the Debtor's business property you have to provide us with the name and address of the business. However, the business must match the name of the Debtor on your judgement unless the Debtor "John Doe", for example, owns the business personally but calls it " ABC Coffee Shop" in which case the business name is: "John Doe, doing business as ABC Coffee Shop". You need to give all the information requested under " A Property Execution".

You need to file this form in the County (Borough) in which the property/business is located which must be within New York City. The Sheriff can not serve an Execution outside the City of New York. Bring or mail this form to:

New York County (Manhattan): 253 Broadway, Room 800, New York, N.Y. 10007. Tel: (212) 240-6700.

Kings County (Brooklyn): Municipal Building, 208 Joralemon Street, 9th Floor, Brooklyn, N.Y. 11201. Tel:(718) 802-3545.

Queens County: 42-71 65th Place, Woodside, N.Y. 11377. Tel: (718) 803-3091.

Bronx County: 332 East 149th Street, Bronx, N.Y. 10452. Tel: (718) 585-1551.

Richmond County (Staten Isl.): 350 St. Marks Place, Room 400 B, Staten Island, N.Y. 10301 Tel: (718) 876-5307.

You are required to pay a $15 fee when you file this form. Make the check payable to: Sheriff, City of New York. It will be added to the amount of the Judgement and reimbursed to you provided a collection of the full judgement amount is made.

4. Should you complete Section B to receive and Income Execution?

If you wish to garnish the Debtor's wages, the Debtor and the employer have to be located within the City of New York. You need to give the Debtor's employer's name and address. An income execution will be served in two stages, each stage requiring a $20 fee. All fees paid by you will be added to the judgement amount.

a.   The Debtor is served with the Execution and then has 20 days to make his or her full payment to the Sheriff, continuing to make payments every month until the Judgement, Fees, and Interest is paid in full. You are required to pay $20 when you file this form.

b.   If, during the first stage, the Debtor fails to pay, the execution is served on the employer who is obligated to withhold the payments from the Debtor's salary and mail them to the Sheriff. Before the Sheriff serves on the employer, you are required to pay an additional $20 fee for this second stage. If the employer is the City of New York, you will need to furnish the Debtor's Social Security Number and pay a $2 fee with a check made out to the City Comptroller.

All Income Executions have to be filed in person or by mail at the address listed below, regardless of the borough the Debtor or employer is located:

Office of the Sheriff, 253 Broadway, Room 800, New York, N.Y. 10007 Tel: (212) 240-6700

FORM 20 SIDE 2

City of New York - Office of the Sheriff

Brooklyn Sheriff

Requisition Request for Small Claims Execution

Read instructions on back of this page before filling out this form.

Plaintiff/Creditor_____DayPhone (___)_____

Address_____City/Zip_____

The Judgment was obtained in the following Court:
☐ Civil Court   ☐ Small Claims Part   Court Index Number:_____

Date of Judgment_____Amount of Judgment_____

Court's Address_____City/Zip_____

Defendant/Debtor_____Soc.Sec.No._____

Address_____City/Zip_____

Attach a copy of your Court Judgment to this application.

A. Property Execution

Debtor's Bank_____ Address_____

Debtor's Business_____Address_____

I hereby direct the Sheriff to place neither custodians in charge nor to remove the property levied upon pursuant to a Property Execution in the above action. It is further understood that the Sheriff is relieved from all liability by reason thereof.

Plaintiff's/Creditor's Signature_____Date_____

B. Income Execution

Debtor's Employer:
Name_____

Address_____City/Zip_____

Do not write below this Line.

Interviewed by_____Mail reviewed by_____Date_____

Case Nr._____Deputy_____

Date(s) Requisition(s) sent to Court:
1. Requisition_____2. Requisition_____

Application returned to Creditor_____
Form SCC7/93

Instructions

1. Why do you need to fill out this form?

After you, the Plaintiff, won a Judgment against the Defendant, the Sheriff can help you collect the money owed to you. However, in order to do so, the Sheriff needs an Execution from the Court. Only an Execution allows the Sheriff to seize the Debtor's property or wages. With the information on this form, the Sheriff can request an Execution from the Court. Please be advised that it may take up to several months until the Court sends the Execution to the Sheriff. Therefore, please wait at least 45 days before calling the Sheriff's office for an update on the status of your case.

If, despite repeated requests, the Court fails to send the Sheriff the Execution, the Sheriff will return this form to you. You may file with the Sheriff at 253 Broadway, Room 600, New York, N.Y. 10007, for a partial refund ($5) of the fee you had paid. If you wish to pursue your matter further, you may have to go to the Court to inquire why they did not provide the Sheriff with the Execution.

2. Will you get the money owed to you?

Once the Court sends the Sheriff your Execution, and, for example, there is no money in the Debtor's bank account for the Sheriff to seize, or if the Debtor's business no longer exists, or if the Debtor is no longer employed, you may not collect anything. It is your responsibility to provide the Sheriff with information about the Debtor's assets. Without asset information we may not be able to collect money for you.

3. Should you complete Section A to receive a Property Execution ?

You should file for a Property Execution if you know that the Debtor has a bank account or an ongoing business. You need to know the bank's name and address. If you want us to levy on the Debtor's business property you have to provide us with the name and address of the business. However, the business must match the name of the Debtor on your Judgment unless the Debtor "John Doe", for example, owns the business personally but calls it "Joe's Coffee Shop" in which case the business name is: "John Doe, doing business as Joe's Coffee Shop". You need to give all the information requested under "A. Property Execution".

You need to file this form in the County (Borough) in which the property/business is located which must be within New York City. The Sheriff can not serve an Execution outside the City of New York. Bring or mail this form to:

New York County (Manhattan): 253 Broadway, Room 600, New York, N.Y. 10013. Tel: (212) 240-6700

Kings County (Brooklyn): Municipal Building, 208 Joralemon Street, 9th Floor, Brooklyn, N.Y. 11201. Tel: (718) 802-3545

Queens County: 42-71 65th Place, Woodside, N.Y. 11377. Tel: (718) 803-3091

Bronx County: 860 River Avenue, Bronx, N.Y. 10452. Tel: (718) 293-3903

Richmond County (Staten Isl.): 350 St. Marks Place, Room 400 B, Staten Island, N.Y. 10301. Tel: (718) 876-5307

You are required to pay a $15 fee when you file this form. Make the check payable to : Sheriff, City of New York. It will be added to the amount of the Judgment and reimbursed to you provided a collection of the full Judgement amount is made.

4. Should you complete Section B to receive an Income Execution ?

If you wish to garnish the Debtor's wages, the Debtor and the employer have to be located within the City of New York. You need to give the Debtor's employer's name and address . An Income Execution will be served in two stages, each stage requiring a $20 fee. All fees paid by you will be added to the judgement amount.

a.   The Debtor is served with the Execution and then has 20 days to make his or her first payment to the Sheriff, continuing to make payments every month until the Judgment, Fees, and Interest is paid in full. You are required to pay $20 when you file this form.

b.   If, during the first stage, the Debtor fails to pay, the execution is served on the employer who is obligated to withhold the payments from the Debtor's salary and mail them to the Sheriff. Before the Sheriff serves on the employer, you are required to pay an additional $20 fee for this second stage. If the employer is the City of New York, you will need to furnish the Debtor's Social Security Number and pay a $2 fee with a check made out to the City Comptroller.

All Income Executions have to be filed in person or by mail at the address listed below, regardless of the borough the Debtor or employer is located :

Office of the Sheriff , 253 Broadway, Room 600, New York, N.Y. 10007 Tel: (212) 240-6700

FORM 21 SIDE 2

Civil Court of the City of New York

COUNTY OF _____ **KINGS** _____

Small Claims _____ Part

Ted Rothstein
                    Claimant(s)/Plaintiff(s),

against

Paul Lapom
                    Defendant(s)/Respondent(s),

Index No. _____ *1122/94* _____

INFORMATION SUBPOENA
AND
RESTRAINING NOTICE

PAUL LAPOM _____
                    (Judgement Debtor)

108 E. 88 St. #12 _____
                    (Address)

New York, NY 10011 _____

S.S. #: _____

THE PEOPLE OF THE STATE OF NEW YORK

TO: _____ *Chemical Bank* _____, the person to be examined and/or restrained;

A Judgment was entered in this court on _____ *3 - 17 - 94* _____, in favor of _____ **CLAIMANT** _____ and

against _____ **DEFENDANT** _____ in the amount of $ _____ *758.00* _____, together with interest,

costs and disbursements for a total of $ _____ *763.58* _____, of which $ _____ *763.58* _____ remains due and unpaid.

INFORMATION SUBPOENA

Because you, the person to whom this subpoena is directed either reside, are regularly employed, or have an office for the regular transaction of business in _____ *Kings* _____ County of the State of New York, you must answer, in writing under oath, separately and fully, each question in the questionnaire accompanying this subpoena, and you must return the answers, together with the original of the questions within seven (7) days after your receipt of the questions and this subpoena, to _____ *TED ROTHSKIN* _____

at _____ *35 REMSEN ST. BROOKLYN NY 11201* _____

False swearing or failure to comply with this Subpoena is punishable as a contempt of court.

RESTRAINING NOTICE

If you owe a debt to the judgment debtor, or are in possession or custody of property in which the judgment debtor has an interest, be advised that in accordance with Section 5222(b) of the Civil Practice Laws and Rules (**which is printed in full on the reverse**) you are hereby forbidden to make or permit any sale, assignment or transfer of, or any interference with, any such property, or pay over or otherwise dispose of any such debt except as provided for in that Section. This notice also covers all property which may in the future come into your possession or custody in which the judgment debtor has an interest, and all debts which may come due in the future from you to the judgment debtor.

Disobedience of this Restraining Notice is punishable as a contempt of court.

July 27, 1995 _____
                    Date

Jack Baer _____
                    Chief Clerk, Civil Court

— SEE REVERSE SIDE —

CIV-SC-60 (Rev. 10/93)

FORM 22 SIDE 1

Civil Court of the City of New York

COUNTY OF _____KINGS_____

Small Claims Part

Ted Rothstein

Claimant(s)/Plaintiff(s)/Petitioner(s),

against

Paul Lapom Defendant(s)/(Respondent(s),

Index No. ___1122/94___

QUESTIONS AND ANSWERS
in connection with
INFORMATION SUBPOENA
regarding

Paul Lapom
(Judgement Debtor)

108 E. 88 th St. #2
(Address)

New York NY 10002

State of New York, County of _____ ss.:

_____, being duly sworn, deposes and says:

(Name of Deponent)

I am the _____ of _____, and acknowledge receipt of an

(Title)   (Name of Organization)

Information Subpoena naming _____ as Judgment Debtor.

The answers below are based upon information contained in the records of the recipient.

#1. Q. Please provide the debtor's full name as indicated on his/her application.
    A.

#2. Q. Please set forth the last known home address and telephone number for the debtor's residence, if different from the address shown above.
    A.

#3. Q. Does the judgment debtor have an acount with your organization and/or are you currently holding any deposits and/or security? If so, what is the account number, and what is/are the amount(s) on deposit?
    A.

#4. Q. Do your records indicate that the debtor is employed? If so, please list the name and address of the employer and the salary as indicated in your records.
    A.

#5. Q. Did the debtor list any bank references on his/her application? If so, set forth the name and address of said bank(s) and account number(s), if available.
    A.

#6. Q. Do your records indicate the location of any other assets of the debtor? If so, please give the location and description of any other assets.
    A.

The answers given to the above questions are true and complete to the best of my knowledge.

Sworn to before me this _____ day of _____, 19_____.

_____
Notary Public

_____
Signature (before a Notary Public)

WHEN COMPLETED, RETURN THE ORIGINAL COPY OF THIS FORM TO: _____

(Judgment Creditor's Name & Address)

CIV-SC-61 (Rev. 3/91)   **DO NOT RETURN THIS FORM TO THE CIVIL COURT**

FORM 22 SIDE 2

McKINNEY'S

CONSOLIDATED LAWS
OF NEW YORK ANNOTATED

Book 29A—Judiciary
Part 2

Court of Claims Act

Uniform Justice Court Act

1996
Cumulative Annual Pocket Part

Replacing prior pocket part in back of volume
copyrighted in 1989

Current Through the Laws of 1995,
Chapters 1 to 3, 6 to 690.

For Later Laws, Consult WESTLAW
or your McKinney's
Session Law News Pamphlets.

For Close of Notes of Decisions and
Information Regarding West's
McKinney's Forms, see Page III.

Includes Commentaries by
David D. Siegel

WEST PUBLISHING CO.
ST. PAUL, MINN.

§ 1802

§ 1802. Parts for the determination of small claims established

Notes of Decisions

Power of court 1

1. Power of court

Civil Court of the City of New York generally does not have jurisdiction over

motion for leave to serve late notice of claim, but Small Claims Part has power to entertain motion to serve late notice. Luria v. New York City Office of Comptroller, 1992, 154 Misc.2d 950, 587 N.Y.S.2d 831.

§ 1803. Commencement of action upon small claims

[See main volume for (a)]

(b) The clerk shall furnish every claimant, upon commencement of the action, with information written in clear and coherent language which shall be prescribed and furnished by the office of court administration, concerning the small claims court. Such information shall include, but not be limited to, an explanation of the following terms and procedures; adjournments, counterclaims, jury trial requests, subpoenas, arbitration, collection methods and fees, the responsibility of the judgment creditor to collect data on the judgment debtor's assets, the ability of the court prior to entering judgment to order examination of or disclosure by, the defendant and restrain him, the utilization of section eighteen hundred twelve of this article concerning treble damage awards and information subpoenas including, but not limited to, specific questions to be used on information subpoenas, and the claimant's right to notify the appropriate state or local licensing or certifying authority of an unsatisfied judgment if it arises out of the carrying on, conducting or transaction of a licensed or certified business or if, such business appears to be engaged in fraudulent or illegal acts or otherwise demonstrates fraud or illegality in the carrying on, conducting or transaction of its business. The information shall be available in English. Large signs in English shall be posted in conspicuous locations in each small claims court clerk's office, advising the public of its availability.

(As amended L.1991, c. 650, § 34.)

Historical and Statutory Notes

1991 Amendments. Subd. (b). L.1991, c. 650, § 34, eff. Nov. 1, 1991 and applicable to all cases begun on or after that date, required informing claimant of judgment creditor's responsibility for collect- ing information on judgment debtor's assets and that court can issue restraining orders and can order prejudgment examination of or disclosure from debtor.

Supplementary Practice Commentaries

by David D. Siegel

1991

The 1991 Amendment Making Court Identify Licensing Authorities and Tell Claimant About Disclosure of Defendant's Assets

☺ The legislature returned in 1991 to what has become the continuing dilemma of getting small claims judgments enforced. A number of amendments of Article 18 in prior years addressed the problem, but apparently didn't do the job. See §§ 1811 to 1814 and the Commentaries on them.

The amendment of § 1803(b) has to do with the defendant's assets. It's the coordinate of a concurrent amendment made in § 1805(a). Under CPLR 5229, a defendant can be examined about its assets after decision

46

§ 1804

☺ (or verdict) even before judgment, and promptly put under a restraint with respect to them. The amendment of § 1805(a) clarifies that CPLR 5229 applies in the small claims part. The amendment of § 1803(b) requires the clerk to advise claimants that this can be done and tells them to compile whatever data they can about a defendant's assets. This is designed to encourage claimants to ask the judge, right at the small claims hearing, to question the debtor about its assets and to supply the court data about those assets so as to facilitate and perhaps even direct the court's questioning. ☺

Practice Commentaries Cited

Cohen v. Banks, Justice Ct., Rockland Co., N.Y., N.Y.Law J., Mar. 1, 1994, p. 27.

Notes of Decisions

Notice 2

2. Notice

Notice sent by certified mail, without contemporaneous service by ordinary

mail, was insufficient to confer jurisdiction over defendant in small claims action, where certified mailing was returned unclaimed. Cohen v. Banks, 1994, 160 Misc.2d 159, 608 N.Y.S.2d 43.

§ 1804. Informal and simplified procedure on small claims

The court shall conduct hearings upon small claims in such manner as to do substantial justice between the parties according to the rules of substantive law and shall not be bound by statutory provisions or rules of practice, procedure, pleading or evidence, except statutory provisions relating to privileged communications and personal transactions or communications with a decedent or mentally ill person. An itemized bill or invoice, receipted or marked paid, or two itemized estimates for services or repairs, are admissible in evidence and are prima facie evidence of the reasonable value and necessity of such services and repairs. Disclosure shall be unavailable in small claims procedure except upon order of the court on showing of proper circumstances. In every small claims action, where the claim arises out of the conduct of the defendant's business at the hearing on the matter, the judge or arbitrator shall determine the appropriate state or local licensing or certifying authority and any business or professional association of which the defendant is a member. The provisions of this act and the rules of this court, together with the statutes and rules governing supreme court practice, shall apply to claims brought under this article so far as the same can be made applicable and are not in conflict with the provisions of this article; in case of conflict, the provisions of this article shall control.

(As amended L.1991, c. 650, § 35.)

Historical and Statutory Notes

1991 Amendments. L.1991, c. 650, § 35, eff. Nov. 1, 1991, and applicable to all cases begun on and after that date, required determination of appropriate li- censing or certifying authority and any applicable business or professional association where the claim arises out of the defendant's business.

Supplementary Practice Commentaries

by David D. Siegel

1991

The 1991 Amendment Requiring Court to Inquire Into Defendant's Licensing

A 1991 amendment of § 1804 requires the court at the hearing to inquire into the licensing circumstances of a business defendant before it,

47

Civil Court of the City of New York

COUNTY OF _____ **KINGS**

Small Claims Part

Ted Rothstein

_____
Claimant(s)/Plaintiff(s)/Petitioner(s),
against

Paul Lapom Defendant(s)/(Respondent(s),

Index No. ___ *112/94*

QUESTIONS AND ANSWERS
In connection with
INFORMATION SUBPOENA

PAUL LAPOM
_____
(Judgement Debtor)

108 E. 88 St. #12

New York, NY 10011

State of New York, County of _____ ss.:

_____, being duly sworn, deposes and says:
(Name of Deponent)

I am the _____ of _____, and acknowledge receipt of an
(Title)   (Name of Organization)

Information Subpoena naming _____ as Judgment Debtor.

The answers below are based upon information contained in the records of the recipient.

#1. Q. Please provide the debtor's full name as indicated on his/her application.
   A.   **NO RECORD**

#2. Q. Please set forth the last known home address and telephone number for the debtor's residence, if different from the address shown above.
   A.   **NO RECORD**

#3. Q. Does the judgment debtor have an acount with your organization and/or are you currently holding any deposits and/or security? If so, what is the account number, and what is/are the amount(s) on deposit?
   A.   **NO RECORD**

#4. Q. Do your records indicate that the debtor is employed? If so, please list the name and address of the employer and the salary as indicated in your records.
   A.   **NO RECORD**

#5. Q. Did the debtor list any bank references on his/her application? If so, set forth the name and address of said bank(s) and account number(s), if available.
   A.   **NO RECORD**

#6. Q. Do your records indicate the location of any other assets of the debtor? If so, please give the location and description of any other assets.
   A.   **NO RECORD**

The answers given to the above questions are true and complete to the best of my knowledge. **CHEMICAL BANKING CORP.**

Sworn to before me this *31* day of *August*, 19*95*   **CENTRAL LEGAL HOLDS & LEVIES DEPT.**

Raipu   ALTUHRD NAHME
_____   Notary Public, State of New York
Notary Public   No. 01R____16   _____
                                         Certified in Kings County   Signature (before a Notary Public)
                                         Commission Expires June 26, 19__   **AUTHORIZED SIGNATURE**

WHEN COMPLETED, RETURN THE ORIGINAL COPY OF THIS FORM TO: _____
                                                              (Judgment Creditor's Name & Address)

CIV-SC-61 (Rev. 3/91)   **DO NOT RETURN THIS FORM TO THE CIVIL COURT**

FORM 24 SIDE 1

Citibank
Customer Account Services
P.O. Box 5870
New York, NY 10163

Ted Rothstein
35 Remsen Street
Brooklyn, NY 11201

CITIBANK●

Civil Court of the City of New York

County of Kings

_____

Ted Rothstein

Plantiff

-Against-

Paul　　Lapom

Defendant

_____

State of New York
County of New York

L. _____er being duly sworn, says

I am an employee of Citibank, N.A. and am authorized to make this affidavit on Citibank's behalf. If necessary, inquiries should be directed to: (212) 613-5531/5519/5520.

We have on our books in the name of Paul　　Lapom　./H.M. Almouch
an account(s) with a balance of $　　0.00.

Payment or delivery of the aforementioned account or property is subject to the following conditions: Signed instructions of _____ Almouch

Sworn to before me,
08/04/95

_____
Signature

Roberta J Notary Public
_____

ALTUHRD NAHME
Notary Public, State of New York
No. 10101010
Qualified in Nassau County
Commission Expires November 30, 1995

LOG NO: 950_____

"Customer Account Services is a department of Citibank, N.A. which performs services for Citibank, N.A.; Citibank, F.S.B.; Citibank (New York State); Citibank (Maine) N.A.; and Citibank (Nevada) N.A."

FORM 24 SIDE 2

Blumbergs Law Products

B 320—Execution Against Property, To Sheriff, Marshal; Notice to Garnishee.
Civil Court. 6 blanks suggested: original; office copy; 3 copies each for debtor and garnishee if officer cannot serve personally. 9-82

© 1974 by JULIUS BLUMBERG, INC., PUBLISHER
62 WHITE STREET, NEW YORK, N. Y. 10013

CIVIL COURT OF THE CITY OF NEW YORK, COUNTY OF **KINGS**

TED ROTHSTEIN

Plaintiff

against

PAUL LAPOM

Defendant

Index No. **SCK 1385/95**

*EXECUTION
WITH NOTICE TO
GARNISHEE*

The People of the State of New York

TO THE SHERIFF OR ANY MARSHAL OF THE CITY OF NEW YORK, GREETING:

WHEREAS, *in an action in the Civil Court of the City of New York, County of* **KINGS**

between

..................Ted Rothstein.................. *as plaintiff and*

Paul Lapom.. *as defendant*

who are all the parties named in said action, a judgment was entered on ....July 20,..................*19* **95**

in favor of ....Ted Rothstein.................., *judgment creditor*

and against ....Paul Lapom.................. *judgment debtor*

whose last known address is ....108 E. 88th St., Apt #2, NY, NY 10012..................

in the amount of $ 947.24.................. including costs, of which $ 947.24.................. together with

interest thereon from.................. July 20,.................. remains due and unpaid;

NOW, THEREFORE, WE COMMAND YOU *to satisfy the said judgment out of the personal property of the above named judgment debtor and the debts due to him; and that only the property in which said judgment debtor who is not deceased has an interest or the debts owed to him shall be levied upon or sold hereunder; AND TO RETURN this execution to the clerk of the above captioned court within 60 days after issuance unless service of this execution is made within that time or within extensions of that time made in writing by the attorney(s) for the judgment creditor*

Notice to Garnishee
TO: Chemical Bank
ADDRESS: 224 Montague St., Brooklyn, NY 11201

WHEREAS, *it appears that you are indebted to the judgment debtor, above named, or in possession or custody of property not capable of delivery in which the judgment debtor has an interest, including, without limitation, the following specified debt and property:*

$947. 24 contained in Paul Lapom's checking account # 26074927

NOW, THEREFORE, YOU ARE REQUIRED *by section 5232(a) of the Civil Practice Law and Rules forthwith to transfer to the said sheriff or marshal all personal property not capable of delivery in which the judgment debtor is known or believed to have an interest now in or hereafter coming into your possession or custody including any property specified in this notice; and to pay to the said sheriff or marshal, upon maturity, all debts now due or hereafter coming due from you to the judgment debtor, including any debts specified in this notice; and to execute any documents necessary to effect such transfer or payment;*

AND TAKE NOTICE *that until such transfer or payment is made or until the expiration of 90 days after the service of this execution upon you or such further time as is provided by any order of the court served upon you whichever event first occurs, you are forbidden to make or suffer any sale, assignment or transfer of, or any interference with, any such property, or pay over or otherwise dispose of any such debt, to any person other than said sheriff or marshal, except upon direction of said sheriff or marshal or pursuant to an order of the court;*

AND TAKE FURTHER NOTICE THAT *at the expiration of 90 days after a levy is made by service of this execution, or of such further time as the court upon motion of the judgment creditor has provided, this levy shall be void except as to property or debts which have been transferred or paid to said sheriff or marshal or as to which a proceeding under sections 5225 or 5227 of the Civil Practice Law and Rules has been brought.*

Dated: August 8, 1995

Ted Rothstein

.... The name signed must be printed beneath.

TED ROTHSTEIN, PRO SE

*Attorney(s) for Judgment Creditor
Office and Post Office Address*

Ted Rothstein, Pro Se
35 Remsen Street
Brooklyn, N.Y. 11201

A notice to judgment debtor in the form presented by CPLR §5222(e) — HAS — HAS NOT — been served on judgment debtor within a year.

FORM 25

Settlement of the Transcript

The transcript must be "settled" by the Judge who heard the case or by agreement of the parties. In this instance the word "settled" is used to mean that the transcript of the minutes of the trial will be examined or reviewed for accuracy.

The **Notice of Settlement of Transcript** form is intended to notify the opposing party or his/her attorney of the date on which the Judge will settle the transcript. The opposing party or his/her attorney must be given at least three days advance notice (eight days if service is by mail) of the scheduled date of such settlement. The person who serves the Notice of Settlement of Transcript must fill out an Affidavit of Service. The Affidavit of Service must be notarized.

The **Notice of Settlement of Transcript** form is to be filled out in triplicate and is distributed as follows.

Page 1, the Original, along with the Transcript of Minutes of the trial (with your objections and/or your proposed corrections, if any) is to be submitted to the Appeals Clerk. The Appeals Clerk will provide them to the trial Judge on the day of the settlement along with the Affidavit of Service.

Page 2, along with a photocopy of the Transcript (with your objections and/or your proposed corrections, if any), must be "served" on the opposing party or his/her attorney by someone over 18 years of age and not a party to the action, notifying him/her of the date on which the Judge will settle the transcript.

Page 3, should be retained by you as your record.

The Appellate Term

After the transcript is settled the Appeals Clerk will prepare a Clerk's Return on Appeal and submit it to the Appellate Term with the transcript, Notice of Appeal, Court Record, and any other related papers.

You must perfect (complete the filing of) your appeal with the Appellate Term of the Supreme Court in accordance with their rules, regulations and instructions.

CIV-GP-67 Outside (Revised 5/92)

THE CIVIL COURT
of
THE CITY OF NEW YORK

INFORMATION REGARDING
AN APPEAL
of
AN ORDER or A JUDGMENT

CIVIL COURT OF THE CITY OF NEW YORK
Appeals Clerk

Room 118	Room 303	Window 9, Basement
111 Centre Street	141 Livingston Street	851 Grand Concourse
New York, N.Y. 10013	Brooklyn, N.Y. 11201	Bronx, N.Y. 10451
(212) 374-4646	(718) 643-5069	(212) 590-3603

Room G-16	Basement
120-55 Queens Blvd.	927 Castleton Avenue
Kews Gardens, N.Y. 11424	Staten Island, N.Y. 10310
(718) 520-3641	(718) 390-5422

FORM 26 SIDE 1

CIVIL COURT OF THE CITY OF NEW YORK

INFORMATION REGARDING AN APPEAL OF AN ORDER OR A JUDGMENT

An appeal cannot be taken from anything other than an Order or a Judgment made by a Judge. Judgments made by an Arbitrator or Referee are not appealable. Where matters have been settled by mutual agreement of the parties, no appeal is possible.

The appeal process may be costly. The Court Reporter (or transcribing service if the minutes were recorded in L&T) is permitted to charge a fee based on the length of the transcript which must be prepared. It is suggested that you contact the Court Reporter or transcribing service to obtain an estimate of the cost of preparing a typewritten transcript of the minutes of the trial. You may consider this information useful in determining whether or not to appeal.

An appeal must be filed within 30 days from the service upon the appellant of the Judgment or Order appealed from and written notice of its entry, (being posted to the records) and must be perfected (completed) within 30 days of filing of Notice of Appeal.

An appeal does not stay (halt) the execution of a Judgment. To stay the enforcement of a Money Judgment either an "Undertaking," by Bond or Certified Check, or an Order from the Appellate Term of the Supreme Court is required. To postpone an eviction pending an appeal may require a Court Order.

An appeal does not mean a new trial or the presenting of new evidence. Rather it is a review of the relevant portion(s) of the court file and the relevant portion(s) of the transcript of the trial minutes by the judges of the Appellate Term of the State Supreme Court.

CIV-GP-67 Inside (Revised 5/92)

PROCEDURE

Filing of Notice of Appeal

The Notice of Appeal forms may be purchased at any stationery store which carries legal forms.

The Notice of Appeal form must be filled out in triplicate.

Page 1, the Original, is to be filed with the Court, along with the fee and an Affidavit of Service form stating that the second page has been served on the opposing party or attorney. Such service may be by mail or personally. The Affidavit of Service form must be notarized.

Page 2, must be "served" on the opposing party or his/her attorney by someone over 18 years of age and not a party to the action.

Page 3, should be retained by you as your record.

Obtaining the Transcript of the Trial

The Appellant (the one who makes the appeal) must order and pay for a transcript of the minutes of the trial from the Court Reporter or transcribing service.

The Appellant must contact the Court Reporter or transcribing service to make arrangements for the actual production of the transcript.

FORM 26 SIDE 2

T 471—Notice of Appeal.   COPYRIGHT 1973 BY JULIUS BLUMBERG, INC., LAW BLANK PUBLISHERS

Blumbergs Law Products

Civil Court City of New York
County of Kings, Small Claims Part

Index No. 12345/96

Rothstein, Ted
    Plaintiff - Appellant

— against —

Nameh, Purson   Defendant - Respondent

NOTICE OF APPEAL

PLEASE TAKE NOTICE, that the above named Plaintiff - Appellant

Ted Rothstein

hereby appeal(s) to the Appellate Term of the Supreme Court

from the decision in the Small Claims Part of the Civil
Court of the City of New York, County of Kings in this action, entered in the office
of the Clerk of said Court

on the 9 day of February 19 96

and from each and every part thereof.
Dated:

Yours, etc., Ted Rothstein
    Ted Rothstein, PRO SE
    ~~Attorney(s) for~~ Plaintiff   and Appellant

To Name, Address of Attorney

Attorney(s) for Defendant   and Respondent;

FORM 27 SIDE 1

161

Civil Court County of New York
County of Kings, Small Claims Part

_____

Rothstein, Ted

      Plaintiff-Appellant   Index No. *12345/95*

           -against-   Affidavit of Service

Nameh, Purson

      Defendant- Respondant

_____

State of New York   )
)SS.

County of Kings   )

Christopher Q   , being duly sworn, disposes and says:

1. That deponent is not a party therein, is over 18 years of age and resides in Brooklyn, N.Y.

2. On February 21st 1996 at 6:05 p.m. at 101 *Some* Street Apartment #1, Brooklyn, N.Y. 11201 deponent serve the within notice of Appeal and Decision on *Nameh, Purson*, the defendant therein named, by delivering there at a true copy to *Nameh, Purson* personally. Deponent knew person served to be the defendant therein.

3. Deponent describes the individual so served as follows: Female, White, 25-30, 5'5"- 5'7", 130-150 pounds, Brown hair

                                   _____
                                   Christopher Q
                                   Lic. # █7300█

*Sworn to before me
this 23rd of February, 1996*

LAWRENCE ████████
Notary Public, State of New York
No. █77202█
Qualified in Queens County
Commission Expires March 30, 19 *97*

CIVIL COURT OF THE CITY OF NEW YORK   Index No. 12345/95

County of Kings Small Claims Part

Rothstein, Ted

)
)
)
)
)
)
)
)
)
)
)
)
)
)

Claimant(s)/ Plaintiff(s)
- against -

Name of Defendant - Respondent

Defendant(s)

NOTICE OF SETTLEMENT

OF TRANSCRIPT

To: Name of Defendant - Respondent

Enclosed is a copy of the transcript of the above trial along with the proposed corrections,

if any, which will be presented to Judge Name of judge who heard your case

by the Appeals Clerk on the date you arranged with the judge's law clerk to settle the minutes

_____Date_____

The Respondent is required to present its objections, if any, to the Appeals Clerk at:

141 Livingston St., Room ###

Building and Room Number

before the above indicated date.

Print Name of Respondent

Name of Defendant - Respondent

Address of Respondent

Address of Defendant - Respondent

Sworn to me before this

12th day of March 19 96

Signature of Small Claims Clerk

Notary Public or Court Employee

Print Name of Appellant

Ted Rothstein

Address of Appellant

35 Remsen St., Bklyn 11201

Ted Rothstein

Signature of Appellant

March 11th, 1996

Dated

CIV-GP (Rev 10/93)

FORM 28 SIDE 1

Civil Court of the City of New York

COUNTY OF _____KINGS_____

Small Claims Part

Index No. 12345/95

Rothstein, Ted
)
Claimant(s)/ Plaintiff(s)
)
- against -
)
Defendant - Respondent
)
Defendant(s)
)

AFFIDAVIT OF SERVICE
OF
NOTICE OF SETTLEMENT

State of New York, County of _Kings_ ss:

Name of person who took mail to post office, being duly sworn, deposes and says:
(Name of Deponent)

I am over 18 years of age and not a party to this action.

At _10:00_ AM/~~PM~~, on _March 11th, 1996_ at _Defendant-Respondent's address_
(Time)   (Date)   (Address)

in the County of _Kings_____, City of New York, I served the annexed NOTICE OF SETTLEMENT on:

1. _____Name of Defendant - Respondent_____
(Name of Person Served)

known to me to be the " _Defendant - Respondent_ " by:
(Plaintiff/Defendant)

☐ (a) Delivering a true copy to him/her at the following address:

_____

Description of Individual Served in Person:		
Sex: _____	~~Color of Skin:~~	Color of Hair: _____
~~Approximate Age:~~ _____	Approximate Weight: _____	~~Approximate Height:~~ _____

☑ (b) Mailing a true copy. Properly sealed and enclosed in a post-paid wrapper, by Certified Mail, Return Receipt Requested, in Post office of the United Stated Postal Service within the State of New York, addressed to the plaintiff/defendant

AND ALSO SERVED THEM ON

2. Marshal _____ by:

☐ (a) delivering a true copy to

_____.

☐ (b) Mailing a true copy. Properly sealed and enclosed in a post-paid wrapper, by Certified Mail, Return Receipt Requested, in Post office of the United Stated Postal Service within the State of New York, addressed to:

Marshal _____ at:

_____

Name of person who took mail to post office
(Signature of Deponent)

Sworn to before me this _12th_ day of _March_____, 19_96_.

Signature of Small Claims Clerk
(Notary Public of Court Employee and Title)

CIV-GP-19 (9/89)

CASE # 96-XXXX K C
FEBRUARY 5, 1997 TERM

At a term of the Appellate Term of the
Supreme Court of the State of New York
for the 2nd and 11th Judicial Districts
held in Kings County, on FEB 18 1997

PRESENT-HON. LEONARD xxxxxxxxxx   JUSTICE PRESIDING
   "   HON. GLORIA xxxxxxxxxxxxx   ASSOCIATE JUSTICE
   "   HON. MICHELLE xxxxxxxxxxxxxxxx,   ASSOCIATE JUSTICE

--x

TED ROTHSTEIN,

                    Appellant,

        -against-

DINAH PADEBIL,

                    Respondent.

--x

       The above named appellant having appealed to this court
from a JUDGMENT of the CIVIL COURT OF THE CITY OF NEW YORK,
KINGS COUNTY entered on FEBRUARY 9, 1996 and the said appeal
having been submitted by APPELLANT IN PERSON and NO BRIEF
SUBMITTED for the respondent and due deliberation having been had
thereon;

       It is hereby ordered and adjudged that the judgment is
unanimously affirmed without costs.

TED. ROTHSTEIN
35 REMSEN STREET
BROOKLYN, NY 11201

                                    John A. Cahill

                                    JOHN A. CAHILL
DINAH PADEBIL   CHIEF CLERK
101 STATE STREET, #1   APPELLATE TERM
BROOKLYN, NY 11201

FORM 29 SIDE 1

165

SUPREME COURT OF THE STATE OF NEW YORK
APPELLATE TERM : 2nd and 11th JUDICIAL DISTRICTS

--x

PRESENT: JUSTICE ONE, JUSTICE TWO, AND JUSTICE THREE

--x

TED ROTHSTEIN,

                    Appellant,

        -against-

                                            NO.   96-XXXX K C

                                            DECIDED

DINAH PADEBIL,

                    Respondent.   FEB 1 8 1997

--x

        Appeal by plaintiff from a small claims judgment
of the Civil Court, Kings County (D. xxxxxxxxx, J.) entered
February 9, 1996 in favor of defendant dismissing the action.

        Judgment unanimously affirmed without costs.

        Substantial justice was done between the parties
in accordance with the rules and principles of substantive
law (see CCA 1804).

FORM 29 SIDE 2

Civil Court of The City of New York
County of New York
Small Claims Part

_____ x

TED ROTHSTEIN,

                                 PLAINTIFF,   **AFFIDAVIT IN**
                                                       SUPPORT OF MOTION
         - AGAINST -   **To Recognize Out of State Judgment**
                                                      INDEX # SC 12345/96

DINAH PAEDEBILL

                                 DEFENDANT.

_____ x

SIR(S):

                PLEASE TAKE NOTICE, that Ted Rothstein says the following under penalty of
perjury.

              The attached judgment was not obtained by default in appearance of the defendant or
by confession of judgment. The judgment is unsatisfied in whole (in part). The amount
remaining unpaid is $ _____. The enforcement of this judgment has not been stayed. The
last know address of the debtor is _____.

Dated: Brooklyn, New York,   Affirmed:
        Date_____

                                             _____
                                           Ted Rothstein
_____   PRO SE
Signature of Notary   35 Remsen Street
                                         Brooklyn, NY
_____   (718) 852-1551
Date

FORM 30

INDIVIDUAL CLAIM COMPLANT FORM

NASSAU COUNTY SMALL CLAIMS:
District County Court House
99 Main St.
Hempstead. NY 11550
Small Claims Court Tel. No. Voice: 516 572 2261

PLAINTIFF'S NAME (please print) _____
(if a partnership name each individual partner)

(if plaintiff is doing business under a trade name, print trade name below)

_____

PLAINTIFF'S ADDRESS _____

_____

NAME OF PERSON OR FIRM YOU ARE SUING (please print) _____

_____

ADDRESS _____

_____

CAUSE OF ACTION (state amount, dates and details) _____

_____

_____

_____

_____

_____

_____

WITH INTEREST FROM _____

_____

    The undersigned acknowledges that ___ he has been informed prior to the commencement of this action, that ___ he shall be deemed to have waived all right to appeal except on the sole ground that substantial justice has not been done.

    The undersigned has also been advised that supporting witnesses, account books, receipts and other documents required to establish the claim herein must be produced at the hearing.

    Plaintiff swears that the institution of this action or proceeding is not prohibited by Section 1809 of the Uniform District Court Act, to wit, that no corporation, and no assignee of any small claim shall institute an action or proceeding under this title.

_____ , being duly sworn, deposes and says that the foregoing statements are true and that ___he is the plaintiff herein.

Sworn to before me this _____
day of _____ , 19____

Clerk or Attorney (if any)

_____
Plaintiff

COMPLETE IN TRIPLICATE

DC 89C   M-433
Revised   10/83

FORM 31

NASSAU COUNTY SMALL CLAIMS

DC 94 M-2056 Revised 10/90

COMMERCIAL CLAIMS COMPLAINT FORM

[ ] Commercial Transaction

[ ] Consumer Transaction

CLAIMANT'S NAME (please print) _____

Address _____

Telephone _____

NAME OF PERSON OR FIRM YOU ARE SUING (please print) _____

_____

Address _____

_____

CAUSE OF ACTION (state amount, dates and details)_____

_____

_____

_____

_____

_____

_____

_____

With Interest From _____

CERTIFICATION (Sec. 1803-A & 1809-A UDCA)

I, _____ (name) am a/an _____

_____ (officer, director or employee) of _____

_____ (claimant-corporation, partnership or association) and have been authorized to represent the claimant in this commercial claim action, which has its principal office in the State of New York. I certify to the truthfulness of the within claim and that no more than five (5) such actions or proceedings (including the instant action or proceeding) have been initiated during the present calendar month. I further certify that I have the requisite authority to bind the corporation, partnership or association in a settlement or trial of any claim or counterclaim.

The undersigned acknowledges that he/she has been informed prior to the commencement of this action, that he/she shall be deemed to have waived all right to appeal except on the sole ground that substantial justice has not been done.

The undersigned has also been advised that supporting witnesses, account books, receipts and other documents required to establish the claim herein must be produced at the hearing.

Date: _____   _____
                                                                        Signature

_____   **COMPLETE IN TRIPLICATE**
     Clerk or Notary

FORM 32

DC 41a

SUFFOLK COUNTY DISTRICT COURT
SMALL CLAIMS COMPLAINT FORM

18-311..11/86ps

DATE _____

RECEIPT NO. _____

FEE PAID _____

INDEX NO. _____

RETURN DATE _____

TIME & DISTRICT _____

PLAINTIFF'S NAME, ADDRESS AND ZIP CODE

DEFENDANT'S NAME, ADDRESS AND ZIP CODE

PRINT   (Last Name)   (First Name)

PRINT   (Last Name)   (First Name)

Tel. No. _____

Tel. No. _____

PRINT   (Last Name)   (First Name)

PRINT   (Last Name)   (First Name)

Tel. No. _____

Tel. No. _____

CAUSE OF ACTION (CHECK ONE)
____ (5) PERSONAL INJURIES
____ (10) PROPERTY DAMAGE
____ (15) LOSS OF PERSONAL PROPERTY
____ (20) GOODS SOLD AND DELIVERED
____ (25) BREACH OF CONTRACT OR WARRANTY
____ (30) RENT DUE
____ (35) WORK, LABOR AND SERVICES
____ (40) MONIES DUE
____ (45) CAR RENTAL EXPENSES

____ (50) PAYMENT OF LOAN
____ (55) RETURN OF SECURITY
____ (60) RETURN OF DEPOSIT
____ (65) UNPAID WAGES
____ (70) REFUND ON DEFECTIVE MERCHANDISE
____ (75) VETERINARY BILL
____ (80) REFUND ON DEFENDANT'S DEFECTIVE WORK, LABOR AND/OR SERVICES
____ (85) ACTION AS SHOWN ON COMPLAINT FORM

STATE AMOUNT, DATES AND DETAILS:

_____

_____

_____

_____

TOTAL AMOUNT $ _____

The undersigned acknowledges that he has been informed prior to the commencement of this action, that he shall be deemed to have waived all right to appeal except on the sole ground that substantial justice has not been done.

The undersigned has also been advised that supporting witnesses, account books, receipts and other documents required to establish the claim herein must be produced at the hearing.

Plaintiff swears that the institution of this action or proceeding is not prohibited by Sec. 1809 of the UDCA, to wit, that no corporation and no assignee of any small claim shall institute an action or proceeding under this title.

Plaintiff further swears that, to the best of his knowledge, the defendant is not in the military service.

DATED: _____

_____
(PLAINTIFF)

_____
(AS AGENT)

_____
(AS PARENT AND NATURAL GUARDIAN)

SUBMIT ORIGINAL AND THREE (3) COPIES

FORM 33 SIDE 1

MAILING INSTRUCTIONS

<u>USE BLACK INK</u>

<u>THE MAXIMUM YOU CAN SUE FOR IS $3000</u>

Instuctions If You Are An <u>Individual</u>

- You are the paintiff, put your last name, first name, address and telephone #. (we cannot accept a P.O. Box)

- Do the same for the defendant (the people you are suing) We cannot accept P.O. Boxes

- Check one cause of action. (if you cannot decide, pick #85).

- State briefly the reason why you are suing.

- Place the total amount your are suing for.

- Sign your name and date it at the bottom.

FILING FEES

$10.00 for claims up to $1,000
$15.00 for claims from 1,000.01 - $3,000.00
Add an extra $2.00 for each additional defendant

We only have DAY COURT here on Wednesday at 9:30 AM and Tuesdays at 9:30 AM
<u>PLEASE SPECIFY WHICH DAY YOU PREFER</u>

PLEASE ENCLOSE A STAMPED SELF-ADDRESSED ENVELOPE.

SEND A CERTIFIED CHECK OR MONEY ORDER ONLY!

THIRD DISTRICT COURT
1850 NEW YORK AVENUE
HUNTINGTON STATION, N.Y. 11746

<u>USE BLACK INK</u>

<u>THE MAXIMUM YOU CAN SUE FOR IS $3000.</u>

Instructions If You Are A <u>Corporation</u>

(You must be a New York State based Corp in order to file in Commercial Claims)

- Fill out and mail the demand letter to the defendant. (Do this only if you are suing an individual. You do not need to do this for another Corp. or Co.)

- Wait 10 days...If you get no response from defendant after those 10 days, file the COMMERCIAL CLAIM APPLICATION.

- Sign and notarize the certification (the certifiction must be notarized only if you are filing by mail) if filing at the court you can sign it in front of a clerk.

- You are the plaintiff, put your full corporate name and address. (we can not accept P.O. boxes).

- Put the defendant's full name and address. (we cannot accept P.O. Boxes).

- Check a cause of action. (if you cannot decide, pick #85).

- State briefly why you are suing.

- Put the total amount you are suing for.

- Sign and date the form at the bottom.

FILING FEES

$20.00 filing fee
<u>$3.16 mailing fee</u>

$23.16 total filing fee

Add an extra $3.16 for each extra defendant

PLEASE ENCLOSE A STAMPED SELF-ADDRESSED ENVELOPE.

SEND A CERTIFIED CHECK OR MONEY ORDER ONLY!

PELHAM JUSTICE COURT

ASSIGNED COURT DATE:

/ /

9:30 AM Wedesday

FILING FEES:

Small Claims - $5.00

Civil - $10.00

SMALL CLAIMS & CIVIL COURT matters are filed
on Tuesdays & Fridays - 9AM thru 11:30 AM

Any person or d/b/a who is over 18 years of
age may bring an action, for money only, in
the SMALL CLAIMS part of the Justice Court.
NO CORPORATIONS, PARTNERSHIPS, ASSOCIATIONS
OR ASSIGNEES may use the SMALL CLAIMS portion
of the Justice Court.

For each additional defendant for SMALL
CLAIMS COURT there is an additional charge
of $3.00 per defendant.

PLAINFIFF: Enter your complete name, address and daytime phone number.

NAME _____

ADDRESS _____

PHONE(S) _____

_____

DEFENDANT(S): Enter the complete name, address, daytime phone number(s)
of the party/parties you want to sue.

NAME _____

ADDRESS _____

PHONE(S) _____

What is the amount of money owed to you by the defendant(s) $_____

THE AMOUNT OWED MAY NOT EXCEED $3,000.00 for either filing.

List a brief description of why this money is owed to you by the defendant

_____

_____

_____

Where did this happen and the approximate date: _____

_____

FEE PAID: _____ cash check

DATE PAID: _____

RECEIPT #: _____

BOOKLET GIVEN ____ ESTIMATE INFO GIVEN ____

INDEX #: _____

_____
Signature of plaintiff

JRC 10/31/95

FORM 34

TOWN JUSTICE COURT
40 GREEN STREET
MOUNT KISCO, NY 10549

<u>SMALL CLAIMS APPLICATION FORM</u>

DATE _____

DEFENDANT'S NAME   _____

ADDRESS   _____

_____

PLAINTIFF'S NAME   _____

ADDRESS   _____

_____

TELEPHONE - HOME   _____

TELEPHONE - BUSINESS   _____

AMOUNT OF ACTION   _____

CAUSE OF ACTION   _____

<u>PLAINTIFF'S SIGNATURE</u>

RETURN THIS APPLICATION WITH $4.84

FORM 35

THE CITY OF WHITE PLAINS

CITY COURT

77 SOUTH LEXINGTON AVENUE
WHITE PLAINS, NY 10601
914-422-6050

JOHN F. HOLDEN, JR.
CITY JUDGE.

ROBERT JAMES FRIEDMAN
CITY JUDGE

ARTHUR C. KELLMAN
CITY JUDGE

JO ANN FRIIA
CITY JUDGE

MARIE KUCHTA
CHIEF CLERK

PATRICIA LUPI
DEPUTY CHIEF CLERK

APPLICATION TO FILE SMALL CLAIM

Filing Fee:

Small Claim - $10.00 for claims up to $1,000; $15.00 for claims from 1,000.01 - $3,000.00

Date _____

Name of Claimant _____

Address _____

_____

Telephone # _____

-against-

Name of Defendant _____

Address (Home or Business/Place of employment)

_____

_____

Amount of Claim $_____ (do not include filing fee)

Nature of Claim (include date of incident)

_____

_____

_____

_____
Signature of Claimant

FORM 36

THE CITY OF WHITE PLAINS

CITY COURT

77 SOUTH LEXINGTON AVENUE
WHITE PLAINS, NY 10601
914-422-6050

JOHN F. HOLDEN, JR.
CITY JUDGE

ROBERT JAMES FRIEDMAN
CITY JUDGE

ARTHUR C. KELLMAN
CITY JUDGE

JO ANN FRIIA
CITY JUDGE

MARIE KUCHTA
CHIEF CLERK

PATRICIA LUPI
DEPUTY CHIEF CLERK

APPLICATION TO FILE COMMERCIAL CLAIM

Filing Fee:

    Comm. Claim - $20.00 filing fee + $2.84 Postage = $22.84

Date _____

Name of Claimant _____

Address (if commercial claim, give principal office address)

_____

Telephone #_____

-against-

Name of Defendant _____

Address (Home or Business/Place of employment)

_____

_____

Amount of Claim $_____ (do not include filing fee)

Nature of Claim (include date of incident)

_____

_____

_____

Certification: (NYCCA 1803-A, UCCA 1803A, UDCA 1803-A)
I hereby certify that no more than five (5) actions or proceeding
(including the instant action or proceeding) pursuant to the
commercial claims procedure has been initiated in the courts of
this state during the present calendar month.

_____   _____
NOTARY OR COURT CLERK   Signature of Claimant

FORM 37

JOHN F. HOLDEN. JR
CITY JUDGE

ROBERT JAMES FRIEDMAN
CITY JUDGE

ARTHUR C KELLMAN
CITY JUDGE

JO ANN FRIIA
CITY JUDGE

THE CITY OF WHITE PLAINS

CITY COURT

77 SOUTH LEXINGTON AVENUE
WHITE PLAINS, NY 10601
914-422-6050

MARIE KUCHTA
CHIEF CLERK

PATRICIA LUPI
DEPUTY CHIEF CLERK

IMPORTANT NOTICE

TO ALL PHYSICIANS, DENTISTS.AND CHIROPRACTORS

SUING FOR SERVICES RENDER

1. IF YOU CONDUCT YOUR PRACTICE AS A PARTNERSHIP OR PROFESSIONAL CORPORATION, YOU MUST BRING THE ACTION AS A COMMERCIAL CLAIM. THE PARTNERSHIP, OR PROFESSIONAL CORPORATION, MAY NOT BRING MORE THAT (5) FIVE COMMERCIAL CLAIMS IN ANY CALENDAR MONTH **IN ANY COMMERCIAL CLAIMS COURT IN THE STATE.** THIS MUST BE CERTIFIED TO THE CLERK OF THE COURT.

2. A COMMERCIAL CLAIMANT SUING FOR PROFESSIONAL SERVICES MUST ALSO CERTIFY TO THE CLERK OF THE COURT THAT AT LEAST (10) DAYS, AND NOT MORE THAN 180 DAYS BEFORE FILING A CLAIMS, A **DEMAND LETTER** WAS SENT, ALONG WITH A COPY OF THE LAST BILL, TO THE PATIENT BY ORDINARY FIRST CLASS MAIL. ASK THE CLERK FOR THE REQUIRED FORM OF THIS DEMAND LETTER. **FAILURE TO SEND THE LETTER AND BILL WILL MAKE THE CLAIM JURISDICTIONAL DEFECTIVE AND IT WILL BE DISMISSED THE COURT.**

3. FINALLY, WHETHER YOU CONDUCT YOUR PRACTICE INDIVIDUALLY AS A PARTNERSHIP, OR A PROFESSIONAL CORPORATION. THE **PERSON WHO PERFORMED THE SERVICES MUST TESTIFY.** THE BOOKKEEPER, OR NURSE ALONE, WILL NOT BE PERMITTED TO TESTIFY REGARDING THE SERVICES RENDER. THE PERSON WHO PERFORMED THE SERVICES MUST ALSO TESTIFY.

CHIEF CLERK OF THE COURT

FORM 38

SMALL CLAIMS
Superior Court of New Jersey
Law Division
Special Civil Part, Small Claims Section

[This brochure is published by the Administrative Office of the Courts Civil Practice Division]

The Small Claims Section is a court in which you may sue someone (the defendant) to collect a small amount of money that you believe is owed to you. Because procedures in Small Claims are simpler than in other courts, persons usually can file and present their cases relatively quickly and inexpensively, and often without an attorney.

This brochure explains how to file a complaint, a counterclaim, or an appeal, and gives general information about Small Claims in New Jersey.

SMALL CLAIMS SECTION

Small Claims is one of three sections of the Superior Court's Special Civil Part. The other two sections are Landlord/Tenant and regular Special Civil Part. [Separate brochures are available for these sections.] Small Claims handles cases in which the demand is not more than $2,000. If the amount of money you are trying to recover is more than $2,000, but less than $10,000, your case should be filed in the regular Special Civil Part. Cases in which damages are more than $10,000 must be filed in the Law Division of the Superior Court.

If you believe you are entitled to damages greater than $2,000 but still wish to sue in Small Claims, you give up your right to recover damages over $2,000. The additional money cannot be claimed later in a separate lawsuit.

TYPICAL CLAIMS FILED

Following is a general list of claims which *can* be filed in Small Claims

- Breach of a written or oral contract.
- Return of money used as a down payment

- Property damage caused by a motor vehicle accident.
- Damage to or loss of property.
- Consumer complaints for defective merchandise or faulty workmanship.
- Payment for work performed.
- Claims based on bad checks.
- Claims for back rent.
- Return of a tenant's security deposit.

Please remember that if you believe you are entitled to damages greater than $2,000 and sue in Small Claims, you can recover damages only up to $2,000.

CLAIMS THAT CANNOT BE FILED

The following is a general list of claims that *cannot* be filed in Small Claims:

- Claims arising from professional malpractice (for example, alleged malpractice by a doctor, dentist, or lawyer).
- Claims for support or alimony from a marital or a domestic dispute.
- Claims arising from a probate matter.

WHERE TO FILE A CLAIM

A complaint must be filed in the Office of the Special Civil Part of the county where at least one defendant lives or where the defendant business is located. If there is more than one defendant, the complaint can be filed in the county where any one of the defendants lives or is located. If none of the defendants lives or is located in New Jersey, the complaint must be filed in the county where the cause of the complaint occurred.

WHO MAY FILE A CLAIM

To sue in Small Claims, a person must be 18 years of age or older. If the person suing is under the age of 18, the complaint must be filed by the parent or guardian.

FILING A COMPLAINT

A Small Claims complaint form is available from the Clerk of the Special Civil Part in the county in which the case will be filed. The complaint can be filed through the mail or in person. When filing a complaint, you, as the plaintiff, must

- Give your full name, address, and telephone number.
- To ensure proper service of the complaint, give the correct name(s) and address(es) of the person(s) named as the defendant(s) in the complaint. It is important that the defendant be properly identified as an individual, a sole proprietorship, a partnership, or a corporation.
- State the amount of money for which you are suing.
- State the reason why the defendant owes you money.
- State whether at the present time there is any other case involving both you and the other party(ies) and, if so, the name of the court.
- Sign the completed form.
- Pay the correct filing and service fees when filing the complaint with the Clerk of the Special Civil Part.

If you are filing a complaint because of a motor vehicle accident, a trial date will not be set unless the defendant notifies the Clerk of the Special Civil Part in writing within 20 (or 35) days from the date the complaint was served that the case will be defended in court. [Defendants living or located outside New Jersey have 35 days to respond to a complaint.] If the defendant responds in writing within the 20 (or 35) days, a trial date will be scheduled. All parties will be notified by the court.

If the defendant does not respond within the 20 (or 35) days, the plaintiff may have a "judgment by default" entered. Through a judgment by default, the court decides the amount of money, if any, to be awarded to a plaintiff because the defendant did not come to court or respond to the complaint in time.

If the complaint is for money damages caused by a motor vehicle accident and the judgment requires a defendant to pay $500 or more, the defendant must pay within 60 days. If the defendant does not pay within the 60 days, the plaintiff may request through the Clerk of the Special Civil Part that the Division of Motor Vehicles stop the defendant's driving privileges until the judgment is paid.

FILING FEES

The cost for filing a complaint in Small Claims is:

- $12.00 for one defendant.
- $2.00 for each additional defendant.
- $3.00 for each defendant served by certified and regular mail. [A fee for mileage may be charged instead of the $3.00 mailing fee if the complaint is served personally by a court officer. Staff of the Special Civil Part can inform you of the mileage fee, if any.]

If you are poor, you may apply to the court to qualify as an indigent and your filing fees may be waived by the judge.

FILING A COUNTERCLAIM

If you have been named as a defendant in a case and you believe the plaintiff (the person who filed the complaint) owes *you* money, you may file a counterclaim. To file a counterclaim, follow the same procedure (outlined above) for filing a complaint, but be sure to do it before the date listed for trial in the summons.

PREPARATION FOR TRIAL

Plaintiff

If you are the plaintiff, you must prove your case. Arrange to have any witnesses and records you need to prove your case at the trial. *A written statement, even if under oath, is not admissible in court.* Only actual testimony in court of what the witness(es) heard or saw will be allowed. Prepare your questions in advance.

Bring to court records of any transactions that may help you prove your case. Such records may include:

- Canceled checks, money orders, sales receipts.
- Bills, contracts, estimates, leases.
- Letters.
- Photographs.
- Other documents proving your claim.

If you are able to settle the case with the defendant before the trial date, call the Special Civil Part Clerk's Office immediately.

Defendant

If you are the defendant, you should prepare your side of the case as the plaintiff prepared his or her case. Bring all necessary witnesses and documents to court with you on the scheduled trial date.

You must come to court at the time and date shown on the summons. If you do not, a default judgment may be entered against you, and you may have to pay the money the plaintiff says you owe.

If you are able to settle the case with the plaintiff before the trial date, call the court immediately to confirm that the case was marked settled.

THE DAY OF TRIAL

The plaintiff and the defendant must come to court at the time and date stated on the summons, unless otherwise notified by the court. Bring all witnesses and evidence needed to present your case.

On the day scheduled for trial, the court may help you settle your case through mediation by a trained mediator. The mediator will try to help the plaintiff and the defendant reach a satisfactory agreement. The mediator is not a judge. If a settlement cannot be reached, your case likely will be heard by the judge on the same day.

If you win your case, consult the Judgment Collection brochure on how to collect your judgment.

RIGHT TO APPEAL

If you, as a plaintiff or a defendant, disagree with the court's decision, you may appeal the case to the Appellate Division of the Superior Court within 45 days from the date of judgment. You must file a Notice of Appeal, a copy of the Request for Transcript, and a Case Information Statement within the 45 days with the Clerk of the Appellate Division (located at the Hughes Justice Complex, Trenton) and deliver copies to:

- All parties to the case who appeared in court.
- The Clerk of the Special Civil Part from which the appeal is taken.
- The judge who decided the case.

You must pay a filing fee of $175 with the Notice of Appeal and deposit $300 with the Clerk of the Appellate Division within 30 days of the Notice of Appeal. This deposit may be used to pay settlement or court costs if the appeal is lost. If the appeal is successful, the deposit will be refunded.

You also must obtain a transcript (a copy of the record of what happened in court) of the trial. The request for a transcript should be made to the Office of the Clerk of the Special Civil Part in the county in which the case was tried. You must deposit with the Clerk the estimated cost of the transcript (as determined by the court reporter, Clerk, or agency preparing it) or $300 for each day or part of a day of the trial. You must file three copies of the transcript with the Office of the Clerk of the Appellate Division. Questions concerning an appeal should be directed to the Office of the Clerk of the Appellate Division at (609)-292-4822, or to an attorney.

SMALL CLAIMS

DEMAND_____

SUMMONS_____

MILEAGE_____

TOTAL_____

From Plaintiff:

_____
Name

_____
Address

_____
City   State   Zip Code

_____
Phone #
                    VS.
To Defendant(s):

_____
Name

_____
Address

_____

$_____, plus costs

_____

_____

_____

_____

DOCKET NUMBER

BERGEN COUNTY SMALL CLAIMS
BERGEN COUNTY COURT HOUSE
10 MAIN STREET, ROOM 430
HACKENSACK, NJ 07601

Phone #'s 646-2240 or
          646-2236

STATE OF NEW JERSEY
SUPERIOR COURT, LAW DIVISION
SPECIAL CIVIL PART
BERGEN COUNTY
SMALL CLAIMS SECTION

CIVIL ACTION

COMPLAINT
( )   Rent
( )   Tort other than MV
( )   Contract
( )   Security Deposit

COMPLAINT

I HEREBY CERTIFY THAT THE MATTER IN CONTROVERSY IS NOT THE SUBJECT OF ANY OTHER COURT ACTION OR ARBITRATION PROCEEDING NOW PENDING OR CONTEMPLATED, AND THAT NO OTHER PARTIES SHOULD BE JOINED IN THIS ACTION

DATE:_____   _____
                                  PLAINTIFF'S SIGNATURE
for office use only: _____
                    SUMMONS
THE STATE OF NEW JERSEY TO:
DEFENDANT, YOU ARE HEREBY SUMMONED TO APPEAR TO ANSWER THE ABOVE COMPLAINT

ON _____ AT 9:00 A.M., 1:30 P.M.
TO BE HELD AT THE BERGEN COUNTY COURTHOUSE, HACKENSACK, NEW JERSEY

_____   _____
   (DATE FILED)   CLERK OF THE SPECIAL CIVIL PART

FORM 40 SIDE 1

ALL PLAINTIFF(S) AND DEFENDANT(S) MUST BRING ALL WITNESSES, PHOTOS, ESTIMATES DOCUMENTS, OTHER EVIDENCE AND AN INTERPRETER, IF NECESSARY, TO THE HEARING. SUBPOENA FORMS ARE AVAILABLE AT THE CLERK'S OFFICE TO REQUIRE THE ATTENDANCE OF WITNESSES. PLAINTIFF WILL USE AN INTERPRETER IN THE _____ LANGUAGE AT THE HEARING.

IF YOU DO NOT HAVE AN ATTORNEY, YOU MAY CALL THE FOLLOWING: 201-488-0044, FOR THE BERGEN COUNTY BAR ASSOCIATION, LAWYER REFERRAL SERVICE.

IF YOU CANNOT AFFORD AN ATTORNEY, YOU MAY CALL THE FOLLOWING: 201-487-2166 FOR THE BERGEN COUNTY LEGAL SERVICES.

SI USTED NO PUEDE PAGAR UN ABOGADO, USTED PUEDE LLAMAR A SERVISIO LEGAIES TELEFONO NO. 201-487-2166

FOR OFFICE USE ONLY

RETURN TO: PROCESS SERVER'S RETURN

P - PERSONAL SERVICE   DATE TIME

M.O.F. - MEMBER OF FAMILY   P_____ M F

CORP. - CORPORATION   P_____ M F

M - MALE   M.O.F._____ H W D S O

F -- FEMALE   M.O.F._____ H W D S O

H W D S O -- HUSBAND/WIFE   CORP._____ P.I.C. OFF.
             DAUGHTER/SON
             OTHER   CORP._____ P.I.C. OFF.

                                 OTHER_____

P.I.C. OFF. -- PERSON IN   OTHER_____
               CHARGE/ OFFICER
                                 DEPT_____

                                 I HERBY CERTIFY THE ABOVE RETURN TO BE
                                 TRUE AND ACCURATE.

                                 _____
                                 COURT OFFICER

SMALL CLAIMS COMPLAINT

Name and Address of Attorney
for Plaintiff:

Superior Court Of New Jersey
Law Division - Special Civil Part
Hudson County
595 Newark Avenue - Seventh Floor
Jersey City , N. J.   07306
201-795-6680

Phone No. _____

From Plaintiff:

Name _____

Address _____

City _____ Zip _____

Phone No. _____

SUPERIOR COURT OF NEW JERSEY
LAW DIVISION,
SPECIAL CIVIL PART

HUDSON COUNTY

SMALL CLAIMS SECTION

V.

CIVIL ACTION

COMPLAINT
( ) Contract
( ) Security Deposit
( ) Rent
( ) Tort other than motor vehicle
     (check only one)

To Defendant :

Name _____

Address _____

City _____ Zip _____

Phone No. _____

COMPLAINT

$_____ , plus costs

Plaintiff says: _____

_____

_____

IMPORTANT: Plaintiffs and defendants must bring all witnesses, photos,
documents, and other evidence to the hearing. Subpoena forms are available
at the Clerk's office to require the attendance of witnesses. Plaintiff will
need an interpreter fluent in the _____ language.

I certify that the matter in controversy is not the subject of any other
court action or arbitration proceeding, now pending or contemplated, and that
no other parties should be joined in this action.

Dated: _____

Plaintiff's Signature
_____

Plaintiff's Name-Typed, Stamped,
or Printed
_____

smallcl.frm

PLEASE NOTIFY COURT OF DISABILITY ACCOMMODATION NEEDS.

SMALL CLAIMS SUMMONS
(Contract – Security Deposit – Rent – Tort)

THE STATE OF NEW JERSEY TO DEFENDANT:

Docket No. _____

NAME: _____

ADDRESS: _____

CITY _____ ZIP _____

HEARING DATE _____

HUDSON COUNTY SUPERIOR COURT
SPECIAL CIVIL PART
595 NEWARK AVENUE – 7TH FLOOR
JERSEY CITY, N.J. 07306
201-795-6680

Demand : $ _____
Summons: $ _____
Service: $ _____
Total : $ _____

DEFENDANT, YOU ARE HEREBY SUMMONED to answer the Civil complaint of the plaintiff at a hearing on _____ at _____ at this court. If you fail to appear and defend against the complaint, a judgement may be entered against you for the relief demanded, plus interest and costs of suit. Please be advised that this matter may be subject to mediation or arbitration.

Date: _____

_____
Clerk of the Special Civil Part

If you do not have an attorney, you may call the following: 201-798-2727 for the Hudson County Lawyer Referral Service.
Si ud. puede pagar los servios de un abogado, pero no conoce a ninguno, puede llamar a las oficinas del Servicio de Referencias de Abogados de la Asociacion de Abogados del Condado local (Telefono: 201-798-2727).
If you cannot afford an attorney, you may call the following: 201-792-6363 for the Hudson County Legal Services.
Si ud. no puede pagar un abogado, ud. puede llamar a Servicios Legales Tele. 201-792-6363.

COURT OFFICER'S RETURN OF SERVICE

Docket No. _____

Date Served _____   Time Served _____
WM   WF   BM   BF   OTHER
Height _____ Weight _____ Age _____ Hair _____

Name of Person Served _____ Relationship _____

Description of Premises _____

I hereby certify the above return to be true and accurate.

_____
Court Officer

CERTIFICATION OF MAILING

I, _____ , hereby certify that on _____ , I mailed a copy of the within summons and complaint by regular and certified mail-return receipt requested.

_____
Employee Signature

summons.scl

FORM 41 SIDE 2

CERTIFICATION OF NON SERVICE

1. Case: Ted Rothstein   vs. Dinah Padebil

    Docket No. SC 003120

2.

Date	Time	Date	Time
11/27/96	2:30 PM	12/2/96	12 NOON
11/30/96	9:30 AM	12/9/96	7:00 PM

3. Reason Process cannot be served:

    (✓)   Tried four times -- no answer

    ( )   Defendant does not reside on premises

    ( )   Defendant receives mail at address, but doesn't reside there

    ( )   Cannot gain entrance: door locked -- fence

    ( )   Dangerous animal prevents service

    ( )   Defendant owns premises, but does not reside there

    ( )   Need Apartment number -- there is no directory or superintendent present
          to lead to defendant

    ( )   Cannot serve at place of business -- was denies access by:
          (Name and describe person)_____
          _____
          _____

4. The premises where service was attempted is described as:_____
    _____
    _____

5. Other:

I CERTIFY THAT THE FOREGOING STATEMENTS MADE BY ME ARE TRUE. I AM AWARE
THAT IF ANY OF THE FOREGOING STATEMENTS MADE BY ME ARE WILLFULLY FALSE
I AM SUBJECT TO PUNISHMENT

_____
DISTRICT COURT OFFICER

WHITE -- ATTORNEY
YELLOW __ OFFICE

FORM 42

SUPERIOR COURT OF NEW JERSEY
SPECIAL CIVIL PART MILEAGE LIST

MUNICIPALITY	FEE	MUNICIPALITY	FEE	MUNICIPALITY	FEE	MUNICIPALITY	FEE
Bartley	8.00	Greystone Park	10.00	Middle Valley	2.00	Port Morris	7.00
Beattystown	11.00	Hackettstown	5.00	Millington	10.00	Prospect Point	9.00
Berkshire Valley	7.00	Hanover - East Hanover	11.00	Milton	4.00	Rainbow Lakes	3.00
Boonton	4.00	Harding Twp.	5.00	Mine Hill	3.00	Randolph	4.00
Boonton Township	6.00	Hibernia	6.00	Montville	6.00	Richard Mine	6.00
Brady Park	9.00	Ironia	2.00	Morris Plains	6.00	Riverdale	10.00
Brookside	5.00	Jefferson	2.00	Morristown/Morris Township	8.00	Rockaway	4.00
Budd Lake	8.00	Kenvil	8.00	Mt. Arlington	6.00	Rockaway Township	5.00
Butler	8.00	Kinnelon	5.00	Mt. Fern	9.00	Rockaway Valley	5.00
Cedar Knolls	2.00	Lake Denmark	4.00	Mt. Freedom	7.00	Roxbury	5.00
Chatham	3.00	Lake Hiawatha	6.00	Mt. Hope	5.00	Schooley's Mountain	10.00
Chatham Township	6.00	Lake Hopatcong	2.00	Mt. Kemble Lake	8.00	Shongum	4.00
Chester-Chester Twp.	7.00	Lake Intervale	8.00	Mt. Olive	4.00	Smoke Rise	9.00
Convent	2.00	Lake Rogerene	5.00	Mt. Tabor	5.00	Stephensburg	12.00
Cozy Lake	11.00	Lake Shawnee	4.00	Mountain Lakes	8.00	Stirling	5.00
Denville	4.00	Lake Telemark	9.00	Naughright	6.00	Succasunna	5.00
Dover	4.00	Landing	7.00	Netcong	7.00	Towaco	6.00
Drakestown	9.00	Ledgewood	9.00	Newfoundland	6.00	Victory Gardens	4.00
Espanong(Lk Hoptacong)	8.00	Lincoln Park	3.00	New Vernon	7.00	Washington Township	10.00
Fairmount	10.00	Long Valley	9.00	Nolan's Point	10.00	Washington Valley	2.00
Flanders	7.00	East Mill Rd (Long Valley)	11.00	Oak Ridge	8.00	Waterloo	8.00
Florham Park	3.00	Longwood Lake	4.00	Parsippany-Troy Hills	10.00	Weldon	9.00
Gillette	5.00	Madison	8.00	Pequannock-Pompton Plains	3.00	Wharton	6.00
Gladstone	7.00	Marcella	6.00	Picatinny	7.00	Whippany	2.00
Green Pond	8.00	Mendham-Mendham Twp.	6.00	Pine Brook	5.00	White Meadow Lake	5.00
Green Village	3.00	Meyersville	10.00	Pleasant Grove	5.00	Woodport	8.00

MILEAGE CHARGE FOR SERVICE OF SUMMONS -- MORIS COUNTY

R. 08/92 Civil Div. # 519

SUPERIOR COURT OF NEW JERSEY
SPECIAL CIVIL PART, HUDSON COUNTY

ON ( ) CONTRACT ( ) TORT ( ) MV

DOCKET NO.

STATEMENT FOR DOCKETING

Plaintiff's Attorney

Plaintiff (s)

--against--

Defendant (s)

Judgment in the above entitled cause was entered in the Superior Court
Special Civil Part, Hudson County in favor of the Plaintiff (s) and against
the defendant (s)

An Execution was issued on ___/___/___ .   Judgment date ___/___/___
and was returned on ___/___/___ .   Judgment amount $_____
monies received by Constable $_____   Costs & Atty. fees $_____
total credits $_____   Execution $_____
                                             Credits, if any $_____
An Execution was issued on ___/___/___   Transcript $_____
and was returned ___/___/___
monies received by Constable $_____
total Credits $_____   Total $_____

I hereby certify that the foregoing reflects the judgment and costs of
record in this court, as of this time.

DATED: _____   _____

            SEAL   CLERK, Special Civil Part

I, the undersigned, am (attorney for)   Total Judgment due $_____
the above named Plaintiff, certify that   Total Credits $_____
at the present time there is due upon   Sub Total $_____
the above mentioned judgment, which is   Interest $_____
about to be docketed in the Superior   Total due this date S_____
Court of New Jersey, as herein set forth.   (being sum less than ten
                                             dollars)

I CERTIFY that the foregoing statements made by me are true. I am aware
that if any of the foregoing statement made by me are willfully false, I
am subject to punishment.

DATED: _____   _____

FORM 44

Attorney for Plaintiff

BERGEN COUNTY SPECIAL CIVIL PART
LAW DIVISION, SUPERIOR COURT
B.C. JUSTICE CENTER ROOM 430
HACKENSACK, N.J. 07601

DOCKET NUMBER _____

CIVIL ACTION

NOTICE OF MOTION FOR WAGE EXECUTION

Plaintiff(s))
)
)
vs.   )
)
)
)
)
Defendant(s))

TO:

TAKE NOTICE that application is being made by the Plaintiff(s) to the above named Court, at

that a WAGE EXECUTION issue against your salary, to be served on your employer,

for: (a) 10% of your gross salary when the same shall equal or exceed $127.50 per week; or (b) 25% of your disposable earnings for that week; or (c) the amount, if any, by which your disposable weekly earnings exceed $127.50 per week, whichever shall be the least. Disposable earnings are defined as that portion of the earnings remaining after the deduction from gross earnings of any amounts erequired by law to be withheld. In the event the disposable earnings so defvened are $127.50 or less, no amount shall be withheld under this Execution. In no event shall more than 10% of gross salary be withheld.

You may notify the Clerk of said Court and the Attorneys for plaintiff, whose address appears above, in writing, within ten days after service of this notice upon you, why such an Order should not be entered, and thereafter the application for the Order will be set down for a hearing of which you will receive notice of the time and place.

If you do not notify the Clerk and the plaintiff, in writing, you will receive no further notice and an Order will be entered as a matter of course.

_____
Attorney for Plaintiff(s)

PROOF OF SERVICE. I served the within Notice upon defendant, on the date stated on the Notice, by certified mail, return receipt requested and by ordinary mail with postage prepaid thereon, at a United States Post Office at   addressed to the defendant(s) last known address, as above set forth. I certify that the foregoing statements made by me are true. I am aware that if any of the foregoing statements made by me are willfully false, I am subject to punishment.

DATED: 19   _____

FORM 45 SIDE 1

Plaintiff _____

_____

        VS.

Defendant _____

_____

STATE OF NEW JERSEY
SUPERIOR COURT, LAW DIVISION
BERGEN COUNTY - SPECIAL CIVIL PART

Docket # _____

ORDER, CERTIFICATION & EXECUTION
AGAINST EARNINGS PURSUANT TO
15 U.S.C. 1673 & N.J.S.A. 2A:17-56

WRIT # _____

NAME & ADDRESS OF EMPLOYER ORDERED TO MAKE DEDUCTIONS:

_____

The Employer is ordered to deduct from the earnings which the designated defendant receives and to pay over to the Court Officer named below, the LESSER of the following: (a) 10% of the gross weekly pay; or (b) 25% of disposable earnings for that week; or (c) the amount, if any, by which the designated defendant's disposable weekly earnings exceed $127.50 per week until the total amount due has been deducted or the complete termination of employment. Upon either of these events, an immediate accounting is to be made to the Court Officer. Disposable earnings are defined as that portion of the earnings remaining after the deduction from gross earnings of any amounts required by law to be withheld. In the event the disposable earnings so defined are $127.50 or less, no amount shall be withheld under this execution. In no event shall more than 10% of gross salary be withheld.
ACCORDING TO LAW, NO EMPLOYER MAY TERMINATE AN EMPLOYEE BECAUSE OF A GARNISHMENT.

CONSTABLE: _____ /FEE: _____]DATE: _____

JUDGMENT DATE: _____ :

Judgment Amount...........$ _____
Costs & Atty's Fees........$ _____
Subsequent Costs..........$ _____
TOTAL....................$ _____
Credits, if any...........$ _____
Subtotal A...............$ _____
Interest..................$ _____
Execution Costs & Mileage.$ _____
Cost of Application.......$ _____
Subtotal B...............$ _____
Court Officer Fee.........$ _____
(10% of first $5,000. - 5% of excess)
TOTAL DUE THIS DATE: $ _____

I CERTIFY that the foregoing statements made by me are true. I am aware that if any of the foregoing statements made by me are willfully false, I am subject to punishment.

DATE: _____

Plaintiff's Attorney:

_____

_____

_____

_____
PRESIDING JUDGE

_____
CHIEF CASE MANAGER

MAKE PAYMENTS AT LEAST MONTHLY TO COURT
OFFICER AS SET FORTH:

_____
COURT OFFICER

_____
Address

I RETURN this execution to the Court
[ ] UNSATISFIED _____

[ ] SATISFIED   [ ] PARTLY SATISFIED

AMOUNT COLLECTED.........$ _____
FEE DEDUCTED.............$ _____
AMOUNT DUE ATTORNEY......$ _____

DATE: _____ / _____
          COURT OFFICER

FORM 45 SIDE 2

Attorney(s):
Office Address & Tel. No.:

Attorney for:
_____
Plaintiff(s)

_____

vs.

_____

Defendant(s)
To (Name of Judgment-Debtor & Address):

SUPERIOR COURT OF NEW JERSEY
LAW DIVISION, SPECIAL CIVIL PART
County

Docket No.

CIVIL ACTION

**NOTICE OF APPLICATION
FOR WAGE EXECUTION**

SPECIMEN

TAKE NOTICE that an application is to be made by the undersigned to the above-named court, located at

New Jersey for a Wage Execution Order to issue against your salary, to be served on your employer,

(name and address of employer),
for: (a) 10% of your gross salary when the same shall equal or exceed the amount of $127.50 per week; or (b) 25% of your disposable earnings for that week; or (c) the amount, if any, by which your disposable weekly earnings exceed $127.50, whichever shall be the least. Disposable earnings are defined as that portion of the earnings remaining after the deduction from the gross earnings of any amounts required by law to be withheld. In the event the disposable earnings so defined are $127.50 or less, no amount shall be withheld under this execution. In no event shall more than 10% of gross salary be withheld. Your employer may not discharge, discipline or discriminate against you because your earnings have been subjected to garnishment.

You may notify the Clerk of the Court and the attorneys for judgment-creditor, whose address appears above, in writing, within ten days after service of this notice upon you, why such an Order should not be issued, and thereafter the application for the Order will be set down for a hearing of which you will receive notice of the date, time and place.

If you do not notify the Clerk of the Court and judgment-creditor attorney in writing of your objection, you will receive no further notice and the Order will be signed by the Judge as a matter of course.

CERTIFICATION OF SERVICE

I served the within Notice upon the judgment-debtor
on this date by sending it simultaneously by regular and certified mail, return receipt requested, to the judgment-debtor's last known address, set forth above. I certify that the foregoing statements made by me are true. I am aware that if any of the foregoing statements made by me are wilfully false, I am subject to the punishment.

Date: ....
                                                                Attorney for Judgment-Creditor or Judgment-Creditor Pro Se

Blumbergs Law Products   T 839— Notice of Application for Wage Execution, N.J. Court Rules, App. XI-1, 9-94   © 1994 BY JULIUS BLUMBERG, INC., PUBLISHER, NYC 10013

FORM 46 SIDE 1

SUPERIOR COURT OF NEW JERSEY
LAW DIVISION, SPECIAL CIVIL PART

County

Street Address of Court

Town, NJ ZIP:
Tel. No. of Court:

Docket No.:

Plaintiff:

- vs. -

Designated Defendant:
Address:
Name and Address of Employer Ordered to Make Deductions:

Order, Certification and Execution

against Earnings pursuant to

15 U.S.C. 1673 and *N.J.S.A. 2A:17-56*

The employer is ordered to deduct from the earnings which the designated defendant receives and to pay over to the court officer named below, the *lesser* of the following: (a) 10% of the gross weekly pay; or (b) 25% of disposable earnings for that week; or (c) the amount, if any, by which the designated defendant's disposable weekly earnings exceed $127.50 per week, until the total amount due has been deducted or the complete termination of employment. Upon either of these events, an immediate accounting is to be made to the court officer. Disposable earnings are defined as that portion of the earnings remaining after the deduction from gross earnings of any amounts required by law to be withheld. In the event the disposable earnings so defined are $127.50 or less, no amount shall be withheld under this execution. In no event shall more than 10% of gross salary be withheld. According to law, no employer may terminate an employee because of a garnishment.

Judgment Date .... _____

Judgment Amount .... $ _____

Costs and Attorney Fees ....

Subseque[nt] [C]o[sts] ....

Total ....

Credits, [if a]ny ...

Subtotal A ....

Interest ....

Executio[n cost] [an]d m[ileage] ....

Costs of Application ....

Subtotal B .... • _____

Court Officer Fee (10% of first $5,000;

5% of excess) .... _____

Total due this date .... $ _____

SPECIMEN

Date: _____

_____
Judge

_____
Clerk of Special Civil Part

Make payments at least monthly to Court Officer as set forth:

_____
Court Officer

_____
Address

ℐ **Return** this execution to the Court

☐ Unsatisfied _____
☐ Satisfied   ☐ Partly Satisfied

Amount Collected .... $ _____
Fee Deducted .... $ _____
Amount Due to Atty .... $ _____

ℐ **Certify** that the foregoing statements made by me are true. I am aware that if any of the foregoing statements made by me are willfully false, I am subject to punishment.

Date: _____

By: _____
    (Typed name of signator)

Firm Name: _____

Address: _____

Date: _____

_____
Court Officer

Blumbergs Law Products **T 847—** Order Certification, and Execution Against Earnings: Superior Court N.J. Court Rules, 1969, Appendix XI-J, 9-94

JULIUS BLUMBERG, INC.,
PUBLISHER, NYC 10013

FORM 46 SIDE 2

NOTICE OF APPEAL

PLEASE PRINT OR TYPE

SUPERIOR COURT OF NEW JERSEY - APPELLATE DIVISION

TITLE OF ACTION AS CAPTIONED BELOW:

(1)

(2)

ATTORNEY OF RECORD

NAME _____

ADDRESS _____

_____

PHONE NO. _____

ATTORNEY FOR _____

ON APPEAL FROM:

(3A) _____
TRIAL COURT/STATE AGENCY

(3B) _____
TRIAL DOCKET OR INDICTMENT NUMBER

(3C) _____
TRIAL COURT JUDGE
CIVIL [ ]   CRIMINAL [ ]   JUVENILE [ ]

NOTICE IS HEREBY GIVEN THAT **(4)** _____

(5) APPEALS TO THE SUPERIOR COURT OF NJ, APPELLATE DIVISION, FROM THE JUDGMENT [ ]   ORDER [ ]

OTHER (SPECIFY) [ ] _____

ENTERED IN THIS ACTION ON **(6)** _____, IN FAVOR OF **(7)** _____.
(DATE)

(8) IF APPEAL IS FROM LESS THAN THE WHOLE, SPECIFY WHAT PARTS OR PARAGRAPHS ARE BEING APPEALED:

_____

_____

_____

_____

(9) ARE ALL ISSUES AS TO ALL PARTIES DISPOSED OF IN THE ACTION BEING APPEALED?   YES [ ]   NO [ ]

IF NOT, IS THERE A CERTIFICATION OF FINAL JUDGMENT ENTERED PURSUANT TO R. 4:42-2?   YES [ ]   NO [ ]

(10) PRIORITY UNDER R. 1:2-5   YES [ ]   NO [ ]   APPLICABLE SECTION UNDER THE RULE _____.

_____

(11) IN CRIMINAL, QUASI-CRIMINAL, AND JUVENILE CASES . . . NOT INCARCERATED [ ]   INCARCERATED [ ]

CONFINED AT _____.

GIVE A CONCISE STATEMENT OF THE OFFENSE AND OF THE JUDGMENT, DATE ENTERED AND ANY

SENTENCE OR DISPOSITION IMPOSED _____

_____

_____

_____

_____

(OVER)

FORM 47 SIDE 1

ATTACH ADDITIONAL SHEETS IF NECESSARY

(12) 1 NOTICE OF APPEAL HAS BEEN SERVED ON:

NAME	DATE OF SERVICE	TYPE OF SERVICE
TRIAL COURT JUDGE _____	_____	_____
TRIAL COURT CLERK/STATE AGENCY _____	_____	_____
ATTORNEY GENERAL OR GOVERNMENTAL OFFICE UNDER R. 2:5-1(h) _____	_____	_____

OTHER PARTIES:

NAME AND DESIGNATION	ATTORNEY NAME, ADDRESS & TELEPHONE NO.	DATE OF SERVICE	TYPE OF SERVICE
(SERVE THIS PARTY WITH TRANSCRIPT)	_____	_____	_____
_____	_____	_____	_____
_____	_____	_____	_____
_____	_____	_____	_____
_____	_____	_____	_____

I HEREBY CERTIFY THAT I HAVE SERVED A COPY OF THIS NOTICE OF APPEAL ON EACH OF THE PERSONS REQUIRED AS INDICATED ABOVE.

_____ _____
(DATE)   SIGNATURE OF ATTORNEY OF RECORD

(13) 2 PRESCRIBED TRANSCRIPT REQUEST FORM HAS BEEN SERVED ON:
        (ALSO INDICATE IF SOUND RECORDED)

NAME	DATE OF SERVICE	AMOUNT OF DEPOSIT
ADMINISTRATIVE OFFICE OF THE COURTS CHIEF, COURT REPORTING SERVICES _____	_____	_____
COURT REPORTER'S SUPERVISOR/ CLERK OF COURT OR AGENCY _____	_____	_____
COURT REPORTER _____	_____	_____
_____	_____	_____

I HEREBY CERTIFY THAT I SERVED THE PRESCRIBED COURT TRANSCRIPT REQUEST FORM ON EACH OF THE ABOVE PERSONS AND PAID THE DEPOSIT AS REQUIRED BY R. 2:5-3(d).

_____ _____
(DATE)   SIGNATURE OF ATTORNEY OF RECORD

(14) 3

I HEREBY CERTIFY THAT:

[ ] THERE IS NO VERBATIM RECORD.

[ ] TRANSCRIPT IS IN THE POSSESSION OF THE ATTORNEY OF RECORD.

[ ] A MOTION FOR ABBREVIATION OF TRANSCRIPT HAS BEEN FILED WITH THE COURT OR AGENCY BELOW.

[ ] A MOTION FOR FREE TRANSCRIPT HAS BEEN FILED WITH THE COURT BELOW.

ADMIN-35
3/96

_____ _____
(DATE)   SIGNATURE OF ATTORNEY OF RECORD

FORM 47 SIDE 2

Pro se

Docket # 12345/97

Name, Address & Telephone #
Ted Rothstein
85 Remsen St
Brooklyn, NY 11201
(718) 852-1551

NOTICE OF MOTION
for
Summary Judgment

Plaintiff
Ted Rothstein
vs.

Dinah Padebil
Defendant

TO: Dinah Padebil the defendant

Take Notice that the undersigned will apply to the above named court at Middlesex County Court House, Kennedy Square, New Brunswick, New Jersey for an order to enter in favor of the Plaintiff a Summary Judgment
                                                                                 upon the following grounds:

A judgment after trial was entered in favor of the Plaintiff in New York State. The judgment has not been stayed

[Send a copy of the Motion for Summary Judgment to the defendant certified mail, return receipt requested.
Send a copy of the Motion and 3 copies of the Order to the Office of the Clerk Special Civil Part]

you may notify the clerk of the Court and the undersigned, in writing within <u>five</u> days after service upon you of this Motion, <u>ten</u> days if Motion is for Summary Judgment, a new trial, or to vacate judgement, that the responding party objects to the entry of the order. The basis of the objection shall be stated with particularity and oral argument may be requested, in which event the clerk may set the Motion down for hearing.

CLERKS ADDRESS Special Civil Part
                P.O. Box 1146
                New Brunswick, New Jersey 08903

Ted Rothstein
Signature

DATED: January 1   1997

If you require any accommodations as a result of a disability, please call (908) 745-3211

FORM 48

Superior Court
Middlesex County
Special Civil Part, Small Claims

_____

TED ROTHSTEIN,

                           PLAINTIFF,   AFFIDAVIT IN
                                                   SUPPORT OF MOTION
                                                   For Summary Judgment
                           - AGAINST -.   DOCKET # SC 12345/96

DINAH PAEDEBILL

                           DEFENDANT.
_____x

SIR(S):
            PLEASE TAKE NOTICE, that Ted Rothstein says the following under penalty of
perjury.

            The attached judgment was not obtained by default in appearance of the defendant or
by confession of judgment. The judgment is unsatisfied in whole (in part). The amount
remaining unpaid is $ _____. The enforcement of this judgment has not been stayed. The
last know address of the debtor is _____.

Dated: Brooklyn, New York,   Affirmed:
        Date_____

                                              _____
                                              Ted Rothstein
_____   PRO SE
Signature of Notary   35 Remsen Street
                                              Brooklyn, NY
_____   (718) 852-1551
Date

FORM 49

Pro se

Name, Address & Telephone #

Ted Rothstein
35 Remsen St.
Brooklyn, NY 11201
(718) 852-1551

_____
Plaintiff

Ted Rothstein
vs.

Dinah Padebit Defendant

Superior Court
Middlesex County, NJ
Special Civil Part

Docket #1234/97

ORDER

This matter having been brought before the Court by ___Ted Rothstein___ the ___Plaintiff___ in this matter by way of motion seeking an order to ___enter in favor of the Plaintiff a Summary judgment :___ ___Note - copy of judgment from New York State___

and the court having reviewed the moving✱ papers, and for good cause having been shown:

It is on this ___1st___ day of ___January___ 199 ___7___

ORDERED that ___Judge's decision is entered here___ .

Further ordered, that a copy of the within order be served upon all parties within seven (7) days from the date hereof.

✱ Legal note : moving papers refer to the Notice of Motion and other papers which support and accompany the Notice of Motion in certain cases.

___Signature of Judge___
Judge

[Send 3 copies of this Order, and 1 copy of the Notice of Motion to the office of the Clerk of the Special Civil Part]

♿ If you require any accommodations as a result of a disability, please call (908) 981-2046

FORM 50

STATE OF CONNECTICUT

SMALL CLAIMS

SUPERIOR COURT G.A. #1

 123 Hoyt St., Stamford, Connecticut 06905   (203)965-5236

INSTRUCTIONS TO THE PLAINTIFF

1. Form must be <u>TYPED</u> and legible. Do not white out any part of claim. Claim must be <u>filed</u> either where the plaintiff resides, the defendant resides or where the transaction took place.
2. You must list first name for defendants (individuals) and not abbreviations, initials or Mr. or Mrs.
3. Box must be checked as to ind., part., or corp.
4. You must include phone numbers, if known.
5. Form must be notarized by you in 2 places <u>BEFORE</u> presenting it to the clerks office.
6. If you are suing an individual, you must fill out the military affidavit and it must be notarized.
7. You must return your correctly completed form to the clerks office with a check in the amount of $30.00 made payable to Superior Court. Make sure you include <u>copies</u> of all bills, contracts or estimates in the amount you are suing for.
8. We will process your claim and will assign a docket number and an answer date which is the date the defendant has to respond to the court in writing with their answer.
9. If the defendant sends us an answer, we will send you a copy. If the defendant contests the claim in his answer, we will set the case down for a court hearing. If the defendant sends us a stipulation, we will send you a copy. If the defendant does not file their answer with us by the answer date, a default judgment <u>may</u> be entered in your favor.
10. You can call the clerks office no sooner than <u>FIVE WORKING DAYS</u> after the answer date if you have not received any correspondence from us.
11. If a court date is set, be fully prepared to defend your suit.
12. You will receive your judgment papers in the mail within two weeks of your trial.
13. If payment is not made in accordance with the terms of the judgment you may file an execution (wage, bank or property), if you know where their assets are. If you do not know where the debtors assets are located, one option is to file an interrogatory, which has a filing fee of $5.00. The cost for filing a wage or property execution is $10.00. All fees paid are made payable to Superior Court.
14. If there is no response to the interrogatory, you may have an examination of judgment debtor and a subpoena issued. You and the defendant will be given a court date, where both parties <u>MUST</u> appear, in which the defendant must explain to the court why the judgment has not been paid and where their assets are.

FORM 51 SIDE 1

Geographical Area Court Locations
Superior Court

Court	Address	Telephone
G.A. 1	115 Hoyt Street (P.O. Box 3281, Ridgeway Station) Stamford, CT 06905	965-5237
G.A. 2	172 Golden Hill Street Bridgeport, CT 06604	579-6562
G.A. 3	146 White Street Danbury, CT 06810	797-4050
G.A. 4	7 Kendrick Avenue Waterbury, CT 06702	596-4050
G.A. 5	106 Elizabeth Street Derby, CT 06418	735-9654
G.A. 6	121 Elm Street New Haven, CT 06510	789-7465
G.A. 7	54 West Main Street Meriden, CT 06450	238-6128
G.A. 9	1 Court Street, Civil Clerk's Office 2nd Floor Middletown, CT 06457-3374	343-6477
G.A. 10	112 Broad Street New London, CT 06320	443-8346
G.A. 11	Municipal Building 172 Main Street Danielson, CT 06239	774-0078
G.A. 12	410 Center Street Manchester, CT 06040	643-6517
G.A. 13	111 Phoenix Avenue Enfield, CT 06082	741-3727
G.A. 14	101 Lafayette Street Hartford, CT 06106	566-1680
G.A. 15	125 Columbus Boulevard New Britain, CT 06051	827-7106
G.A. 16	105 Raymond Road West Hartford, CT 06107	236-5166
G.A. 17	Municipal Building 131 North Main Street (P.O. Box 1400) Bristol, CT 06010	582-8111
G.A. 18	80 Doyle Road (P.O. Box 667) Bantam, CT 06750	567-3942
G.A. 19	55 West Main Street (P.O. Box 980) Rockville, CT 06066	872-4548
G.A. 20	17 Belden Avenue (P.O. Box 2225) Norwalk, CT 06852-2225	846-4206
G.A. 21	1 Courthouse Square Norwich, CT 06360	887-3731
G.A. 22	14 West River Street Milford, CT 06460	874-1116

FORM 51 SIDE 2

The Towns of Connecticut and the Geographic Area Superior Court Which has Jurisdiction Over Them When a Small Claims Court Action is Initiated Against an Individual or Corporation That Lives, Works or Transacts Business in One of These Towns

COURT DISTRICTS BY TOWN

Town	Geographical Area	Judicial District	Town	Geographical Area	Judicial District
Andover	19	Tolland	Franklin	21	New London
Ansonia	5	Ansonia-Milford	Glastonbury	12	Hartford-New Britain
Ashford	11	Windham	Goshen	18	Litchfield
Avon	16	Hartford-New Britain	Granby	13	Hartford-New Britain
Barkhamsted	18	Litchfield	Greenwich	1	Stamford-Norwalk
Beacon Falls	5	Ansonia-Milford	Griswold	21	New London
Berlin	15	Hartford-New Britain	Groton	10	New London
Bethany	6	New Haven	Guilford	8	New Haven
Bethel	3	Danbury	Haddam	9	Middlesex
Bethlehem	18	Litchfield	Hamden	7	New Haven
Bloomfield	16	Hartford-New Britain	Hampton	11	Windham
Bolton	19	Tolland	Hartford	14	Hartford-New Britain
Bozrah	21	New London	Hartland	18	Litchfield
Branford	8	New Haven	Harwinton	18	Litchfield
Bridgeport	2	Fairfield	Hebron	19	Tolland
Bridgewater	18	Litchfield	Kent	18	Litchfield
Bristol	17	Hartford-New Britain	Killingly	11	Windham
Brookfield	3	Danbury	Killingworth	9	Middlesex
Brooklyn	11	Windham	Lebanon	21	New London
Burlington	17	Hartford-New Britain	Ledyard	10	New London
Canaan	18	Litchfield	Lisbon	21	New London
Canterbury	11	Windham	Litchfield	18	Litchfield
Canton	16	Hartford-New Britain	Lyme	10	New London
Chaplin	11	Windham	Madison	8	New Haven
Cheshire	7	New Haven	Manchester	12	Hartford-New Britain
Chester	9	Middlesex	Mansfield	19	Tolland
Clinton	9	Middlesex	Marlborough	12	Hartford-New Britain
Colchester	21	New London	Meriden	7	New Haven
Colebrook	18	Litchfield	Middlebury	4	Waterbury
Columbia	19	Tolland	Middlefield	9	Middlesex
Cornwall	18	Litchfield	Middletown	9	Middlesex
Coventry	19	Tolland	Milford	22	Ansonia-Milford
Cromwell	9	Middlesex	Monroe	2	Fairfield
Danbury	3	Danbury	Montville	21	New London
Darien	1	Stamford-Norwalk	Morris	18	Litchfield
Deep River	9	Middlesex	Naugatuck	4	Waterbury
Derby	5	Ansonia-Milford	New Britain	15	Hartford-New Britain
Durham	9	Middlesex	New Canaan	20	Stamford-Norwalk
Eastford	11	Windham	New Fairfield	3	Danbury
East Granby	13	Hartford-New Britain	New Hartford	18	Litchfield
East Haddam	9	Middlesex	New Haven	6	New Haven
East Hampton	9	Middlesex	Newington	15	Hartford-New Britain
East Hartford	12	Hartford-New Britain	New London	10	New London
East Haven	8	New Haven	New Milford	18	Litchfield
East Lyme	10	New London	Newtown	3	Danbury
Easton	2	Fairfield	Norfolk	18	Litchfield
East Windsor	13	Hartford-New Britain	North Branford	8	New Haven
Ellington	19	Tolland	North Canaan	18	Litchfield
Enfield	13	Hartford-New Britain	North Haven	7	New Haven
Essex	9	Middlesex	North Stonington	10	New London
Fairfield	2	Fairfield	Norwalk	20	Stamford-Norwalk
Farmington	16	Hartford-New Britain			

Town	Geographical Area	Judicial District
Norwich	21	New London
Old Lyme	10	New London
Old Saybrook	9	Middlesex
Orange	5	Ansonia-Milford
Oxford	5	Ansonia-Milford
Plainfield	11	Windham
Plainville	17	Hartford-New Britain
Plymouth	17	Hartford-New Britain
Pomfret	11	Windham
Portland	9	Middlesex
Preston	21	New London
Prospect	4	Waterbury
Putnam	11	Windham
Redding	3	Danbury
Ridgefield	3	Danbury
Rocky Hill	15	Hartford-New Britain
Roxbury	18	Litchfield
Salem	21	New London
Salisbury	18	Litchfield
Scotland	11	Windham
Seymour	5	Ansonia-Milford
Sharon	18	Litchfield
Sherman	3	Danbury
Shelton	5	Ansonia-Milford
Simsbury	13	Hartford-New Britain
Somers	19	Tolland
Southbury	4	Waterbury
Southington	17	Hartford-New Britain
South Windsor	12	Hartford-New Britain
Sprague	21	New London
Stafford	19	Tolland
Stamford	1	Stamford-Norwalk
Sterling	11	Windham
Stonington	10	New London
Stratford	2	Fairfield
Suffield	13	Hartford-New Britain
Thomaston	18	Litchfield
Thompson	11	Windham
Tolland	19	Tolland
Torrington	18	Litchfield
Trumbull	2	Fairfield
Union	19	Tolland
Vernon	19	Tolland
Voluntown	21	New London
Wallingford	7	New Haven
Warren	18	Litchfield
Washington	18	Litchfield
Waterbury	4	Waterbury
Waterford	10	New London
Watertown	4	Waterbury
Westbrook	9	Middlesex
West Hartford	16	Hartford-New Britain
West Haven	22	Ansonia-Milford
Weston	20	Stamford-Norwalk
Westport	20	Stamford-Norwalk
Wethersfield	15	Hartford-New Britain
Willington	19	Tolland
Wilton	20	Stamford-Norwalk
Winchester (Winsted)	18	Litchfield
Windham	11	Windham
Windsor	13	Hartford-New Britain
Windsor Locks	13	Hartford-New Britain
Wolcott	4	Waterbury
Woodbridge	6	New Haven
Woodbury	4	Waterbury
Woodstock	11	Windham

FORM 52 SIDE 2

**SMALL CLAIM
AND NOTICE OF SUIT**
JD CV 40 Rev 4-95
C G S § 51-15 51-193L, 52-549a b c
Pr Bk § 347 et seq

STATE OF CONNECTICUT
SUPERIOR COURT
SMALL CLAIMS SESSION

(Name, address and zip code)

TO:

Defendant
#1.

Defendant
#2.

IND   PART   CORP
☐   ☐   ☐
(°X° ONE)

IND   PART   CORP
☐   ☐   ☐
(°X° ONE)

DOCKET NO.

Hearing required if   ☐ YES
defendant defaults   ☐ NO

CONTINUANCES

ATTY. FOR DEF.

TELEPHONE NO.

2 YOU ARE THE DEFENDANT AND **YOU ARE BEING SUED** BY THE FOLLOWING PLAINTIFF(S):

NAME ADDRESS ZIP CODE AND TELEPHONE NO

NAME ADDRESS ZIP CODE AND TELEPHONE NO

ATTORNEY FOR PLAINTIFF (Name address and zip code)

TELEPHONE NO

(°X° ONE) ☐ IND ☐ PART ☐ CORP   (°X° ONE) ☐ IND ☐ PART ☐ CORP

THE ABOVE PLAINTIFF(S) **CLAIMS YOU OWE** ➡
PLUS COSTS, FOR THE FOLLOWING REASONS:

AMOUNT DUE
$

TOWN WHERE TRANSACTION OCCURRED

← FIRST FOLD

1.

2.

☐ "X" here and complete the Military Service Affidavit below if the defendant(s) is are an individual(s) or partnership
The undersigned, being duly sworn, deposes and says that the above amount is now due from the defendant(s) to plaintiff(s) in accordance with the above claim

SIGNED (Plaintiff or Plaintiff's Attorney)

TYPE IN NAME OF PERSON SIGNING AT LEFT

TITLE OF PERSON SIGNING (if applicable)

DATE ENTERED

SUBSCRIBED AND SWORN TO BEFORE ME ON (Date)

SIGNED (Comm Notary Comm of Sup Ct)

The undersigned deposes and says   **MILITARY SERVICE AFFIDAVIT**

☐ that the undersigned is unable to determine whether or not the defendant(s) in this action are in the military or naval service of the United States

☐ that no defendant in this action is in the military or naval service of the United States, and that, to the personal knowledge of the undersigned *(state facts showing defendant is not in such service)*

SIGNATURE AND TITLE

ON (Date)

SIGNED (Comm Notary Comm of Sup Ct)

Subscribed and sworn to before me:

ANSWER DATE

SMALL CLAIMS TELEPHONE NO.

COURT LOCATION SMALL CLAIMS
☐ GEOGRAPHICAL AREA _____   ☐ HOUSING SESSION

SIGNED Cm

JUDGMENT FOR:	☐ PLAINTIFF	☐ DEFENDANT
AFTER DEFAULT:	☐ WITH HEARING IN DAMAGES	☐ WITHOUT HEARING
	☐ BY STIP- ULATION	☐ AFTER TRIAL

ON (Date): _____ WITH PAYMENTS OF

$ _____ PER _____ COMMENCING _____

☐ WITHDRAWN   ☐ DISMISSED
☐ TRANSFER TO REGULAR DOCKET ON _____
☐ JUDGMENT OPENED ON: _____
☐ SEE NEW JUDGMENT

DISPOSITION (For Court Use)

Damages	$ _____	Entry Fee	$ _____
Interest	$ _____	Service	$ _____
Atty Fees	$ _____	Other	$ _____
TOT DAM.	$ _____	TOT. COST	$ _____
☐ SEE OTHER SIDE	TOT DAM. AND COSTS	$ _____

SIGNED (Judge Magistrate or Clerk)

SC

DOCKET NO

FORM 53

SMALL CLAIM
AND NOTICE OF SUIT
JD-CV-40 Rev. 12-93
C.G.S. § 51-15, 51-193L, 52-549e,b,c
Pr. Bk. § 547 et seq.

STATE OF CONNECTICUT
SUPERIOR COURT
SMALL CLAIMS SESSION

DOCKET NO.

Hearing required if
defendant defaults
☐ YES
☐ NO

CONTINUANCES

(Name, address and zip code)

TO:
Defendant
#1.

_FULL NAME OF DEFENDANT
STREET ADDRESS
CITY & STATE & ZIP CODE
PHONE #

IND PAID CORP
☐ ☐ ☐
("X" ONE)

1.
Defendant
#2.

_IF THERE IS ANOTHER DEFENDANT
FILL OUT THIS BOX. IF THERE
IS A THIRD PERSON, PLEASE
PUT OVER HERE----------------→

IND PAID CORP
☐ ☐ ☐
("X" ONE)

ATTY. FOR DEF.

TELEPHONE NO

2. YOU ARE THE DEFENDANT AND **YOU ARE BEING SUED** BY THE FOLLOWING PLAINTIFF(S):

NAME, ADDRESS, ZIP CODE AND TELEPHONE NO

YOURSELF
NAME
ADDRESS
CITY & STATE & ZIP CODE
PHONE #
("X" ONE) ☐ IND. ☐ PART. ☐ CORP.

NAME, ADDRESS, ZIP CODE AND TELEPHONE NO

("X" ONE) ☐ IND ☐ PART ☐ CORP

ATTORNEY (OR PLAINTIFF (if any) (name, address and telephone)

TELEPHONE NO

THE ABOVE PLAINTIFF(S) **CLAIMS YOU OWE →**
PLUS COSTS, FOR THE FOLLOWING REASONS:

AMOUNT DUE
$AMOUNT

TOWN WHERE TRANSACTION OCCURRED
TRANSACTION TOWN

$2,500.00 is maximum

EXPLAIN WHY YOU ARE SUING

1.

2.   IF THE DEFENDANT IS A CORPORATION, DO NOT FILL OUT THE BOX BELOW.
     IF THE DEFENDANT IS AN INDIVIDUAL, PLEASE COMPLETE

☐ "X" here and complete the Military Service Affidavit below if the defendant(s) is/are an individual(s) or partnership.
The undersigned, being duly sworn, deposes and says that the above amount is now due from the defendant(s) to plaintiff(s) in accordance with the above claim.

SIGNED (Plaintiff or Plaintiff's Attorney)	TYPE IN NAME OF PERSON SIGNING AT LEFT	TITLE OF PERSON SIGNING (if applicable)
YOU SIGN HERE	TYPE FULL NAME	TYPE YOUR TITLE HERE
DATE ENTERED	SUBSCRIBED AND SWORN TO BEFORE ME ON (Date)	SIGNED (Clerk, Notary, Comm. of Sup. Ct.)
LEAVE BLANK	NOTARY MUST DATE	NOTARY SIGNATURE

The undersigned deposes and says: **MILITARY SERVICE AFFIDAVIT**

☐ that the undersigned is unable to determine whether or not the defendant(s) in this action are in the military or naval service of the United States.

☐ that no defendant in this action is in the military or naval service of the United States, and that, to the personal knowledge of the undersigned *(state facts showing defendant is not in such service):*

YOU MUST STATE TO THE BEST OF YOUR KNOWLEDGE THAT THE ABOVE DEFENDANT IS NOT
IN THE MILITARY SERVICE, SUCH AS: 1. EMPLOYMENT 2. WHERE THEY RESIDE
3. THEY MAY BE ABOVE THE AGE
SIGNATURE AND TITLE _____ YOU SIGN HERE _____

Subscribed and sworn to before me:	ON (Date) NOTARY DATE	SIGNED (Clerk, Notary, Comm. of Sup. Ct.) NOTARY SIGNATURE
ANSWER DATE	SMALL CLAIMS TELEPHONE NO. 965-5236	COURT LOCATION - SMALL CLAIMS COURT ☒ GEOGRAPHICAL AREA __1__ ☐ HOUSING SESSION 123 HOYT ST., STAMFORD, CT. 06905

SIGNED (Clerk, Notary, Comm. of Sup. Ct.)

DISPOSITION (For Court Use)

JUDGMENT FOR: ☐ PLAINTIFF   ☐ DEFENDANT
AFTER DEFAULT: ☐ WITH HEARING IN DAMAGES   ☐ WITHOUT HEARING
☐ BY STIP- ULATION   ☐ AFTER TRIAL
ON (Date): _____ WITH PAYMENTS OF
$_____ PER _____ COMMENCING _____

☐ WITHDRAWN   ☐ DISMISSED
☐ TRANSFER TO REGULAR DOCKET ON: _____
☐ JUDGMENT OPENED ON: _____
☐ SEE NEW JUDGMENT

Damages	$ _____	Entry Fee	$ _____
Interest	$ _____	Service	$ _____
Atty. Fees	$ _____	Other	$ _____
TOT. DAM.	$ _____	TOT. COST	$ _____

☐ SEE OTHER SIDE   TOT. DAM. AND COSTS $ _____
SIGNED (Judge, Magistrate or Clerk)

SC

DOCKET NO.

COURT ORIGINAL

FORM 54

STATE OF CONNECTICUT

SMALL CLAIMS

SUPERIOR COURT G.A. #1

 115 Hoyt St., Stamford, Connecticut 06905   (203)965-5236

SHERIFF LISTING

BRIDGEPORT
TERRY L. BROWN
(203)332-9231
   .   367-6408

GERALD V. CAPPIELLO, JR.
(203)332-9252
1-800-512-2411

THOMAS FRAHER
(203)333-5759

SARA LADEN
(203)332-7557

PAUL M. POST
(203)372-5624

EDDIE RODRIQUEZ, SR.
(203)372-3378

WILLIE J. SMITH
(203)374-6844
   371-9012

CHARLES VALENTINO
(203)333-2866
   366-0382

DANBURY
ROGER F. DELSIN
(203)744-0741
   748-3951

STEVEN PICHIARALLO
(203)792-5234

EDWARD W. PLATE
(203)743-3991

GARY D. RENZ
(203)743-5875

J. STEPHEN WOODS
(203)790-7656

FAIRFIELD
RONALD Z. KADAR
(203)255-6944
   260-1785

JOAN A. SWANSON
(203)255-0659

GREENWICH
JACK BART
(203)531-5791

SIEGRUN G. POTTGEN
(203)531-1174
   531-7898

MONROE
ALBERT CALIENDO
(203)268-7158
   556-0133 (car)

JOHN J. COTTER, JR.
(203)367-7766
   556-5775

RICHARD A. ORR
(203)268-9669
   556-1040(car)

ROBERT ZWIERLEIN
(203)261-2268
   261-0633

NEWTOWN
FRANK DeLUCA
(203)426-4848

NORWALK
LAWRENCE F. CAFERO
(203)853-4054

ALAN FREEDMAN
(203)853-6667

TRUMBULL
GEORGE F. HAMMEL
(203)268-6322
   373-8045

DONALD W. MATTICE
(203)268-1353

WESTPORT
FAUSTO CARUSONE
(203)222-5106
   367-6408

E. KEITH MAKOWSKI
(203)838-6611
   838-8768

RICHARD MOCCIA
(203)846-0490

WILLIAM D. WIEST
(203)838-1019
   556-2218(car)

REDDING
CHARLES J. ALLARD
(203)938-3367

RIDGEFIELD
JAMES E. SULLIVAN
(203)438-9885

SHELTON
RICHARD J. CHAFFEE, SR.
(203)929-5414

PATRICIA A. RANDALL
(203)929-6386
   365-3519

STAMFORD
MARK PESIRI
(203)323-6127

PAUL VERILLE
(203)327-0816

ANTHONY D. VERRICO
(203)327-7018

STRATFORD
THOMAS W. ALLEN
(203)377-3514

THOMAS R. ENGLISH, JR.
(203)378-4340
   381-8440

EDWARD J. FENNELL
(203)375-8033
   556-2887

FORM 55 SIDE 1

Sheriff's Office Locations

Sheriff's Offices	Telephone
Superior Court 1061 Main Street Bridgeport, CT 06604	579-6239
Superior Court 101 Lafayette Street Hartford, CT 06106	566-4930
Superior Court West Street, P.O. Box 735 Litchfield, CT 06759	567-0844
Superior Court 1 Court Street, 2nd Floor Middletown, CT 06457-3375	343-6550
Superior Court 235 Church Street, P.O. Box 200 New Haven, CT 06510	789-7883
Superior Court 70 Huntington Street, P.O. Box 671 New London, CT 06320	443-5400
Superior Court 155 Church Street Putnam, CT 06260	928-5181
Superior Court 69 Brooklyn Street, P.O. Box 316 Rockville, CT 06066	872-3878
Superior Court 300 Grand Street Waterbury, CT 06702	596-4016

COUNTY SHERIFFS

FAIRFIELD COUNTY
579-6239

HARTFORD COUNTY
566-4930

LICHFIELD COUNTY
567-0844

MIDDLESEX COUNTY
344-2964

NEW HAVEN COUNTY
789-7883

NEW LONDON COUNTY
443-5400

TOLLAND COUNTY
872-3878

WINDHAM COUNTY
928-5181

CONSTABLES

STAMFORD
JON T. GALLUP
(203)969-0232

RALPH T. SERAFINO, JR.
(203)323-3753

WAGE EXECUTION PROCEEDINGS
APPLICATION, ORDER, EXECUTION
JD-CV-3 Rev. 1-91
Gen. Stat. 31-58(j), 52-361a, 52-365d(e)
29 U.S.C. 206(a)(1)

STATE OF CONNECTICUT
SUPERIOR COURT

EMPLOYER: SEE REVERSE SIDE FOR INSTRUCTIONS
INSTRUCTIONS

JUDGMENT CREDITOR OR ATTORNEY
1. Prepare original and four copies.
2. Attach form JD-CV-3a to one copy of this form.
3. Present original and 3 copies to clerk of court.
4. Retain one copy for your file.

CLERK
1. Issue execution by signing original and 2 copies.
2. Retain remaining copy for court file.
3. Enter any court ordered limitation at the bottom of section II on reverse side.

SHERIFF
1. Leave 2 signed copies with employer.
2. Make return on signed original.
3. Leave 1 copy of Modification and Exemption Claim form (JD-CV-3a) with employer and fill in "Date of Service" on form.

NAME AND MAILING ADDRESS OF JUDGMENT CREDITOR OR ATTORNEY
(To be completed by Plaintiff)

APPLICATION

ADDRESS OF COURT *(Number, street and town)* ☐ G.A. ☐ J.D. ☐ Housing Session	DATE OF JUDGMENT	DOCKET NO.
AMOUNT OF WEEKLY PAYMENTS ORDERED *(Employers must pay amount of execution calculated on the reverse side of this form)* $ — COMMENCEMENT DATE — TOTAL AMOUNT PAID TO DATE $		DATE OF LAST PAYMENT
NAME(S) OF JUDGMENT CREDITOR(S) — OF *(Street and Town)* — NAME(S) OF JUDGMENT DEBTOR(S)		OF *(Street and Town)*
EMPLOYER OF JUDGMENT DEBTOR *(If known)* — OF *(Street and Town)*		TELEPHONE NO.

1. AMOUNT OF JUDGMENT *(In words)(Including damages and, where applicable, prejudgment interest and attorney fees)*   DOLLARS $

2. AMOUNT OF COSTS IN OBTAINING JUDGMENT *(In words)*   DOLLARS $

3. TOTAL JUDGMENT AND COSTS *(In words)(Add lines 1 and 2)*   DOLLARS $

4. TOTAL PAID ON ACCOUNT *(In words)*   DOLLARS $

5. TOTAL UNPAID JUDGMENT *(In words)(Subtract line 4 from line 3)*   DOLLARS $

6. APPLICATION FEE FOR WAGE EXECUTION *(In words)(If not waived by the court)*   DOLLARS $

7. TOTAL OF LINES 5 AND 6 *(In words)*   DOLLARS $

SIGNED *(Judgment Creditor or Attorney)*	DATE APPLICATION SIGNED
ADDRESS OF PERSON SIGNING	TELEPHONE NO.

EXECUTION

To: Any Proper Officer:

    WHEREAS the above-named Judgment Creditor(s) recovered judgment against the above-named Judgment Debtor(s) for the above Amount of Judgment, as appears of record, whereof execution remains to be done on the Total Shown in line 7 above,

    AND WHEREAS, pursuant to statute, the said court entered an order that said judgment be paid in weekly payments,

    AND WHEREAS, the said Judgment Debtor(s) failed to comply with said order for weekly payments, as appears of record by application of said Judgment Creditor(s) moving that this execution issue on said Total in line 7 above.

    These are, therefore, by authority of the State of Connecticut, to command you, that of any amount of any debt accruing by reason of personal services due any said Judgment Debtor as may not exceed the Amount of Execution calculated on the reverse side of this form, within your precincts, you cause to be levied, paid, and satisfied unto the said Judgment Creditor(s), with interest from the said Date of Judgment on the Total in line 5 above, to the date when this execution is satisfied, and your own fees.

    Make service hereof within one year of this date, and due return hereof with your doings thereon, within thirty days from satisfaction hereof.

SIGNED *(Assistant Clerk of said court)*	ON *(Date)*

(over)

FORM 56 SIDE 1

IMPORTANT NOTICE TO EMPLOYER

You are being served with a wage execution, a court order requiring you to withhold non-exempt wages from a person employed by you. This execution is being served upon you because your employee, the Judgment Debtor (on reverse side), has had a judgment entered against him by the Superior Court requiring him to pay damages to the Judgment Creditor (on reverse side) and has not made payment of the total amount of the judgment plus any court costs as shown on reverse side. This notice is to inform you of the actions you must take in order to comply with the law regarding wage executions. Please read each section carefully.

I. YOU MUST NOTIFY THE EMPLOYEE — Your employee has certain legal rights which may allow him to request the court to change or stop this execution upon his wages. A notice of his rights and how to get a hearing in court is attached to the second copy of the wage execution given to you by the officer. You must complete your portion of the wage execution and your portion of the exemption and modification claim form and DELIVER OR MAIL, POSTAGE PREPAID, A COPY OF THESE PAPERS TO YOUR EMPLOYEE IMMEDIATELY so that your employee can make any claims allowed by law.

II. EXECUTION NOT EFFECTIVE FOR 20 DAYS — This execution is not effective until after 20 days from the day the officer served these papers on you. No money should be deducted from your employee's wages until the first wages you pay to your employee after the 20-day period ends.

If your employee elects within the 20-day period to make a claim to the court that his wages are partially or totally exempt from execution to pay this judgment or he seeks to have the amount of this execution changed, wages are not to be withheld from the employee until the court decides the claims or determines the rights of your employee in this case.

If you are not notified that your employee has filed papers with the court, the execution is to be enforced after 20 days from the date of service on you.

III. STAY OF EXECUTION — No earnings claimed to be exempt or subject to a claim for modification may be withheld from any employee until determination of the claim by the court.

IV. ONLY ONE EXECUTION ISSUED UNDER GEN. STAT. 52-361a TO BE SATISFIED AT A TIME — You must make deductions from your employee's wages and pay over the withheld money against only one execution issued under Gen. Stat. 52-361a at a time. If you are served with more than one execution issued under Gen. Stat. 52-361a against this employee's wages, the executions are to be satisfied in the order in which you are served

with them. *(Wage executions and earnings assignments for support of a family, issued under C.G.S. § 52-362a or c, take precedence over this execution. Family support wage executions and earnings assignments are issued on Form JD-FM-1.)*

V. MAXIMUM AMOUNT DEDUCTED — The maximum amount which can be legally withheld from your employee's wages is 25% of his disposable earnings for each week. The amount to be withheld to pay this execution may be less than 25%, but it can never be more. The computations you complete below will allow you to calculate the exact amount which should be withheld from this employee's wages.

Unless the court orders that this execution is to be for a smaller amount, you must withhold and pay over the maximum amount which you figure out using the computations below. Your employee has a right to request the court to reduce the amount withheld, but until you receive notice that the court has agreed to allow the amount to be reduced, you must withhold the maximum amount.

VI. YOUR DUTY TO COMPLY WITH THIS EXECUTION — You have a legal duty to make deductions from your employee's wages and pay any amounts deducted as required by this execution. If you do not, legal action may be taken against you. If you are found to be in contempt of a court order, you may be held liable to the Judgment Creditor for the amounts of wages which you did not withhold from your employee.

VII. DISCIPLINE AGAINST YOUR EMPLOYEE — You may not discipline, suspend or discharge your employee because this wage execution has been served upon you. If you do unlawfully take action against your employee, you may be liable to pay him all of his lost earnings and employment benefits from the time of your action to the time that the employee is reinstated.

The law allows you to take disciplinary measures against the employee if you are served with more than 7 wage executions against his wages in any calendar year.

SECTION I. COMPUTATION OF EMPLOYEE'S DISPOSABLE EARNINGS

"DISPOSABLE EARNINGS" means that part of the earnings of an individual remaining after the deduction from those earnings of amounts to be withheld for payment of federal income and employment taxes, normal retirement contributions, union dues and initiation fees, group life insurance premiums, health insurance premiums, federal tax levies, and state income tax deductions authorized pursuant to section 12-34b *(income tax deduction for out-of-state residents employed in Connecticut).*

1. Employee's gross compensation per week .... _____
2. Federal income tax withheld .... _____
3. Federal employment tax .... _____
4. Normal retirement contribution .... _____
5. Union dues and initiation fees .... _____
6. Group life insurance premium .... _____
7. Health insurance premium .... _____
8. Other federal tax levies .... _____
9. State income tax withheld .... _____
10. Total allowable deductions (Add lines 2-9) .... _____
11. WEEKLY DISPOSABLE EARNINGS (Subtract line 10 from line 1) ....

SECTION II. COMPUTATION OF AMOUNT OF EXECUTION

To be calculated by employer	COL. 1	COL. 2
A-1. Weekly disposable earnings *(from line 11 above)*	$	
A-2. 25% of disposable earnings for week		$
B-1. Weekly disposable earnings *(from line 11 above)*	$	
B-2. Forty times the HIGHER of the current federal minimum hourly wage OR state full minimum fair wage.	$	
Amount by which line B-1 exceeds B-2		$
AMOUNT OF EXECUTION *(Lesser of the two amounts in column 2 subject to any court ordered limitation set forth in the box below if a lesser amount.)*		$

COURT ORDERED LIMITATION *(If any, to be entered by clerk)*

FORM 56 SIDE 2

WAGE EXECUTION PROCEEDINGS
APPLICATION, ORDER, EXECUTION
JD-CV-3 Rev. 1-91
Gen. Stat. 31-58(j), 52-361a, 52-365d(e)
29 U.S.C. 206(a)(1)

STATE OF CONNECTICUT
SUPERIOR COURT

EMPLOYER: SEE REVERSE SIDE FOR INSTRUCTIONS

INSTRUCTIONS

JUDGMENT CREDITOR OR ATTORNEY
1. Prepare original and four copies.
2. Attach form JD-CV-3a to one copy of this form.
3. Present original and 3 copies to clerk of court.
4. Retain one copy for your file.

CLERK
1. Issue execution by signing original and 2 copies.
2. Retain remaining copy for court file.
3. Enter any court ordered limitation at the bottom of section II on reverse side.

SHERIFF
1. Leave 2 signed copies with employer.
2. Make return on signed original.
3. Leave 1 copy of Modification and Exemption Claim form (JD-CV-3a) with employer and fill in "Date of Service" on form.

NAME AND MAILING ADDRESS OF JUDGMENT CREDITOR OR ATTORNEY
(To be completed by Plaintiff)

John Smith
32 Oak Lane
Hartford, CT 06106

ADDRESS OF COURT *(Number, street and town)* ☒ G.A. ☐ J.D. ☐ Housing Session	DATE OF JUDGMENT	DOCKET NO.
GA 6 121 Elm Street., New Haven 06510	November 1, 1993	SC6-99999

AMOUNT OF WEEKLY PAYMENTS ORDERED $ 15.00 *(Employers must pay amount of execution calculated on the reverse side of this form)*	COMMENCEMENT DATE 11/22/93	TOTAL AMOUNT PAID TO DATE $ 0	DATE OF LAST PAYMENT 0

NAME(S) OF JUDGMENT CREDITOR(S) John Smith	OF *(Street and Town)* 32 Oak Lane Hartford	NAME(S) OF JUDGMENT DEBTOR(S) Paul Doe	OF *(Street and Town)* 16 Elm Street New Haven

EMPLOYER OF JUDGMENT DEBTOR *(If known)* Acme Manufacturing	OF *(Street and Town)* 22 Sycamore Lane, Branford	TELEPHONE NO. 933-3333

APPLICATION

1. AMOUNT OF JUDGMENT *(In words)(Including damages and, where applicable, prejudgment interest and attorney fees)* One Thousand	DOLLARS	$1,000.00
2. AMOUNT OF COSTS IN OBTAINING JUDGMENT *(In words)* Thirty	DOLLARS	$ 30.00
3. TOTAL JUDGMENT AND COSTS *(In words)(Add lines 1 and 2)* One thousand thirty	DOLLARS	$1,030.00
4. TOTAL PAID ON ACCOUNT *(In words)* Zero	DOLLARS	$ 0
5. TOTAL UNPAID JUDGMENT *(In words)(Subtract line 4 from line 3)* One thousand thirty	DOLLARS	$1,030.00
6. APPLICATION FEE FOR WAGE EXECUTION *(In words)(If not waived by the court)* Ten	DOLLARS	10.00
7. TOTAL OF LINES 5 AND 6 *(In words)* One thousand forty	DOLLARS	1,040.00

SIGNED *(Judgment Creditor or Attorney)*	DATE APPLICATION SIGNED November 27, 1993

ADDRESS OF PERSON SIGNING 32 Oak Lane, Hartford, 06106	TELEPHONE NO. 866-6666

EXECUTION

To: Any Proper Officer:

WHEREAS the above-named Judgment Creditor(s) recovered judgment against the above-named Judgment Debtor(s) for the above Amount of Judgment, as appears of record, whereof execution remains to be done on the Total Shown in line 7 above,

AND WHEREAS, pursuant to statute, the said court entered an order that said judgment be paid in weekly payments,

AND WHEREAS, the said Judgment Debtor(s) failed to comply with said order for weekly payments, as appears of record by application of said Judgment Creditor(s) moving that this execution issue on said Total in line 7 above.

These are, therefore, by authority of the State of Connecticut, to command you, that of any amount of any debt accruing by reason of personal services due any said Judgment Debtor as may not exceed the Amount of Execution calculated on the reverse side of this form, within your precincts, you cause to be levied, paid, and satisfied unto the said Judgment Creditor(s), with interest from the said Date of Judgment on the Total in line 5 above, to the date when this execution is satisfied, and your own fees.

Make service hereof within one year of this date, and due return hereof with your doings thereon, within thirty days from satisfaction hereof.

SIGNED *(Assistant Clerk of said court)*	ON *(Date)*

(over)

FORM 57

EXEMPTION AND MODIFICATION CLAIM FORM
WAGE EXECUTION
JD-CV-3a Rev. 9-87
C.G.S. § 31-58(j), 52-212, 52-350a,
52-352b, 52-361a, 52-361b
29 U.S.C. 206(a)(1)

STATE OF CONNECTICUT

SUPERIOR COURT

NAME AND ADDRESS OF JUDGMENT DEBTOR OR ATTORNEY
(To be completed by Plaintiff)

⌐   ⌐

L   ⌐

INSTRUCTIONS

TO SHERIFF: Complete section II below and make service on employer in accordance with the instructions on form JD-CV-3.
TO EMPLOYER: Complete Section III below and immediately deliver to employee.

Fold

SECTION I *(Plaintiff to complete this section and attach to one copy of the wage execution application (JD-CV-3)).*

NAME AND ADDRESS OF COURT

NAME OF JUDGMENT DEBTOR	DOCKET NO.

NAME AND ADDRESS OF JUDGMENT CREDITOR OR ATTORNEY	TELEPHONE NO.

SECTION II *(To be completed by sheriff)*

DATE OF SERVICE OF WAGE EXECUTION ON EMPLOYER	NAME OF SHERIFF

SECTION III *(Employer to complete this section and immediately send one copy of this form and the Wage Execution form (JD-CV-3) to the judgment debtor pursuant to General Statutes section 52-361a (d).*

NAME AND ADDRESS OF EMPLOYER	TEL. NO. OF PAYROLL DEPT.

DATE OF DELIVERY OR MAILING TO JUDGMENT DEBTOR	TOTAL AMOUNT OF WAGE EXECUTION	AMOUNT TO BE TAKEN OUT FROM WEEKLY EARNINGS

SECTION IV   **NOTICE TO JUDGMENT DEBTOR**

As the result of a judgment entered against you, the attached execution has been issued against wages earned by you from the employer named above. In compliance with this execution, beginning 20 days from the Date of Service of Wage Execution on Employer indicated above, the employer will remove from your weekly earnings an amount of money which leaves you with the greater of seventy-five percent of your disposable earnings OR forty times the higher of the minimum hourly wage prescribed by federal law or state law. On the reverse side of this form are those sections of the general statutes which your employer must follow in determining the weekly amount that may be taken out of your wages to satisfy the wage execution. If you determine that your employer has not calculated the weekly amount correctly, you should bring this to your employer's attention.

YOUR EARNINGS MAY BE EXEMPT FROM EXECUTION — Any wages earned by a public assistance recipient under an incentive earnings or similar program are exempt from execution. (Gen. Stat. § 52-352b(d))

HOW TO CLAIM AN EXEMPTION ALLOWED BY LAW — If you wish to claim that your earnings are exempt by law from execution you must fill out and sign the Claim of Exemption on the reverse side of this page and return this exemption and modification claim form to the Superior Court at the above address.

Upon receipt of this form the clerk of the Superior Court will notify you and the judgment creditor of the date on which a hearing will be held by the court to determine the issues raised by your claim. If this form is received by the court no later than 20 days from the Date of Service of Wage Execution on Employer indicated above, the employer will not begin withholding your earnings until after your claim is determined by the court. A claim may also be filed after the 20 day period. No earnings claimed to be exempt may be withheld from any employee until determination of the claim.

MODIFICATION OF EXECUTION — If you have reasonable cause to believe that you are entitled to a modification of the wage execution and wish to have the execution so modified, you must fill out the Claim for Modification on the reverse side of this page and return this exemption and modification claim form to the Superior Court at the above address.

Upon receipt of this form the clerk of Superior Court will notify you and the judgment creditor of the date on which a hearing will be held by the court to determine the issues raised by your claim. If this form is received by the court no later than 20 days from the Date of Service of Wage Execution on Employer indicated above, the employer will not begin withholding your earnings until after your claim is determined by the court. A claim may also be filed after the 20 day period. No earnings subject to a claim for modification may be withheld from any employee until determination of the claim

SETTING ASIDE JUDGMENT — If the judgment was rendered against you because of your failure to appear in court, you may, pursuant to section 52-212 of the general statutes, within four months of the date judgment was rendered and upon belief that you have reasonable cause, move the court to set aside the judgment entered against you.

(SEE OTHER SIDE)

FORM 58

**EXEMPTION AND MODIFICATION CLAIM FORM
WAGE EXECUTION**
JD-CV-3a Rev. 9-87
C.G.S. § 31-58(i), 52-212, 52-350a,
52-352b, 52-361a, 52-361b
29 U.S.C. 206(a)(1)

STATE OF CONNECTICUT
SUPERIOR COURT

NAME AND ADDRESS OF JUDGMENT DEBTOR OR ATTORNEY
(To be completed by Plaintiff)

Paul Doe
16 Elm Street
New Haven, CT 06510

INSTRUCTIONS
TO SHERIFF: Complete section II below and
make service on employer in accordance
with the instructions on form JD-CV-3.
TO EMPLOYER: Complete Section III below
and immediately deliver to employee.

Fold

SECTION I *(Plaintiff to complete this section and attach to one copy of the wage execution application (JD-CV-3)).*

NAME AND ADDRESS OF COURT
Superior Court GA6 121 Elm Street, New Haven, CT 06510

NAME OF JUDGMENT DEBTOR	DOCKET NO.
Paul Doe	SC6-99999

NAME AND ADDRESS OF JUDGMENT CREDITOR OR ATTORNEY	TELEPHONE NO.
John Smith 32 Oak Lane, Hartford, 06106	866-6666

SECTION II *(To be completed by sheriff)*

DATE OF SERVICE OF WAGE EXECUTION ON EMPLOYER	NAME OF SHERIFF

SECTION III *(Employer to complete this section and immediately send one copy of this form and the Wage Execution form (JD-CV-3) to the judgment debtor pursuant to General Statutes section 52-361a (d).*

NAME AND ADDRESS OF EMPLOYER	TEL. NO. OF PAYROLL DEPT.

DATE OF DELIVERY OR MAILING TO JUDGMENT DEBTOR	TOTAL AMOUNT OF WAGE EXECUTION	AMOUNT TO BE TAKEN OUT FROM WEEKLY EARNINGS

SECTION IV

NOTICE TO JUDGMENT DEBTOR

As the result of a judgment entered against you, the attached execution has been issued against wages earned by you from the employer named above. In compliance with this execution, beginning 20 days from the Date of Service of Wage Execution on Employer indicated above, the employer will remove from your weekly earnings an amount of money which leaves you with the greater of seventy-five percent of your disposable earnings OR forty times the higher of the minimum hourly wage prescribed by federal law or state law. On the reverse side of this form are those sections of the general statutes which your employer must follow in determining the weekly amount that may be taken out of your wages to satisfy the wage execution. If you determine that your employer has not calculated the weekly amount correctly, you should bring this to your employer's attention.

YOUR EARNINGS MAY BE EXEMPT FROM EXECUTION — Any wages earned by a public assistance recipient under an incentive earnings or similar program are exempt from execution. (Gen. Stat. § 52-352b(d))

HOW TO CLAIM AN EXEMPTION ALLOWED BY LAW — If you wish to claim that your earnings are exempt by law from execution you must fill out and sign the Claim of Exemption on the reverse side of this page and return this exemption and modification claim form to the Superior Court at the above address.

Upon receipt of this form the clerk of the Superior Court will notify you and the judgment creditor of the date on which a hearing will be held by the court to determine the issues raised by your claim. If this form is received by the court no later than 20 days from the Date of Service of Wage Execution on Employer indicated above, the employer will not begin withholding your earnings until after your claim is determined by the court. A claim may also be filed after the 20 day period. No earnings claimed to be exempt may be withheld from any employee until determination of the claim.

MODIFICATION OF EXECUTION — If you have reasonable cause to believe that you are entitled to a modification of the wage execution and wish to have the execution so modified, you must fill out the Claim for Modification on the reverse side of this page and return this exemption and modification claim form to the Superior Court at the above address.

Upon receipt of this form the clerk of Superior Court will notify you and the judgment creditor of the date on which a hearing will be held by the court to determine the issues raised by your claim. If this form is received by the court no later than 20 days from the Date of Service of Wage Execution on Employer indicated above, the employer will not begin withholding your earnings until after your claim is determined by the court. A claim may also be filed after the 20 day period. No earnings subject to a claim for modification may be withheld from any employee until determination of the claim

SETTING ASIDE JUDGMENT — If the judgment was rendered against you because of your failure to appear in court, you may, pursuant to section 52-212 of the general statutes, within four months of the date judgment was rendered and upon belief that you have reasonable cause, move the court to set aside the judgment entered against you.

(SEE OTHER SIDE)

FORM 59

BANK EXECUTION PROCEEDINGS
APPLICATION AND EXECUTION
JD-CV-24 Rev. 10-94
Gen. Stat. 52-367a, 52-367b, P.A. 94-141

STATE OF CONNECTICUT
SUPERIOR COURT
(See reverse side for instructions to banking institution)
INSTRUCTIONS

PLAINTIFF OR ATTORNEY
1. Prepare on typewriter.
2. Complete the application section; make original and 4 copies.
3. Put an "X" in the appropriate box of the "execution" section below, if box A is chosen, complete section 1 of the Exemption Claim Form, JD-CV-24a and attach to this form.
4. Present original and 3 copies to clerk of court.

CLERK
1. Check the file to ensure that the information provided on the application is correct.
2. Sign original execution.
3. Return original and 2 copies to applicant.
4. Retain a copy for file.

NAME AND ADDRESS OF COURT	☐ JUDICIAL DISTRICT ☐ HOUSING SESSION	☐ G.A. ____	DOCKET NO.

APPLICATION

NAME AND MAILING ADDRESS OF JUDGMENT CREDITOR OR ATTORNEY
(To be completed by plaintiff)

⌐　　　　　　　　　¬

└　　　　　　　　　┘

NAME(S) OF JUDGMENT CREDITOR(S)	OF *(Town)*	NAME(S) AND ADDRESS(ES) OF JUDGMENT DEBTOR(S)

DATE OF JUDGMENT	AMOUNT OF DAMAGES	AMOUNT OF COSTS	AMOUNT OF DAMAGES AND COSTS ALREADY PAID *(if any)*

TOTAL UNPAID DAMAGES AND COSTS $	TOTAL UNPAID DAMAGES AND COSTS *(in words)*

SIGNED *(Plaintiff or attorney)*	DATE SIGNED	ADDRESS OF PERSON SIGNING	TELEPHONE NO.

EXECUTION

TO ANY PROPER OFFICER,

Whereas on said Date of Judgment the above-named Judgment Creditor(s) recovered judgment against the above-named Judgment Debtor(s) before the above-named court for the amount of damages and costs stated above, as appears of record, whereof execution remains to be done. These are, therefore, BY AUTHORITY OF THE STATE OF CONNECTICUT TO COMMAND YOU:

☐ **A. IF JUDGMENT DEBTOR IS A NATURAL PERSON**

Within seven days from your receipt of this execution, make demand upon the main office of any banking institution having its main office within your county, or if such main office is not within your county and such banking institution has one or more branch offices within your county, upon an employee of such a branch office, such employee and such branch office having been designated by the banking institution in accordance with regulations adopted by the banking commissioner, for payment to you pursuant to section 52-367b (b) of the general statutes of any nonexempt debt due said Judgment Debtor(s), which sum shall not exceed the total unpaid damages and costs on said judgment as stated above, plus interest on the unpaid amount of said judgment from its date until the time when this execution shall be satisfied, plus your own fee. After having made such demand you are directed to serve a true and attested copy of this execution, together with the attached affidavit and exemption claim form, with your doings endorsed thereon, with the banking institution officer upon whom such demand was made. Said sum shall be received by you and applied on this execution in accordance with the provisions of section 52-367b of the general statutes.

☐ **B. OTHER**

Make demand upon the main office of any banking institution having its main office within your county, or if such main office is not within your county and such banking institution has one or more branch offices within your county, upon an employee of such a branch office, such employee and such branch office having been designated by the banking institution in accordance with regulations adopted by the banking commissioner, for payment to you of any debt due said Judgment Debtor(s), which sum shall not exceed the total unpaid damages and costs on said judgment as stated above, plus interest on the unpaid amount of said judgment from its date until the time when this execution shall be satisfied, plus your own fees. Said sum shall be received by you and applied on this execution. After having made such demand you are directed to serve a true and attested copy hereof, with your doings thereon endorsed, with the banking institution officer upon whom such demand was made.

HEREOF FAIL NOT, AND MAKE DUE RETURN OF THIS WRIT WITH YOUR DOINGS THEREON, ACCORDING TO LAW.

SIGNED *(Assistant Clerk)*	ON *(Date)*

FORM 60

BANK EXECUTION PROCEEDINGS
APPLICATION AND EXECUTION
JD-CV-24   Rev. 8-91
Gen. Stat. 52-367a, 52-367b

STATE OF CONNECTICUT
SUPERIOR COURT
(See reverse side for instructions to banking institution)
INSTRUCTIONS

PLAINTIFF OR ATTORNEY
1. Prepare on typewriter.
2. Complete the application section; make original and 4 copies.
3. Put an "X" in the appropriate box of the "execution" section below, if box A is chosen, complete section 1 of the Exemption Claim Form, JD-CV-24a and attach to this form.
4. Present original and 3 copies to clerk of court.

CLERK
1. Check the file to ensure that the information provided on the application is correct.
2. Sign original execution.
3. Return original and 2 copies to applicant.
4. Retain a copy for file.

NAME AND ADDRESS OF COURT		JUDICIAL DISTRICT ☐ HOUSING SESSION ☐	☒ G.A. __6__	DOCKET NO.
Superior Court 121 Elm Street, New Haven				SC6-99999

NAME AND MAILING ADDRESS OF JUDGMENT CREDITOR OR ATTORNEY
(To be completed by plaintiff)

⌐　　　　　　　　　　　　　¬

　　John Smith
　　32 Oak Lane
　　Hartford, CT 06106

∟　　　　　　　　　　　　　⌟

APPLICATION

NAME(S) OF JUDGMENT CREDITOR(S)	OF (Town)	NAME(S) AND ADDRESS(ES) OF JUDGMENT DEBTOR(S)
John Smith	Hartford	Paul Doe, 16 Elm Street, New Haven, CT 06510

DATE OF JUDGMENT	AMOUNT OF DAMAGES	AMOUNT OF COSTS	AMOUNT OF DAMAGES AND COSTS ALREADY PAID (if any)
November 1, 1993	$1000.00	$30.00	0

TOTAL UNPAID DAMAGES AND COSTS	TOTAL UNPAID DAMAGES AND COSTS (in words)		
$ 1030.00	One thousand thirty dollars		

SIGNED (Plaintiff or attorney)	DATE SIGNED	ADDRESS OF PERSON SIGNING	TELEPHONE NO.
	11/29/93	32 Oak Lane, Hartford, CT 06106	866-6666

EXECUTION

TO ANY PROPER OFFICER,

Whereas on said Date of Judgment the above-named Judgment Creditor(s) recovered judgment against the above-named Judgment Debtor(s) before the above-named court for the amount of damages and costs stated above, as appears of record, whereof execution remains to be done. These are, therefore, BY AUTHORITY OF THE STATE OF CONNECTICUT TO COMMAND YOU:

☐ A. *IF JUDGMENT DEBTOR IS A NATURAL PERSON*

Within seven days from your receipt of this execution, make demand upon the main office of any banking institution having its main office within your county, or if such main office is not within your county and such banking institution has one or more branch offices within your county, upon an employee of such a branch office, such employee and such branch office having been designated by the banking institution in accordance with regulations adopted by the banking commissioner, for payment to you pursuant to section 52-367b (b) of the general statutes of any nonexempt debt due said Judgment Debtor(s), which sum shall not exceed the total unpaid damages and costs on said judgment as stated above, plus interest on the unpaid amount of said judgment from its date until the time when this execution shall be satisfied, plus your own fee. After having made such demand you are directed to serve a true and attested copy of this execution, together with the attached affidavit and exemption claim form, with your doings endorsed thereon, with the banking institution officer upon whom such demand was made. Said sum shall be received by you and applied on this execution in accordance with the provisions of section 52-367b of the general statutes.

☐ B. *OTHER*

Make demand upon the main office of any banking institution having its main office within your county, or if such main office is not within your county and such banking institution has one or more branch offices within your county, upon an employee of such a branch office, such employee and such branch office having been designated by the banking institution in accordance with regulations adopted by the banking commissioner, for payment to you of any debt due said Judgment Debtor(s), which sum shall not exceed the total unpaid damages and costs on said judgment as stated above, plus interest on the unpaid amount of said judgment from its date until the time when this execution shall be satisfied, plus your own fees. Said sum shall be received by you and applied on this execution. After having made such demand you are directed to serve a true and attested copy hereof, with your doings thereon endorsed, with the banking institution officer upon whom such demand was made.

HEREOF FAIL NOT, AND MAKE DUE RETURN OF THIS WRIT WITH YOUR DOINGS THEREON, ACCORDING TO LAW.

SIGNED (Assistant Clerk)	ON (Date)

FORM 61

EXEMPTION CLAIM FORM
BANK EXECUTION
JD-CV-24a   Rev. 3-93
Gen. Stat. 31-58(j), 52-350a, 52-352b, 52-361a, 52-367b
29 U.S.C. 206(a)(1), P.A. 92-215(a)

STATE OF CONNECTICUT
SUPERIOR COURT

NAME AND ADDRESS OF JUDGMENT DEBTOR OR ATTORNEY
(To be completed by plaintiff)

SECTION I *(To be completed by plaintiff)*
NAME AND ADDRESS OF COURT *(No., Street, Town and Zip Code)*

Fold

NAME OF JUDGMENT DEBTOR	DATE EXECUTION ISSUED	DOCKET NO.

SECTION II *(To be completed by banking institution — see instructions on back)*
NAME AND ADDRESS OF BANKING INSTITUTION TO WHICH EXEMPTION CLAIM *(IF ANY)* IS TO BE RETURNED | DATE OF MAILING TO JUDGMENT DEBTOR

DESCRIPTION OF ACCOUNT(S) AND AMOUNT(S) REMOVED PURSUANT TO EXECUTION

SECTION III   **NOTICE TO JUDGMENT DEBTOR**

As the result of a judgment entered against you, the attached execution has been issued against funds deposited by you in the banking institution named above. In compliance with this execution, the banking institution has removed from the account(s) enumerated above the amount of money indicated above.

THE MONEY IN YOUR ACCOUNT(S) MAY BE EXEMPT FROM EXECUTION — The money in your account(s) may be protected from execution by state statutes or by other laws or regulations of this state or of the United States. A checklist and a description of the exemptions established by law are set forth on the reverse side of this page.

HOW TO CLAIM AN EXEMPTION ESTABLISHED BY LAW — If you wish to claim that the money in your account(s) is exempt by law from execution, you must fill out and sign before a proper official the Affidavit of Claim of Exemption below and mail or deliver this exemption claim form to the banking institution at the above address. This form must be received by the banking institution no later than 15 days from the DATE OF MAILING TO JUDGMENT DEBTOR indicated above.

Upon receipt of this form the bank will forward it to the Superior Court and the court clerk will notify you and the judgment creditor of the date on which a hearing will be held by the court to determine the issues raised by your claim.

SECTION IV   **AFFIDAVIT OF CLAIM OF EXEMPTION ESTABLISHED BY LAW**

I, the judgment debtor named above, hereby claim and certify under the penalty of false statement that the money in the above account(s) is exempt by law from execution as follows:

ACCOUNT NUMBER	DESCRIBE CLAIMED EXEMPTION ESTABLISHED BY LAW
AMOUNT CLAIMED TO BE EXEMPT	

ACCOUNT NUMBER	DESCRIBE CLAIMED EXEMPTION ESTABLISHED BY LAW
AMOUNT CLAIMED TO BE EXEMPT	

☐ Additional sheet(s) attached hereto and made a part hereof *(If necessary)*.

SIGNED **X**	DATE SIGNED	STATE OF CONNECTICUT, COUNTY OF } ss
COMPLETE MAILING ADDRESS OF JUDGMENT DEBTOR		SUBSCRIBED AND SWORN TO BEFORE ME THIS
		_____ DAY OF _____, 19_____.
TELEPHONE NO.		NOTARY PUBLIC, COMMISSIONER OF SUPERIOR COURT **X**

FORM 62

EXEMPTION CLAIM FORM
BANK EXECUTION
JD-CV-24a   Rev. 8-91
Gen. Stat. 31-58(j), 52-350a, 52-352b, 52-361a, 52-367b
29 U.S.C. 206(a)(1), P.A. 91-239

STATE OF CONNECTICUT
SUPERIOR COURT

NAME AND ADDRESS OF JUDGMENT DEBTOR OR ATTORNEY
(To be completed by plaintiff)

Paul Doe
16 Elm Street
New Haven, CT 06510

SECTION I *(To be completed by plaintiff)*

NAME AND ADDRESS OF COURT *(No., Street, Town and Zip Code)*
Superior Court, GA 6   121 Elm Street, New Haven, CT 06510

NAME OF JUDGMENT DEBTOR	DATE EXECUTION ISSUED	DOCKET NO.
Paul Doe	11/30/93	SC6-99999

SECTION II *(To be completed by banking institution — see instructions on back)*

NAME AND ADDRESS OF BANKING INSTITUTION TO WHICH EXEMPTION CLAIM *(IF ANY)* IS TO BE RETURNED	DATE OF MAILING TO JUDGMENT DEBTOR

DESCRIPTION OF ACCOUNT(S) AND AMOUNT(S) REMOVED PURSUANT TO EXECUTION

SECTION III   **NOTICE TO JUDGMENT DEBTOR**

   As the result of a judgment entered against you, the attached execution has been issued against funds deposited by you in the banking institution named above. In compliance with this execution, the banking institution has removed from the account(s) enumerated above the amount of money indicated above.

   THE MONEY IN YOUR ACCOUNT(S) MAY BE EXEMPT FROM EXECUTION — The money in your account(s) may be protected from execution by state statutes or by other laws or regulations of this state or of the United States. A checklist and a description of the exemptions established by law are set forth on the reverse side of this page.

   HOW TO CLAIM AN EXEMPTION ESTABLISHED BY LAW — If you wish to claim that the money in your account(s) is exempt by law from execution, you must fill out and sign before a proper official the Affidavit of Claim of Exemption below and mail or deliver this exemption claim form to the banking institution at the above address. This form must be received by the banking institution no later than 15 days from the DATE OF MAILING TO JUDGMENT DEBTOR indicated above.

   Upon receipt of this form the bank will forward it to the Superior Court and the court clerk will notify you and the judgment creditor of the date on which a hearing will be held by the court to determine the issues raised by your claim.

SECTION IV   **AFFIDAVIT OF CLAIM OF EXEMPTION ESTABLISHED BY LAW**

   I, the judgment debtor named above, hereby claim and certify under the penalty of false statement that the money in the above account(s) is exempt by law from execution as follows:

ACCOUNT NUMBER	DESCRIBE CLAIMED EXEMPTION ESTABLISHED BY LAW
AMOUNT CLAIMED TO BE EXEMPT	

ACCOUNT NUMBER	DESCRIBE CLAIMED EXEMPTION ESTABLISHED BY LAW
AMOUNT CLAIMED TO BE EXEMPT	

☐ Additional sheet(s) attached hereto and made a part hereof *(If necessary).*

SIGNED	DATE SIGNED	STATE OF CONNECTICUT, COUNTY OF } ss
X		

COMPLETE MAILING ADDRESS OF JUDGMENT DEBTOR	SUBSCRIBED AND SWORN TO BEFORE ME THIS
	_____ DAY OF _____, 19 _____.
TELEPHONE NO.	NOTARY PUBLIC, COMMISSIONER OF SUPERIOR COURT
	X

FORM 63

FORM UCC-1 / UNIFORM COMMERCIAL CODE / FINANCING STATEMENT / STATE OF CONNECTICUT / REV 11/94
PLEASE TYPE OR PRINT - SEE REVERSE SIDE FOR COMPLETE INSTRUCTION

1. REQUESTING PARTY: Cust. ID# _____	SPACE FOR OFFICE USE ONLY
NAME ADDRESS CITY STATE ZIP	

2. SPECIAL DEBTOR/COLLATERAL INFORMATION - CHECK AND COMPLETE IF APPLICABLE

____ a. Debtor is a transmitting utility as defined in section 42a-9-402 of the Connecticut General Statutes.
____ b. Debtor does not have an interest of record. The name of the owner of such interest is _____
____ c. Products of collateral are claimed and thus covered.
____ d. (The Collateral is crops) The below described crops are growing or are to be grown on: (describe the real estate below or on a separate sheet) ·
____ e. (The below goods are to become fixtures) Describe the real estate below or on a separate sheet and file a financing statement on real estate records.
____ f. Party named in secured party block is a LESSOR and party named in debtor block is LESSEE.
____ g. Party named in secured party block is a CONSIGNOR and party named in debtor block is CONSIGNEE.

3. DEBTOR'S EXACT LEGAL NAME - Attach 8 1/2" x 11" sheet to present additional debtor information.   ☐ Check here for additional debtors.

	LAST NAME	FIRST NAME	MIDDLE NAME	SUFFIX	S.S. NUMBER
IF INDIVIDUAL					
-OR-	NAME			TAXPAYER I.D.#	
IF BUSINESS					

MAILING ADDRESS (Street or P.O. Box)	CITY	STATE	COUNTRY	POSTAL CODE

4. SECURED PARTY'S FULL LEGAL NAME - Attach 8 1/2" x 11" sheet to present additional secured party information in conformity with the statement below.

	LAST NAME	FIRST NAME	MIDDLE NAME	SUFFIX	S.S. NUMBER
IF INDIVIDUAL					
-OR-	NAME			TAXPAYER I.D.#	
IF BUSINESS					

MAILING ADDRESS (Street or P.O. Box)	CITY	STATE	COUNTRY	POSTAL CODE

5. (IF APPLICABLE) ASSIGNEE'S FULL LEGAL NAME

	LAST NAME	FIRST NAME	MIDDLE NAME	SUFFIX	S.S. NUMBER
IF INDIVIDUAL					
-OR-	NAME			TAXPAYER I.D.#	
IF BUSINESS					

MAILING ADDRESS (Street or P.O. Box)	CITY	STATE	COUNTRY	POSTAL CODE

6. THIS FINANCING STATEMENT COVERS THE FOLLOWING TYPES (or items) OF PROPERTY (Describe):

NUMBER OF ADDITIONAL SHEETS PRESENTED _____

_____   _____
SIGNATURE OF DEBTOR (or Assignor)   SIGNATURE OF SECURED PARTY (or Assignee)

INSTRUCTIONS FOR COMPLETION OF FORM UCC-1

Please read and comply with the following itemized instructions.

1. **RETURN COPY TO:** Please provide the mailing address to which the return copy should be sent.

2. **SPECIAL DEBTOR/COLLATERAL INFORMATION:** Read each statement carefully and place a check mark next to any applicable statements.

3. **DEBTOR INFORMATION:** Please provide full legal name(s) and distinguish between debtors who are individuals and debtors which are businesses by completing the appropriate blocks. Records in the Office of the Secretary of the State will reflect the distinction of debtor type made by the filer. Note that the address blocks apply to both individuals and businesses.

4. **SECURED PARTY INFORMATION:** Please provide full legal name(s) and distinguish between secured parties who are individuals and secured parties which are businesses by completing the appropriate blocks. Records in the Office of the Secretary of the State will reflect the distinction of secured party type made by the filer. Note that the address blocks apply to both individuals and businesses.

5. **ASSIGNEE INFORMATION:** Complete only to reflect an assignment in the original financing statement. Please provide full legal name(s) and distinguish between assignees who are individuals and assignees which are businesses by completing the appropriate blocks. Records in the Office of the Secretary of the State will reflect the distinction of assignee type made by the filer. Note that the address blocks apply to both individuals and businesses.

6. **STATEMENT OF COLLATERAL:** Please provide a description of the property used as collateral for the debt. A statement of the total number of attached sheets must be made under this heading.

GENERAL INFORMATION
Please note the following:

a. Pertinent signatures should be provided at the bottom of the form.

b. If additional space is needed please attach an 8 1/2 x 11 piece of paper and make the appropriate reference on the form.

c. The UCC-1 form has two parts, an original and a carbonless copy. The original will be filed and the copy returned to the filer. Please do not detach the copy.

FORM UCC-1 / UNIFORM COMMERCIAL CODE / FINANCING STATEMENT / STATE OF CONNECTICUT / REV 11/94
PLEASE TYPE OR PRINT - SEE REVERSE SIDE FOR COMPLETE INSTRUCTION

1. REQUESTING PARTY: Cust. ID# _____	SPACE FOR OFFICE USE ONLY
NAME ADDRESS CITY STATE ZIP *Leave Blank*	

2. SPECIAL DEBTOR/COLLATERAL INFORMATION - CHECK AND COMPLETE IF APPLICABLE   *LEAVE BLANK*

____ a.   Debtor is a transmitting utility as defined in section 42a-9-402 of the Connecticut General Statutes.
____ b.   Debtor does not have an interest of record. The name of the owner of such interest is _____
____ c.   Products of collateral are claimed and thus covered.
____ d.   (The Collateral is crops) The below described crops are growing or are to be grown on: (describe the real estate below or on a separate sheet) ·
____ e.   (The below goods are to become fixtures) Describe the real estate below or on a separate sheet and file a financing statement on real estate records.
____ f.   Party named in secured party block is a LESSOR and party named in debtor block is LESSEE.
____ g.   Party named in secured party block is a CONSIGNOR and party named in debtor block is CONSIGNEE

3. DEBTOR'S EXACT LEGAL NAME - Attach 8 1/2" x 11" sheet to present additional debtor information.   ☐ Check here for additional debtors.

	LAST NAME	FIRST NAME	MIDDLE NAME	SUFFIX	S.S. NUMBER
IF INDIVIDUAL	*Defendant's Last Name*	*Defendant's First Name*			*Social Security #*
-OR- IF BUSINESS	NAME *If defendant is business list name of business here*			TAXPAYER I.D.# *Taxpayer I.D. # of business*	

MAILING ADDRESS (Street or P.O. Box) *Defendant mailing address*	CITY	STATE	COUNTRY	POSTAL CODE

4. SECURED PARTY'S FULL LEGAL NAME - Attach 8 1/2" x 11" sheet to present additional secured party information in conformity with the statement below.

	LAST NAME	FIRST NAME	MIDDLE NAME	SUFFIX	S.S. NUMBER
IF INDIVIDUAL	*Plaintiff's Last Name*	*Plaintiff's First Name*			*Social Security #*
-OR- IF BUSINESS	NAME			TAXPAYER I.D.#	

MAILING ADDRESS (Street or P.O. Box) *Plaintiff mailing address*	CITY	STATE	COUNTRY	POSTAL CODE

5. (IF APPLICABLE) ASSIGNEE'S FULL LEGAL NAME

	LAST NAME	FIRST NAME	MIDDLE NAME	SUFFIX	S.S. NUMBER
IF INDIVIDUAL	*Leave Blank*				
-OR- IF BUSINESS	NAME			TAXPAYER I.D.#	

MAILING ADDRESS (Street or P.O. Box) *Leave Blank*	CITY	STATE	COUNTRY	POSTAL CODE

6. THIS FINANCING STATEMENT COVERS THE FOLLOWING TYPES (or items) OF PROPERTY (Describe):

Description of property owned by debtor. If no known property leave space blank.

NUMBER OF ADDITIONAL SHEETS PRESENTED _____

_____	*Plaintiff's Signature* _____
SIGNATURE OF DEBTOR (or Assignor)	SIGNATURE OF SECURED PARTY (or Assignee)

FORM 65

FORM B9A
6/90

United States Bankruptcy Court

9████ (ash)
Case Number

Southern District of New York (White Plains)

Cred.id:9█████3

NOTICE OF COMMENCEMENT OF CASE UNDER CHAPTER 7 OF THE BANKRUPTCY CODE, MEETING OF CREDITORS, AND FIXING OF DATES
(Individual or Joint Debtor No Asset Case)

In re (Name of Debtor) ████████	Address of Debtor ████████ Mt. Vernon, NY 10553	
	Date Case Filed (or Converted) 9/13/95	
Name and Address of Attorney for Debtor ████████ Bronx, NY 10461	Name and Address of Trustee J███████ 3████████Road Suite 102 White Plains, NY 10603	
Telephone Number (212) 597-████		Telephone Number (914) 328-████

☐ This is a converted case originally filed under chapter _____ on _____ (date).

DATE, TIME, AND LOCATION OF MEETING OF CREDITORS

October 23, 1995 at 10:00 am, U.S. Bankruptcy Court, 300 Quarropas Street, White Plains, NY 10601-5008

DISCHARGE OF DEBTS

Deadline to File a Complaint Objecting to Discharge of the Debtor or to Determine Dischargeability of Certain Types of Debts: 12/22/95

AT THIS TIME THERE APPEAR TO BE NO ASSETS AVAILABLE FROM WHICH PAYMENT MAY BE MADE TO UNSECURED CREDITORS. DO NOT FILE A PROOF OF CLAIM UNTIL YOU RECEIVE NOTICE TO DO SO.

COMMENCEMENT OF CASE. A petition for liquidation under Chapter 7 of the Bankruptcy Code has been filed in this court by or against the person or persons named above as the debtor, and an order for relief has been entered. You will not receive notice of all documents filed in this case. All documents filed with the court, including lists of the debtor's property, debts and property claimed as exempt, are available for inspection at the clerk's office of the bankruptcy court, at the below address, during posted business hours.

CREDITORS MAY NOT TAKE CERTAIN ACTIONS. A creditor is anyone to whom the debtor owes money or property. Under the Bankruptcy Code, the debtor is granted certain protection against creditors. Common examples of prohibited actions by creditors are contacting the debtor to demand repayment, taking action against the debtor to collect money owed to creditors or taking property of the debtor, and starting or continuing foreclosure actions, repossessions, or wage deductions. If unauthorized actions are taken by a creditor against a debtor, the court may penalize that creditor. A creditor considering taking action against the debtor or the property of the debtor should review Section 362 of the Bankruptcy Code and may wish to seek legal advice. The staff of the clerk's office of the bankruptcy court is not permitted to give legal advice.

MEETING OF CREDITORS. The debtor (both husband and wife in a joint case) is required to appear on the date, time and location of the meeting of creditors set forth above for the purpose of being examined under oath. Failure by the debtor to appear, or timely pay filing fees, may result in the dismissal of the case without further notice. Attendance by creditors at the meeting is welcomed, but not required. At the meeting the creditors may elect a trustee other than the one named above, elect a committee of creditors, examine the debtor, and transact such other business as may properly come before the meeting. The meeting may be continued or adjourned from time to time by notice at the meeting, without further written notice to the creditors.

LIQUIDATION OF THE DEBTOR'S PROPERTY. The trustee will collect the debtor's property and convert any that is not exempt into money. However, it appears from the schedules of the debtor that there are no assets from which any distribution can be paid to creditors at this time. If at a later date it appears that there are assets from which a distribution may be paid, the creditors will be notified and may file a proof of claim, but are not required to do so.

EXEMPT PROPERTY. Under state and federal law, the debtor is permitted to keep certain money or property as exempt. If a creditor believes that an exemption of money or property is not authorized by law, the creditor may file an objection. An objection must be filed not later than 30 days after the conclusion of the meeting of creditors.

DISCHARGE OF DEBTS. The debtor is seeking a discharge of debts. A discharge means that certain debts are unenforceable against the debtor personally. Creditors whose claims against the debtor are discharged may never take action against the discharged debts. If a creditor believes that the debtor should not receive any discharge of debts under Section 727 of the Bankruptcy Code or that a debt owed to the creditor is not dischargeable under Section 523(a)(2), (4), (6) or (15) of the Bankruptcy Code, timely action must be taken in the bankruptcy court by the deadline set forth above labeled "Discharge of Debts." Creditors considering taking such action may wish to seek legal advice.

APPOINTMENT OF TRUSTEE. The United States Trustee appoints the above individual as the interim trustee. The trustee shall serve under a blanket bond. The trustee may abandon property of the estate with notice of abandonment to the court, 11 U.S.C. Section 554 (a). Further notice will be provided on request only. Any non-exempt property scheduled, but not administered, will be deemed abandoned, 11 U.S.C Section 554(c).

DO NOT FILE A PROOF OF CLAIM UNLESS YOU RECEIVE A COURT NOTICE TO DO SO

Address of the Clerk of the Bankruptcy Court	For the Court: Cecelia G. Morris
300 Quarropas Street White Plains, NY 10601-5085	*Clerk of the Bankruptcy Court*
	09/20/95 *Date*

FORM 66

B18 (Official Form 18)
(6/91)

United States Bankruptcy Court

Eastern District of New York (Brooklyn)

In re

Sophia ████████, 5██████52, aka
Sophia ████████████████████

Bankruptcy Case No. 95-█████-mah

DISCHARGE OF DEBTOR

It appears that a petition commencing a case under title 11, United States Code, was filed by or against the person named above on 7/27/95, that an order for relief was entered under chapter 7, and that no complaint objecting to the discharge of the debtor was filed within the time fixed by the court [or that a complaint objecting to discharge of the debtor was filed and, after due notice and hearing, was not sustained].

IT IS ORDERED THAT:

1. The above-named debtor is released from all dischargeable debts.

2. Any judgment heretofore or hereafter obtained in any court other than this court is null and void as a determination of the personal liability of the debtor with respect to any of the following:

   (a) debts dischargeable under 11 U.S.C. § 523;

   (b) unless heretofore or hereafter determined by order of this court to be nondischargeable, debts alleged to be excepted from discharge under clauses (2), (4), (6) and (15) of 11 U.S.C. § 523 (a);

   (c) debts determined by this court to be discharged.

3. All creditors whose debts are discharged by this order and all creditors whose judgments are declared null and void in paragraph 2 above are enjoined from instituting or continuing any action or employing any process or engaging in any act to collect such debts as personal liabilities of the above-named debtor.

BY THE COURT

Dated: _____4/16/96_____   _____Marvin A. Holland_____
                                                         United States Bankruptcy Judge

LAW OFFICES OF

*MEMBER OF N.Y. & N.J. BARS

Please respond to the office indicated

[]

August 23, 1995

Ronald Moses, City Marshall
Attn. Income executions
116 John Street, 15th.Floor
New York, New York 10038

Re. Bankruptcy Case No.
    Our Client - Sophia
    Your File No - 8   8

Dear Sir,

        Please be advised that our client filed a Chapter 7
bankruptcy petition on July 27, 1995 in which Ted Rothstein, DDS
is listed as an unsecured creditor. - see enclosed documents.

Please cease income execution and refund all monies taken since
this date.

If you have any questions, please do not hesitate to call me.

                    Very Truly Yours,

                        Thomas P. McNu   Esq.

FORM 67 SIDE 2

CASE INFORMATION SHEET

The undersigned is the attorney for the judgment creditor. The enclosed judgment is a true and complete copy of the judgment on file with the court where it was entered. Kerry H. Lutz, Esq. is authorized to act of counsel to this firm only for the purpose of signing all restraining notices and information subpoenas to be served upon the designated banks.

CASE DATA

Plaintiff(s): _____

Defendant(s): _____

Court: _____ County: _____

Index No: _____ Judgment Date: _____

Judgment $: _____ Judgment $ Owed: _____

Counties to search: _____

DEBTOR DATA

Debtor #1

Name: _____

Address: _____

SS # (if known): _____ Date of Birth: _____

Corporate Taxpayer ID # (if known): _____

Debtor #2

Name: _____

Address: _____

SS # (if known): _____ Date of Birth: _____

Corporate Taxpayer ID # (if known): _____

ATTORNEY OR PRO SE INFORMATION

Signed: _____ Date: _____

Attorney: _____

Law Firm: _____

Address: _____

City: _____ State: _____ Zip: _____

Phone: _____ Fax: _____

LUTZ ASSET RESEARCH

330 WEST 42ND STREET

30TH FLOOR

NEW YORK, N.Y. 10036-6902

June 17, 1996   (212) 760-0242

(212) 760-0243

Kerry H. Lutz, Esq.
330 West 42nd Street
New York, NY   10036

Re: TED ROTHSTEIN v. PAUL LAPOM

Dear Attorney:

Restraining notices on the above matter were sent to banks in following counties:
NEW YORK•KINGS

To date we have not located any of the debtor's accounts
If we learn of any accounts, we will immediately notify you by telephone.

We're sorry our efforts didn't bear fruit this time, however, our system can't find what can't be found.

If you have heard anything to the contrary from any bank or the debtor, please advise us, so that we may update our records.

Thanks for using our service.

Very truly yours,

M

M :kl

CIVIL COURT OF THE CITY OF NEW YORK
141 LIVINGSTON STREET
BROOKLYN, NEW YORK 11201

EXEMP. COPY RECEIPT FEE $10.00

11/2/92 RECEIPT # 2253

JUDGMENT

After

Inquest (Trial) Arbitration

INDEX # 1349/92.

Judgment is rendered in favor of _____ *Ted Rothstein, D.D.S.*

Address: *35 Remsen Street*

Brooklyn, New York 11210

against _____ for $ *3,548.89* with $ *118 50* Interest

Address: *40-54 W. Shula Parkway*

Bronx, New York 10468

and Disbursements in the sum of $ *180 00 XXX* amounting in all to:

Three thousand eight hundred & forty-seven. 39/xxx Dollars [*$3847 39/xxx*]

Dated New York City, *SEP 28 1992* , 19___ .

_____
C l e r k

The defendant is a civilian and not in military
service. From conversations had with the
defendant as well as knowledge of the defendant's
present whereabouts, plaintiff knows that
defendant is not in military service
T.R.

FORM 69 SIDE 1

No. **2253**

EXEMPLIFICATION OF A RECORD IN
THE CIVIL COURT OF THE CITY OF NEW YORK

CERTIFICATION OF THE CHIEF CLERK

I, _____**JACK BAER**_____, Chief Clerk of the Civil Court of the City of New York, do hereby certify that the attached is a true copy of the records filed in this Court and that they are legally kept in my possession:

_____ 11/20/92 _____ _Jack Baer_

Clerk of County   Dated   Chief Clerk of the Civil Court
Verification

CERTIFICATION OF A JUDGE OF THE CIVIL COURT OF THE CITY OF NEW YORK

I, _____**LIOS ARNIO**_____, a Judge of the Civil Court of the City of New York, do hereby certify that _____**JACK BAER**_____, whose name is subscribed above, is the Chief Clerk of the Civil Court of the City of New York, that the signature on the above attestation is genuine, and that the affixed seal is the Seal of the Civil Court of the City of New York.

DEC 15 1992
_____   **LIOS ARNIO**
Dated   Judge of the Civil Court of the City of New York

===

SUMMARY OF RECORD

Title of action or proceeding:

Ted Rothstein, D.D.S ,Plaintiff/~~Claimant~~/~~Petitioner~~

against

Dinah Padebil ,Defendant/~~Respondent~~

Judgment entered: ☒ after trial on the merits

            ☐ after Inquest before the Court   **SEE ATTACHED JUDGMENT**

            ☐ by the Clerk pursuant to CPLR 3215

in favor of: _Ted Rothstein, D.D.S_

and against: _Dinah Padebil_ for:

Damages	$ 3,548.89
Interest	118.50
Costs	
Disbursements	180.00
Other_____	
Total Judgment	$ 3847.39

FORM 69 SIDE 2

Civil Court of the City of New York

Index No. S.C. _867/96_

COUNTY OF _KINGS_

Small Claims/Commercial Claims Part

Ted Rothstein

Claimant(s),

against

Dinah Padebil

Defendant(s),

NOTICE OF JUDGMENT

DECISION: After Trial/~~Inquest~~, the decision in the above action is as follows:

A. ☐ Judgment and Award in favor of_____

_____

_____

_____

Award amount ....$ _____

Interest ....$ _____

Disbursements.................$ _____

TOTAL JUDGMENT ....$ __Ø__

(Information below and on the reverse side applies to all parties when an award has been granted.)

B. ☒ Judgment in favor of Defendant, dismissing claim. No monetary award.

_____

_____

_____

(Information below and on the other side is not applicable.)

Date: **DEC 2 1996**

By: ___JUDGE ANA JOHN___

J.C.C./~~Arbitrator~~

INFORMATION FOR THE JUDGMENT DEBTOR

(the party against whom a money judgement has been entered)

YOU HAVE A LEGAL OBLIGATION TO PAY THIS JUDGMENT.
YOU MUST PRESENT PROOF TO THE COURT UPON SATISFACTION OF THE JUDGMENT.

Your failure to pay the judgment may subject you to any one or any combination of the following:

a) garnishment of wage(s) and/or bank account(s);

b) lien, seizure and/or sale of real property and/or personal property, including automobile(s);

c) suspension of motor vehicle registration, and/or drivers license, if the underlying claim is based on judgment debtor's ownership or operation of a motor vehicle;

d) revocation, suspension, or denial of renewal of any applicable business license or permit;

e) investigation and prosecution by the State Attorney General for fradulent or illegal business practices;

f) a penalty equal to three times the amount of the unsatisfied judgment plus attorney's fees if there are unpaid claims.

If you did not appear in court on the day the Hearing was held, you are a defaulting party. A judgment may have been taken against you even though you were not in court. If that is so, you may apply to the court in writing and ask to have the default judgment opened. You must give the judge a reasonable excuse for your failure to appear in court and show that you have a meritorious defense. The Judge may open your default judgment and give you another chance to go to court.

("Information for the Judgment Creditor" is on the reverse side.)

THE JUDGMENT IS VALID FOR A PERIOD OF 20 YEARS. IF THE JUDGMENT IS NOT COLLECTED UPON THE FIRST ATTEMPT, FURTHER ATTEMPTS TO COLLECT MAY BE MADE AT A LATER DATE.

CIV-SC-92 (Revised 5/92)

FORM 70

AFTERWORD

There you have it: a guide to assist you in taking action and putting money back in your pocket—where it belongs.

It is my hope that this guide will embolden you to begin using the small claims court.

Taking a new pathway for many can be a frightening experience. There are numerous excuses that you can entertain, should you decide not to take this route even though you have a new map in hand. There may be some surprises, for no doubt the map maker has probably overlooked some of the pitfalls.

The reader who is too timid to travel this new road, and who rationalizes his/her decision with a litany of excuses, will derive none of the possible benefits and be left with only the excuses. As Robert Frost said: "Two roads diverged in a wood, and I—I took the one less traveled by, and that has made all the difference."

The "principle of the thing" for me, just like the fabled Don Quixote, is the underpinning of the need to right a perceived wrong and seek justice. Forms 29 and 70 are decisions from cases that I recently lost. Nevertheless, I could not have lived happily with myself had I not acted on the courage of my convictions.

Even though I lost those cases, the emotional closure that ensued enabled me to purge myself of the matters and to move on without anger. I recommend this type of catharsis as medicine for self-healing.

Should any reader have comments or experiences in small claims court they would like to relate, the author would be pleased to hear them. Perhaps they will be incorporated into a second edition of the guide.

BIBLIOGRAPHY/SOURCES OF INFORMATION

Black's Law Dictionary. 6th ed. Edited by Henry Campbell Black. St. Paul: West Publishing Co., 1991.

BNA's Directory of State and Federal Courts, Judges and Clerks, a State-by-State and Federal Listing, 1997 ed. Compiled by Judith A. Miller with the Bureau of National Affairs Library Staff. Washington, D.C.: Bureau of National Affairs, 1997.

BRB Publications Inc. *County Court Records (Sourcebook of), A Sourcebook From The Public Record Research Library.* 2nd ed. Tempe: BRB Publications Inc., 1995.

Casenotes Legal Briefs (Contracts). Edited by Dana Blatt and Norman Goldenberg. Beverly Hills: Casenotes Publishing Co., Inc., 1997.

Connecticut. Judicial Branch Superior Court. *The Samll Claims Process.* Hartford: Judicial Branch Superior Court, 1994.

Culligan, Joseph J. *You, Too, Can Find Anybody.* Miami: Hallmark Press, Inc., 1995.

Hansell, Saul. "We Like You. We Care About You. Now Pay Up." *New York Times,* 26 Jan. 1997.

Internet: Nolo Press (Self-Help Law Center): http://www.nolo.com; by phone (800) 992-6656 and (800) 728-3555.

Internet: Population Statistics: http://www.cenus.gov/population/www/estimates.

Internet: Dr. Ted Rothsetein: http://www.drted.com.

Kelsea, Wilber W. *Small Claims Court Without a Lawyer.* Napperville: Source Books Trade, 1992.

Lebovits, Gerald, and Mark Snyder. "Practitioner's Guide to Small Claims Part." *New York Law Journal,* 25 Feb. 1997.

Looseleaf Law Publications. *Civil Practice Law and Rules (CPLR).* Flushing: Looseleaf Law Publications, 1993.

New York State Bar Association. *New York Appellate Practice: How to Take a Civil Appeal in New York State.* New York: Record Press International, 1989.

New York State Bar Association. *Preparing for and Trying the Civil Law Suit.* New York: New York State Bar Association, 1991.

New York State Unified Court System. *Guide for the Use of the Commercial Claims Part.* New York: New York State Unified Court System, 1994.

Siegel, David D. *Practitioner's Handbook for Appeals to the Court of Appeals.* 2nd ed. New York: New York State Bar Association, 1991.

Siegel, David D. "Small Claims." Chap. 21 in *New York Practice.* 2nd ed. St. Paul: West Publishing Co., 1991.

Small Claims Guide for Towns and Village Courts. 16th ed. Revised by Herbert A. Kline, Esq. Binghamton: Gould Publications, 1994.

Warner, Ralph. *Everybody's Guide to Small Claims Court.* 5th ed. Berkeley: Nolo Press, 1991.

West Publishing Co. *McKinney's Consolidated Laws of New York.* Book 29A, *Judiciary Court Acts.* St. Paul: West Publishing Co., 1995.

INDEX

NOTES

NOTES

NOTES

NOTES

NOTES

NOTES

NOTES

NOTES

NOTES

Printed in the United States
1190500001B/172

9 780764 191572